William Spohn Baker

Character Portraits of Washington

As Delineated by Historians, Orators and Divines...

William Spohn Baker

Character Portraits of Washington
As Delineated by Historians, Orators and Divines...

ISBN/EAN: 9783744677523

Printed in Europe, USA, Canada, Australia, Japan

Cover: Foto ©ninafisch / pixelio.de

More available books at **www.hansebooks.com**

First in
War-first in
Peace-&first in
the hearts of his
Countrymen.
SACRED TO THE MEMORY OF
GENERAL GEORGE WASHINGTON, L.L.D.
Born Feb:r 11th (O.S.) 1732; Died Dec:r 14, 1799.

·CHARACTER

PORTRAITS OF WASHINGTON

AS DELINEATED BY

HISTORIANS ORATORS AND DIVINES

SELECTED

AND ARRANGED IN CHRONOLOGICAL ORDER WITH
BIOGRAPHICAL NOTES AND REFERENCES

BY

W. S. BAKER

Author of the " Engraved Portraits of Washington,"
" Medallic Portraits of Washington," &c., &c.

PHILADELPHIA
ROBERT M. LINDSAY
1887

PREFACE.

It is the purpose of these pages to exhibit the character of Washington as understood and portrayed by some of the best writers and thinkers; as well by contemporaries, whose personal knowledge and convictions lend additional value, as by those of a later day, whose careful study and critical analysis render their testimony of equal weight and importance. These tributes, scattered throughout many publications, have been brought together, so that all may become familiar with the details of a character, which, in its gradual development, reached the highest degree of excellence humanity can attain.

The character of Washington is a national possession. To its courage and perseverance we owe the successful issue of our war for independence; to its integrity and judgment, the permanence of our constitutional experiment; and, to its firmness and patriotism, our position as a nation. All Americans should study and venerate it. At all times and places, in peace and in war, in tumult and in quiet, its contemplation will be a benefit, its example an influence, and its imitation an assistance. "God be praised, that character is ours forever!"

W. S. BAKER.

Philadelphia, Nov. 1st, 1886.

CONTENTS.

The frontispiece is a reproduction of the rare allegorical print published with the funeral oration by Henry Lee. Quarto. Philadelphia: 1800.

(7)

JAMES THACHER.

1778.

THE personal appearance of our Commander in Chief, is that of the perfect gentleman and accomplished warrior. He is remarkably tall, full six feet, erect and well proportioned. The strength and proportion of his joints and muscles, appear to be commensurate with the pre-eminent powers of his mind. The serenity of his countenance, and majestic gracefulness of his deportment, impart a strong impression of that dignity and grandeur, which are his peculiar characteristics, and no one can stand in his presence without feeling the ascendancy of his mind, and associating with his countenance the idea of wisdom, philanthrophy, magnanimity, and patriotism. There is a fine symmetry in the features of his face, indicative of a benign and dignified spirit. His nose is straight, and his eyes inclined to blue. He wears his hair in a becoming cue, and from his forehead it is turned back and powdered in a manner which adds to the military air of his appearance. He displays a native gravity, but devoid of all appearance of ostentation. His uniform dress is a blue coat, with two brilliant epaulettes, buff coloured under clothes, and a three cornered hat, with a black cockade. He is constantly equipped with an elegant small sword, boots, and spurs, in readiness to mount his noble charger. There is not in the present age, perhaps, another man so eminently qualified to discharge the arduous duties of the exalted station he is called to

2

(9)

sustain, amidst difficulties which to others would appear insurmount-able, nor could any man have more at command the veneration and regard of the officers and soldiers of our army, even after defeat and misfortune. This is the illustrious chief, whom a kind Providence has decreed as the instrument to conduct our country to peace and to in-dependence.

His Excellency, made a visit to our hospital; his arrival was scarcely-announced, before he presented himself at our doors. Dr. Williams and myself had the honor to wait on this great and truly good man, through the different wards, and to reply to his inquiries relative to the condition of our patients. He appeared to take a deep interest in the situation of the sick and wounded soldiers, and inquired particularly as to their treatment and comfortable accommodations.

JAMES THACHER, M.D., was born at Barnstable, Mass., February 14th, 1754, and died at Plymouth, May 24th, 1844. He joined the Revolutionary army at Cambridge in June, 1775, as surgeon's mate under Dr. John Warren, was promoted to surgeon and served through the war, being present at many of the principal battles. Dr. Thacher kept a diary of the war, which was published at Boston in 1823, with the title: "A Military Journal during the American Revolutionary War, from 1775 to 1783," 8vo., a work of considerable historical value. The extract above given, is his entry on the occasion of Washington's visit to the military hospital at Robinson's house, near West Point, in October, 1778, and as a description of his personal appearance, very properly serves as an introduction to the "Character Portraits of Washington."

JOHN BELL.

1779.

GENERAL WASHINGTON having never been in Europe, could not possibly have seen much military service when the armies of Britain were sent to subdue us; yet still, for a variety of reasons, he was by much the most proper man on this continent, and probably any where else, to be placed at the head of an American army. The very high estimation he stood in for integrity and honour, his engaging in the cause of his country from sentiment and a conviction of her wrongs, his moderation in politics, his extensive property, and his approved abilities as a commander, were motives which necessarily obliged the choice of America to fall upon him. That nature has given him extraordinary military talents will hardly be controverted by his most bitter enemies; and having been early actuated with a warm passion to serve his country in the military line, he has greatly improved them by unwearied industry, and a close application to the best writers upon tactics, and by a more than common method and exactness: and, in reality, when it comes to be considered that at first he only headed a body of men intirely unacquainted with military discipline or operations, somewhat ungovernable in temper, and who at best could only be stiled an alert and good militia, acting under very short enlistments, uncloathed, unaccoutred, and at all times very ill supplied with ammunition and artillery; and that with such an army he withstood the ra-

(11)

vages and progress of near forty thousand veteran troops, plentifully provided with every necessary article, commanded by the bravest officers in Europe, and supported by a very powerful navy, which effectually prevented all movements by water; when, I say, all this comes to be impartially considered, I think I may venture to pronounce, that general Washington will be regarded by mankind as one of the greatest military ornaments of the present age, and that his name will command the veneration of the latest posterity.

I would not mention to you the person of this excellent man, were I not convinced that it bears great analogy to the qualifications of his mind. General Washington is now in the forty-seventh year of his age; he is a tall well-made man, rather large boned, and has a tolerably genteel address: his features are manly and bold, his eyes of a bluish cast and very lively; his hair a deep brown, his face rather long and marked with the small pox; his complexion sun-burnt and without much colour, and his countenance sensible, composed, and thoughtful; there is a remarkable air of dignity about him, with a striking degree of gracefulness: he has an excellent understanding without much quickness; is strictly just, vigilant, and generous; an affectionate husband, a faithful friend, a father to the deserving soldier; gentle in his manners, in temper rather reserved; a total stranger to religious prejudices, which have so often excited Christians of one denomination to cut the throats of those of another; in his morals irreproachable; he was never known to exceed the bounds of the most rigid temperance: in a word, all his friends and acquaintance universally allow, that no man ever united in his own person a more perfect alliance of the virtues of a philosopher with the talents of a general.

Candour, sincerity, affability, and simplicity, seem to be the striking features of his character, till an occasion offers of displaying the most determined bravery and independence of spirit.

Such, my good friend, is the man, to whom America has intrusted her important cause. Hitherto she has had every reason to be satisfied with her choice; and most ungrateful would she be to the great Disposer of human events, were she not to render him unremitting thanks for having provided her with such a citizen at such a crisis. Most nations have been favoured with some patriotic deliverer: the Israelites had their Moses; Rome had her Camillus; Greece her Leonidas; Sweden her Gustavus; and England her Hambdens, her Russels, and her Sydneys: but these illustrious heroes, though successful in preserving and defending, did not, like Washington, form or establish empires, which will be the refuge or asylum of Liberty banished from Europe by luxury and corruption. Must not, therefore, your heart beat with conscious pride at the prospect of your friend's being ranked among (if not above) those illustrious patriots? at the enchanting thought, that He, whom you know and love, shall be acknowledged by present and future generations as their great deliverer, and the chief instrument in the hands of the Almighty for laying the foundation of that freedom and happiness, which, I trust, await the future myriads of this vast continent?

THE "Sketch of General Washington's Life and Character," from which we make the foregoing extract, is contained in a letter from "a gentleman of Maryland," to a friend in Europe, dated May 3, 1779, and published in London the following year, annexed to "A poetical epistle to his Excellency George Washington, Esq., Commander in Chief of the Armies of the United States of America, from an inhabitant of the State of Maryland." The author of the Epistle, was Charles Henry Wharton, D.D., at the time a resident of Worcester, England, and the publication, was " for the charitable purpose of raising a few guineas to relieve, in a small measure, the distresses of some hundreds of American prisoners, *now* suffering confinement in the gaols of England."   The sketch which is probably the first attempt at a Biography of Washington, made in America, was also printed in the *London Chronicle*, July 22, 1780, and a portion of it in the *Westminster Magazine*, for the following month.   In this country it was reprinted in the *Massachusetts Magazine*, March 1791, where the name of the author, JOHN BELL, ESQ., of Maryland, first appears, of whom, however, we have no information other than the statement in the preface to the *Epistle* to Washington, that he was "connected and intimate in the family of that great man."

CLAUDE C. ROBIN.

1781.

I HAVE seen General Washington, that most singular man—the soul and support of one of the greatest revolutions that has ever happened, or can happen. I fixed my eyes upon him with that keen attention which the sight of a great man always inspires. We naturally entertain a secret hope of discovering in the features of such illustrious persons some traces of that excellent genius which distinguishes them from, and elevates them above their fellow mortals.

Perhaps the exterior of no man was better calculated to gratify these expectations than that of General Washington. He is of a tall and noble stature, well proportioned, a fine, cheerful, open countenance, a simple and modest carriage; and his whole mien has something in it that interests the French, the Americans, and even enemies themselves in his favor. Placed in a military view, at the head of a nation where each individual has a share in the supreme legislative authority, and where coercive laws are yet in a great degree destitute of vigor, where the climate and manners can add but little to their energy, where the spirit of party, private interest, slowness and national indolence, slacken, suspend and overthrow the best concerted measures; although so situated, he has found out a method of keeping his troops in the most absolute subordination; making them rivals in praising him; fearing him even when he is silent, and retaining their full confi-

(15)

dence in him after defeats and disgrace. His reputation has, at length, arisen to a most brilliant height; and he may now grasp at the most unbounded power, without provoking envy or exciting suspicion. He has ever shown himself superior to fortune, and in the most trying adversity has discovered resources till then unknown; and, as if his abilities only increased and dilated at the prospect of difficulty, he is never better supplied than when he seems destitute of every thing, nor have his arms ever been so fatal to his enemies, as at the very instant when they had thought they had crushed him for ever. It is his to excite a spirit of heroism and enthusiasm in a people, who are by nature very little susceptible of it; to gain over the respect and homage of those whose interest it is to refuse it, and to execute his plans and projects by means unknown even to those who are his instruments; he is intrepid in dangers, yet never seeks them but when the good of his country demands it, preferring rather to temporize and act upon the defensive, because he knows such a mode of conduct best suits the genius and circumstances of the nation, and that all he and they have to expect, depends upon time, fortitude, and patience: he is frugal and sober in regard to himself, but profuse in the public cause; like Peter the Great, he has by defeats conducted his army to victory; and like Fabius, but with fewer resources and more difficulty, he has conquered without fighting, and saved his country.

Such are the ideas that arise in the mind, at the sight of this great man, in examining the events in which he had a share, or in listening to those whose duty obliges them to be near his person, and consequently best display his character. In all these extensive states they consider him in the light of a beneficent God, dispensing peace and happiness around him. Old men, women, and children, press about him when he accidentally passes along, and think themselves happy, once in their lives, to have seen him—they follow him through the towns with torches, and celebrate his arrival by public illuminations. The Americans, that cool and sedate people, who in the midst of their most trying difficulties, have attended only to the directions and impulses of plain method and common sense, are roused, animated, and inflamed at the very mention of his name: and the first songs that sentiment or gratitude has dictated, have been to celebrate General Washington.

Anné Robin, one of the chaplains to the French army in America, wrote while in this country, a series of thirteen letters, which were published at Paris, in 1782, and afterwards translated and published at Philadelphia, in 1783, with the title "New Travels through North America, in a series of letters exhibiting the history of the victorious campaign of the allied armies under his Excellency Gen. Washington, and the Count de Rochambeau, in the year 1781." 8vo. The Abbé arrived at Boston in June (1781), and joined the French troops at Providence, the two armies uniting at Philipsburg (near Dobbs' Ferry N. Y.) the following month. The letter from which our extract is made, is dated "Camp at Philipsburg, August 4, 1781." The letters, covering as they do one of the most important military movements of the war, the march to Yorktown, and the siege and final surrender of the British army, make the volume a valuable contemporary record, while apart from our quotation, the remarks of the writer upon the genius, temper, and customs of the people, are extremely interesting.

PRINCE DE BROGLIE.

1782.

GENERAL WASHINGTON is now about forty-nine years of age. He is tall, nobly built and very well proportioned. His face is much more agreeable than represented in his portrait. He must have been much handsomer three years ago, and although the gentlemen who have remained with him during all that time say that he seems to have grown much older, it is not to be denied that the General is still as fresh and active as a young man.

His physiognomy is mild and open. His accost is cold although polite. His pensive eyes seem more attentive than sparkling; but their expression is benevolent, noble, and self-possessed. In his private conduct, he preserves that polite and attentive good breeding which satisfies everybody, and that dignified reserve which offends no one. He is a foe to ostentation and to vain-glory. His temper is always even. He has never testified the least humor. Modest even to humility, he does not seem to estimate himself at his true worth. He receives with perfect grace all the homages which are paid him, but he evades them rather than seeks them. His company is agreeable and winning. Always serious, never abstracted, always simple, always easy and affable without being familiar, the respect which he inspires is never oppressive. He speaks but little in general, and that in a subdued tone, but he is so attentive to what is said to him,

(18)

that being satisfied he understands you perfectly, one is disposed to dispense with an answer. This behaviour has been very useful to him on numerous occasions. Nobody has greater necessity than he to act with circumspection, and to carefully weigh his words.

To an unalterable tranquility of soul he joins a most exact judgment, and the utmost with which he has been reproached is a little tardiness in his determination and even in the execution of his decisions, when once he has made them.

His courage is calm and brilliant, but to appreciate in a satisfactory manner the real extent of his talents and his ability as a great and warlike captain, I think one should have seen him at the head of a greater army, with greater means than he has had, and opposed to an enemy less his superior.

At least one cannot fail to give him the title of an excellent patriot, of a wise and virtuous man, and one is in fact tempted to ascribe to him all good qualities, even those that circumstances have not yet permitted him to develop.

Mr. Washington's first military services were against the French in the War for Canada. He had no opportunity for distinguishing himself, and after the defeat of Braddock, the war having crossed the river St. Lawrence, and the Virginia militia of which he was Colonel having been sent home, he was not kept in active service; whereupon he retired to his plantation where he lived like a philosopher.

His estate was quite distant from the seat of the English government, the real hot-bed of the insurrection; and his wise character witheld him still further from mixing in its movements, so that he had but little share in the first troubles.

On the breaking out of hostilities with the mother-country, every body wished a chief who joined a profound sagacity to the advantage of having had military experience. All eyes turned toward Washington, and he was unanimously called to the command of the army. The course of events justified the choice. Never was there a man better fitted to command the Americans, and his conduct throughout developed the greatest foresight, steadiness and wisdom.

Mr. Washington received no pay as General; refused it as not needing it. The expenses of his table only are paid by the State. Every day he has about thirty persons to dinner. He gives good military fare, and is very civil towards all the officers admitted to his table. It is ordinarily the moment of the day when he is most cheerful.

At desert he eats an enormous quantity of nuts, and when the conversation is entertaining he keeps eating through a couple of hours, from time to time giving sundry healths, according to the English and American custom. It is what they call "toasting." They always begin by drinking to the United States of America; after that to the king of France, then to the Queen of France, then to the success of the allied armies, after which, what they call a sentiment is sometimes given; for example, to our success over our enemies and with the beauties—to our triumphs in war and in love.

I toasted very often with the General, and amongst others on one occasion I proposed to drink to the Marquis de Lafayette, whom he regards as his own child. He accepted with a benevolent smile, and had the politeness to respond by proposing the health of my father and my wife.

General Washington appeared to me to maintain a perfect demeanor towards the officers of his army. He treats them with great politeness, but they are far from attempting any familiarity with him. All of them, on the contrary, exhibit towards their General an air of respect, of confidence and of admiration.

CLAUDE VICTOR, PRINCE DE BROGLIE, was born at Paris in 1757, and entered the army at the age of fourteen. At the age of twenty-five he became a colonel, and was ordered to America to take command of the regiment Saintonge, which had distinguished itself in the siege of Yorktown. He sailed July 15, 1782, with Count de Ségur, on board the frigate *La Gloire*, and after an eventful voyage, landed on the 13th of September, near Dover, Delaware. having been intercepted in the Bay by an English squadron. After spending a few days in Philadelphia, the Prince hastened to join his regiment then in camp at Crampond, nine miles from Peekskill on the Hudson, and two days after his arrival was presented to Washington and dined with him at his Headquarters at Verplanck's Point. He returned to France with his regiment, sailing from Boston, December 24th, of the same year. The Prince espoused the popular cause in the revolution and accepted a command in the army of the Rhine, but resigned after Aug. 10, 1792. He was arrested Dec. 28, 1793, and after a trial before the revolutionary tribunal, condemned and guillotined June 27, 1794. The Prince kept a journal of his visit to the United States, from a translation of which, published in Vol. I, pp. 180, etc. of the *Magazine of American History* (1877), our extract is made. The translation was made from the original MS. in possession of his grandson, the present Duc de Broglie, by Elise W. Balch, daughter of Thomas Balch, deceased (1877), author of " Les Francais en Amérique pendant La Guerre De L'Indépendance Des Etats-Unis, 1777-1783." Paris, 1872.

JOSEPH MANDRILLON.

1784.

WHY did I not receive from nature the genius and eloquence of the celebrated orators of Greece and Rome! Why can I not for a moment snatch their pencils to trace rapidly the portrait of the greatest man that America has ever produced, and one of the most celebrated that ever existed! With what energy, with what enthusiasm would I not speak of his brilliant virtues! Who is the man that would be jealous of the homage I pay him? Who is the man that would tax me with flattery?

We are no longer in those barbarous ages in which men offered incense to tyrants, in which they dared to give the name of hero to men addicted to every vice, and whom they dreaded too much to offend. We are no longer in those ages when cruel sovereigns had writers in their pay to palliate their crimes, and to magnify their supposed virtues. Our more enlightened age presents to us in history sovereigns and men, such as they have been; truth is its character. The public veneration for General Washington is the precious fruit of the most severe examination of his conduct. Jealous of his glory and the good opinion of his contemporaries, he enjoys them without arrogance and without presumption; and if he does himself the justice to believe that he merits his celebrity, he knows also that posterity, which raises and demolishes statues, will never sully the trophies

(22)

erected to him. Nothing but the hand of an illiterate barbarian, or of a savage ignorant of history, with the stroke of a hatchet would break his statue, supposing it to be that of a despot. But when from among the debris of the inscription, one could put together nothing but the name of Washington, the chief of this barbarian or of this savage, whose knowledge of the American revolution comes from tradition, would take vengeance on him for this attempt, causing the monument to be again put in place, on its base will be read: ignorance had overthrown it, and justice again raised it up: mortals revere his memory!

Having been the soul and support of one of the greatest events of the century, it is just that Washington should pass his days without a cloud, in the bosom of repose, of honor and public veneration. Nature sometimes places the soul of a hero in a feeble body; but when we speak of the brilliant actions of a man whose features and stature we are ignorant of, we are inclined to paint him as endowed with every valuable gift of nature, and please ourselves with believing that his features bear the image of that genius which distinguishes him above his fellow men. No person is better calculated to sustain this opinion than Washington. Imposing in size, noble and well proportioned, a countenance open, calm and sedate, but without any one striking feature, and when you depart from him, the remembrance only of a fine man will remain, a fine figure, an exterior plain and modest, a pleasing address, firm without severity, a manly courage, an uncommon capacity for grasping the whole scope of a subject, and a complete experience in war and politics; equally useful in the cabinet and in the field of Mars, the idol of his country, the admiration of the enemy he has fought and vanquished; modest in victory, great in the reverse;

why do I say reverse! very far from being subdued he has made every misfortune contribute to his success.   He knows to obey as well as to command, he never made use of his power or the submission of his army to derogate from the authority of his country or to disobey its commands. With a perfect knowledge of man, he knew how to govern freemen in peace, and by his example, his activity, his energy, he taught them to love glory and danger, notwithstanding the inclemency of the climate and the rigors of winter. The soldier jealous of his praises, feared even his silence; never was general better served and obeyed. More careful of his country's glory than his own, he risked nothing to chance; his operations, marked by prudence, had always the welfare of his country for their sole object; he appeared unwilling to possess glory but from her alone: his maxim was always to gain time, to act on the defence; without attacking his enemies in front, he knew how to harass them, to exhaust their forces by excursions, by surprises, of which only a great man can value the utility. Like Camillus he forsook the charms of rural life and flew to the assistance of his country; like Fabius he saved it by procrastinating; like Peter the Great he triumphed over his enemies by the experience acquired through defeat. There is not a man, not even a monarch in Europe who would not envy the glory of having acted such a part as Washington. It is said the king of Prussia sent him a sword with only this direction. *The greatest general of the old world to the greatest general of the new.*

If ever mortal enjoyed his whole reputation during his lifetime, if ever a citizen has found in his own country a reward for his services and abilities, it is my hero; every where fêted, admired, caressed, he every where sees hearts eager to render him homage; if he enters a town, or if he passes through a village, old and young men, women and children, all follow him with acclamations; all load him with blessings; in every heart he has a temple consecrated to respect and friendship. How I love to imagine to myself the French general, (M. de Rochambeau) equally the idol and the hero of his army, saying at table as he sat near Washington, that he had never known what true glory was, nor a truly great man, until he became acquainted with him. When America, overthrown by the dreadful revolutions of nature shall no longer exist, it will be remembered of Washington, that he was the defender of liberty, the friend of man, and the avenger of an oppressed people.

JOSEPH MANDRILLON was born at Bourg-en-Bresse, France, in 1742. Having embraced the mercantile profession, he established himself at Amsterdam, from whence he made a voyage to the United States, and afterwards published the results of his observations in a 12mo. Volume, entitled "Le Spectateur Américain," Amsterdam, 1784. Our translation of his Portrait of Washington is from a copy of the book, presented by him to the "American Philosophical Society," of which he was elected a member, January 22d, 1785. A contemporary translation was published in the *Columbian Magazine*, January 1787. After his return to Holland, his opposition to the Stadtholder made him unpopular, and he went to France. The independence of his character caused him to be suspected by Robespierre, and he was guillotined January 7th, 1794.

MARQUIS DE CHASTELLUX.

1786.

HERE would be the proper place to give the portrait of General Washington: but what can my testimony add to the idea already formed of him? The continent of North America, from Boston to Charles Town, is a great volume, every page of which presents his eulogium. I know, that having had the opportunity of a near inspection, and of closely observing him, some more particular details may be expected from me; but the strongest characteristic of this respectable man is the perfect union which reigns between the physical and moral qualities which compose the individual, one alone will enable you to judge of all the rest. If you are presented with medals of Cæsar, of Trajan, or Alexander, on examining their features, you will still be led to ask what was their stature, and the form of their persons; but if you discover, in a heap of ruins, the head or the limb of an antique *Apollo*, be not curious about the other parts, but rest assured that they all were conformable to those of a God. Let not this comparison be attributed to enthusiasm! It is not my intention to exaggerate, I wish only to express the impression General Washington has left on my mind; the idea of a perfect whole, that cannot be the produce of enthusiasm, which rather would reject it, since the effect of proportion is to diminish the idea of greatness. Brave without temerity, laborious without ambition, generous without prodi-

(26)

gality, noble without pride, virtuous without severity; he seems always to have confined himself within those limits, where the virtues, by clothing themselves in more lively, but more changeable and doubtful colours, may be mistaken for faults. *This is the seventh year that he has commanded the army, and that he has obeyed the Congress; more need not be said, especially in America, where they know how to appreciate all the merit contained in this simple fact.* Let it be repeated that Conde was intrepid, Turenne prudent, Eugene adroit, Catinat disinterested. It is not thus that Washington will be characterized. It will be said of him, AT THE END OF A LONG CIVIL WAR, HE HAD NOTHING WITH WHICH HE COULD REPROACH HIMSELF. If any thing can be more marvellous than such a character, it is the unanimity of the public suffrages in his favour. Soldier, magistrate, people, all love and admire him; all speak of him in terms of tenderness and veneration. Does there then exist a virtue capable of restraining the injustice of mankind; or are glory and happiness too recently established in America, for Envy to have deigned to pass the seas?

In speaking of this perfect whole of which General Washington furnishes the idea, I have not excluded exterior form. His stature is noble and lofty, he is well made, and exactly proportioned; his physiognomy mild and agreeable, but such as to render it impossible to speak particularly of any of his features, so that in quitting him, you have only the recollection of a fine face. He has neither a grave nor a familiar face, his brow is sometimes marked with thought, but never with inquietude; in inspiring respect, he inspires confidence, and his smile is always the smile of benevolence.

But above all, it is in the midst of his General Officers, that it is interesting to behold him. General in a republic, he has not the imposing stateliness of a Marechal de France who gives the *order;* a hero in a republic, he excites another sort of respect, which seems to spring from the sole idea, that the safety of each individual, is attached to his person. As for the rest, I must observe on this occasion, that the General Officers of the American army, have a very military and a very becoming carriage; that even all the officers, whose characters were brought into public view, unite much politeness to a great deal of capacity; that the headquarters of this army, in short, neither present the image of want, nor inexperience. When one sees the battalion of the General's guards encamped within the precincts of his house; nine waggons, destined to carry his baggage, ranged in his court; a great number of grooms taking care of very fine horses belonging to the General Officers and their Aides de Camp; when one observes the perfect order that reigns within these precincts, where the guards are exactly stationed, and where the drums beat an alarm, and a particular retreat, one is tempted to apply to the Americans what Pyrrhus said of the Romans : *Truly these people have nothing barbarous in their discipline!*

FRANCOIS JEAN, MARQUIS DE CHASTELLUX was born at Paris, in 1734, and died there October 28, 1788. He was elected in 1775, one of the forty members of the French Academy, and in 1780 came to America as a Major General in the French army under the Count de Rochambeau. He gained the particular friendship of Washington, of whom he was a great admirer, and while on a tour through the country, passed several days with him at his headquarters near Passaic Falls, N. J., in the latter part of November, 1780. The well-known pen-portrait of Washington, in his " Voyage dans l'Amérique Septentrionale dans les Années 1780-2," Paris 1786, and which we quote from a translation published at London in 1787, closes his relation of this visit. The translator, George Greive, an Englishman, who was in

America in 1781-2, and frequently in the company of Washington, referring in a note (vol. 1, p. 139) to this portrait, says: "It is impossible for any man who has had the happiness to approach the General, not to admire the accuracy of this description, and the justness and happiness with which it is developed, or to read it without the strongest emotion. It is here above all, the translator must apologize to his author; it is not possible to do justice to the original, to feel all its elegance it must be read in the language in which it was written. Posterity, future historians, will be grateful to the Marquis de Chastellux for this exquisite portrait; every feature, and every tint of which will stand the test of the severest scrutiny, and be handed down to distant ages in never fading colours."

JEDIDIAH MORSE.

1789.

No person who had not the advantage of being present when
General Washington received the intelligence of peace, and who did
not accompany him to his domestic retirement, can describe the relief
which that joyful event brought to his labouring mind, or the supreme
satisfaction with which he withdrew to private life. From his triumphant entry into New York, upon the evacuation of that city by
the British army, to his arrival at Mount Vernon, after the resignation
of his commission to Congress, festive crowds impeded his passage
through all the populous towns; the devotion of a whole people pursued him with prayers to Heaven for blessings on his head, while
their gratitude sought the most expressive language of manifesting
itself to him as their common father and benefactor. When he became a private citizen, he had the unusual felicity to find, that his
native state was among the most zealous in doing justice to his
merits ; and that stronger demonstrations of affectionate esteem (if
possible) were given by the citizens of his neighborhood, than by any
other description of men on the continent. But he has constantly
declined accepting any compensation for his services, or provision for
the augmented expenses which have been incurred by him in consequence of his public employment, although proposals have been made

(30)

in the most delicate manner, particularly by the states of Virginia and Pennsylvania.

The virtuous simplicity which distinguishes the private life of General Washington, though less known than the dazzling splendor of his military achievements, is not less edifying in example, or worthy the attention of his countrymen. The conspicuous character he has acted on the theatre of human affairs, the uniform dignity with which he sustained his part, amidst difficulties of the most discouraging nature, and the glory of having arrived through them at the hour of triumph, have made many official and literary persons, on both sides of the ocean, ambitious of a correspondence with him. These correspondencies unavoidably engross a great portion of his time; and the communications contained in them, combined with the numerous periodical publications and news-papers which he peruses, render him as it were the *focus of political intelligence for the new world.* Nor are his conversations with well informed men less conducive to bring him acquainted with the various events which happen in different countries of the globe. Every foreigner of distinction, who travels in America, makes it a point to visit him. Members of Congress and other dignified personages do not pass his house, without calling to pay their respects. As another source of information, it may be mentioned, that many literary productions are sent to him annually, by their authors in Europe; and that there is scarcely one work written in America on any art, science, or subject, which does not seek his protection, or which is not offered to him as a token of gratitude. Mechanical inventions are frequently submitted to him for his approbation, and natural curiosities presented for his investigation. But the multiplicity of epistolary applications, often on the remains of some business which happened when he was Commander-in-Chief, sometimes on subjects foreign to his situation, frivolous in their nature, and intended merely to gratify the vanity of the writers, by drawing answers from him, is truly distressing, and almost incredible. His benignity in answering, perhaps increases the number. Did he not husband every moment to the best advantage, it would not be in his power to notice the vast variety of subjects that claim his attention. Here a minuter description of his domestic life may be expected.

To apply a life, at best but short, to the most useful purposes, he lives as he ever has done, in the unvarying habits of regularity, temperance, and industry. He rises, in winter as well as summer, at the dawn of day; and generally reads or writes some time before breakfast. He breakfasts about seven o'clock on three small Indian hoecakes, and as many dishes of tea. He rides immediately to his different farms, and remains with his labourers until a little past two o'clock, when he returns and dresses. At three he dines, commonly on a single dish, and drinks from half a pint to a pint of Madeira wine. This, with one small glass of punch, a draught of beer, and two dishes of tea (which he takes half an hour before sun-setting) constitutes his whole sustenance till the next day. Whether there be company or not, the table is always prepared, by its elegance and exuberance, for their reception; and the General remains at it for an hour after dinner, in familiar conversation and convivial hilarity. It is then that every one present is called upon to give some absent friend as a toast; the name not unfrequently awakens a pleasing remembrance of past events, and gives a new turn to the animated colloquy. General Washington is more chearful than he was in the army. Although his temper is rather of a serious cast, and his countenance commonly carries the impression of thoughtfulness, yet he perfectly relishes a pleasant story, an unaffected sally of wit, or a burlesque description, which surprises by its suddenness and incongruity with the ordinary appearance of the object described. After this sociable and innocent relaxation, he applies himself to business, and about nine o'clock retires to rest. This is the *rotine*, and this the hour he observes, when no one but his family is present; at other times, he attends politely upon his company until they wish to withdraw.

Notwithstanding he has no offspring, his actual family consists of eight persons.* It is seldom alone. He keeps a pack of hounds, and in the season indulges himself with hunting once in a week; at which diversion the gentlemen of Alexandria often assist.

Agriculture is the favourite employment of General Washington, in which he wishes to pass the remainder of his days. To acquire and communicate practical knowledge, he corresponds with Mr. Arthur Young, who has written so sensibly on the subject, and also with many agricultural gentlemen in this country. As improvement is known to be his passion, he receives envoys with rare seeds and results of new projects from every quarter. He likewise makes copious notes, relative to his own experiments, the state of the seasons, the

---

* *The family of* General Washington, *in addition to the General and his Lady, consists of* Major George Washington (*Nephew to the General and late Aid de Camp to the Marquis de la Fayette*) *with his wife, who is a niece to the General's Lady*—Col. Humphreys, *formerly Aid de Camp to the General*—Mr. Lear, *a gentleman of liberal education, private Secretary to the General—and two Grand Children of Mrs. Washington.*

5

nature of soils, the effects of different kinds of manure, and such other topics as may throw light on the farming business.

On Saturday in the afternoon, every week, reports are made by all his overseers, and registered in books kept for the purpose: so that at the end of the year, the quantity of labour and produce may be accurately known. Order and economy are established in all the departments within and without doors. His lands are enclosed in lots of equal dimensions, and crops are assigned to each for many years. Every thing is undertaken on a great scale; but with a view to introduce or augment the culture of such articles as he conceives will become most beneficial in their consequence to the country. He has raised this year, two hundred lambs, sowed twenty seven bushels of flax seed, and planted more than seven hundred bushels of potatoes. In the meantime, the publick may rest persuaded, that there is manufactured under his roof, linen and woolen cloth, nearly or quite sufficient for the use of his numerous household.

EXTRACT from a Biographical Sketch of Washington by, JEDIDIAH MORSE, D.D., in his " American Geography or a view of the present situation of the United States of America." Elizabeth-Town, (N. J.) 1789: 8vo. Dr. Morse, of whom a brief notice will be found on a succeeding page, prepared at New Haven in the twenty-third year of his age, (1784), a small geography for the use of schools, which was the first work of the kind in America. This was followed by larger geographies and gazetteers of the United States, from materials obtained by travelling and correspondence—especially that of Jeremy Belknap, the historian; Thomas Hutchins, the geographer; and Ebenezer Hazard. For thirty years no important competitor appeared in this field of literature, and translations of his works were made into the French and German languages. He has been termed the " father of American geography."

WILLIAM P. CAREY.

1789.

ABOVE the cruel views of a conqueror, who, actuated by the lust of fame, shuts his ears to the supplications of pity, and hardening his heart for the work of devastation, wars to establish a shining infamy, by the destruction of his fellow-creatures on the smoking ruins of desolated kingdoms, the great Washington fought to befriend and save mankind, in defence of whatever is most dear to the generous breast of enlightened patriotism. Distinguished, in an eminent degree, for the great qualities of the Macedonian and Swedish heroes, yet unsullied by the savage cruelty and intemperance of the one, or mad ambition and obstinacy of the other, he possessed the rare gift of uniting all the sublime talents requisite in the founder of a mighty empire, with the polished refinements of civilized society, and the softest feelings of humanity. A stranger to profusion, yet generous in every instance where liberality was a virtue; during the late troubles, his fortune was employed in succouring merit, rewarding bravery, promoting discipline in the soldiery, and subordination to the new established government, in the citizens. At a time when the calamities incident to a state of civil warfare, fell heavy on all ranks, but principally on the middle class of his countrymen, his beneficence, which seemed to shun the public eye, would in all probability be lost in oblivion, but for the voice of those whom he freed from the accu-

(35)

mulated miseries of famine, sickness, and imprisonment. Many of his good deeds are passed over by the writers of his time, amidst the striking details of battles, of sieges, and military manœuvres, with which the general curiosity is often more pleased, than with the less glaring portrait of private virtue. Born with abilities to unite the jarring interests of a number of states, and be the leader of a brave and injured people, nature has not been less favorable to him in corporeal than in mental endowments. His person is majestic and striking, his physiognomy is pre-possessing, and strongly expressive of the noble qualities of his soul: the dignity of his appearance inspires an awe, which keeps the unacquainted beholder at a respectful distance, until the easy politeness of his manner, formed to gain the affections without artifice, and the modest frankness of his conversation, fraught with judicious reflexions, founded on a thorough knowledge of human nature, insensibly banish the coldness of reserve, and induce the philosopher, the soldier, and polished gentleman, to quit his company with regret, filled with sentiments of enthusiastic reverence and admiration. * * * *

Having equalled the greatest heroes of antiquity in glory, the illustrious Washington surpassed them in virtue and exemplary moderation; when his fellow-soldiers laid aside the sword to add lustre to the arts—to cultivate their native fields, and to enrich the United States, by a beneficial commerce—when the childless father, the lone orphan, and the widowed mourner, restored to the bosom of peace, and the blessings of plenty, forgot their sorrows, and ceased to weep over the manes of their slaughtered relations—the American hero resigned his command; he refused the liberal rewards offered him by his grateful country; he was contented with the just approbation of a virtuous conscience, and quitting the splendid honors of a public life, he retired to the station of a private citizen.

In whatever light we view the character of this truly great man, we are struck with fresh cause for esteem and admiration: we every moment discover new and shining traits of humanity, of wisdom, and disinterested heroism: we see united in him the distinguished virtues of a good citizen, an experienced general, an upright senator, and a wise politician; we behold him rising superior to every mean consideration of self-love, hazarding his fortunes in the cause of freedom, chearfully submitting to bear the name of rebel, and braving an ignominious death, to which he would inevitably have fallen a sacrifice, had Britain triumphed in the contest: we behold him furnishing an example the most glorious to the world, the most animating to the nations which yet groan beneath the arm of oppression, an example the most interesting to humanity, and capable of nerving the palsied arm of age, or even of cowardice itself: we behold him like another Aaron, the sacred delegate of heaven, leading to the field a brave but ill appointed and new-raised army, to contend with the ablest generals and best disciplined troops of the mightiest empire in the universe: we behold him often without money, and ill supplied with provisions, braving the accumulated severities of an American winter's campaign, inuring his soldiers to fatigue, and training them by the practice of military evolutions, to defeat the attacks of a powerful enemy: we view him stedfastly pursuing the great line of conduct which he had marked out at the commencement of hostilities, mitigating the calamities of war, preventing the effusion of human blood, wasting the forces of his adversaries, tiring out the British nation by avoiding a decisive action, and finally triumphing over every obstacle which seemed insurmountably to oppose the progress of his arms, and the freedom of his country. The rash and unthinking, who estimate a commander by the multitudes whom he has destroyed, by the cities which he has sacked, and the provinces which he has desolated, may choose some ferocious conqueror for the idol of their reverence. The philanthropist, who laments the miseries which fall on mankind, by the usurpation and ambition of kings, and the philosopher, who judges of the abilities of a general by the tenor of his plans; and their consistence with his situation and resources, will not hesitate to pronounce the Great Washington equal, if not superior to the most shining characters in ancient or modern history.

WILLIAM PAULETT CAREY, a native of Ireland, was born in 1768. He became a resident of England, and distinguished himself as an able advocate of political reform, and as the author of many critical and poetical contributions to the periodicals of the day. He died in 1830. The sketch from which we make the above extract, was written in Dublin for a periodical entitled the *Miscellanist*, and was subsequently printed May, 1789, in Vol. V. of the *American Museum*, published at Philadelphia, by his brother Mathew Carey, the eminent philanthropist, writer and publisher of that city. It will also be found in *Washingtoniana*, Baltimore, 1800.

BRISSOT DE WARVILLE.

1791.

SCARCELY had I arrived at Alexandria, (Nov. 1788,) when I hastened to pay a visit to Mount Vernon, the beautiful seat of General Washington, which is situated at the distance of ten miles lower on the river. To arrive at it, you must cross a great deal of wood, and after passing two eminences, you discover a delightful and elegantly simple habitation. Before it there is a lawn, kept in excellent order. On one side are the stables, and on the other a green-house and buildings, in which the negroes are employed. In a kind of farm-yard you perceive turkeys, geese, ducks, and other kinds of poultry. From this mansion, which commands a view of the Potowmac, there is a most enchanting prospect; on this side there is a very high and extensive portico. The distribution of the whole edifice is very judicious and convenient. On the outside it is covered with a kind of varnished plaster, which renders it impenetrable to water. The General did not arrive till the evening. He returned very much fatigued, from a tour into part of his estates through which he was making a road. You have often heard him compared to Cincinnatus; the comparison is just. This celebrated General is at present only a plain farmer, continually employed in looking after his farm, as he calls it; in improving the cultivation of it, and in building barns. He showed me one which he had erected. It is an immense

(39)

building, about an hundred feet long, and proportionably broad. It was intended to contain his grain, his potatoes, turnips, etc. Around it he has caused stables to be constructed for all his cattle, horses, and asses, the breed of which, unknown in this country, he is endeavoring to increase. This building is so properly laid out, that a man may fill the rack in a short time, without any danger. The General told me that he had built it after a plan sent to him by that celebrated English farmer Arthur Young; but that he had made considerable improvements. This building is of brick, made upon the spot. Except the joists and shingles which cover the roof, and which he was obliged to purchase, because he was pressed for time, all the materials were procured in the neighborhood. He told me that this barn cost him no more than three hundred pounds: In France it would have cost more than 80.000 livres. This year he had sown seven hundred bushels of potatoes. All this was new in Virginia, where the people have neither barns nor provisions for their cattle.

His horses, asses, and mules, were ranging about in the adjacent pastures. He told us that he intended to give to his country the example of forming artificial meadows, which are there so rare, yet so necessary, as the cattle in winter are often in want of provisions. His mules thrive extremely well. He had a superb stallion, which will preserve the breed of horses in that province. He showed us two beautiful mules, one of which was brought from Malta, and the other from Spain.

His three hundred negroes were distributed in log houses, scattered over his estate, which, in this place, contains about ten thousand acres.

Colonel Humphreys, the poet, who lives with him as his secretary, assured me that his various estates, in different places, contain more than two hundred thousand acres.

The General sent to England for an experienced English farmer, together with his family, and has entrusted him with the management of his whole farm.

In the General's house every thing is simple. His table is good, but void of pomp; regularity appears throughout all of his domestic economy. Mrs. Washington presides over the whole, and unites to the qualities of an excellent farmer's wife, that simple dignity which ought to characterize a woman whose husband has acted so distinguished a part. She is remarkable also for that politeness, and attention to strangers, which render hospitality so sweet. The same virtues are conspicuous in her interesting niece, who unfortunately appears not to enjoy good health.

You have often heard me blame M. Chatellux for putting too much sprightliness in the character he has drawn of this general. To give pretensions to the portrait of a man who has none is truly absurd. The General's goodness appears in his looks. They have nothing of that brilliancy which his officers found in them when he was at the head of his army; but in conversation they become animated. He has no characteristic traits in his figure, and this has rendered it always so difficult to describe it: there are few portraits which resemble him. All his answers are pertinent; he shows the utmost reserve, and is very diffident; but, at the same time, he is firm and unchangeable in whatever he undertakes. His modesty must be very astonishing,

6

especially to a Frenchman.* He speaks of the American war as if he had not directed it; and of his victories with an indifference which strangers even would not affect. I never saw him divest himself of that coolness by which he is characterized, and become warm but when speaking of the present state of America. The divisions of his country harrow up his soul; he sees the necessity of collecting all the friends of liberty around one central point, and of giving energy to government. He is still ready to sacrifice that repose which forms his happiness. There is no happiness, said he to me, in grandeur, and the tumults of life. This philosopher was so convinced of the above truth, that from the moment of his retreat he entirely gave up political correspondence, and renounced all his places—and notwithstanding this self denial, disinterestedness, and modesty, this astonishing man has enemies. He has been attacked in newspapers, and accused of ambition and forming intrigues, when his whole life, and all America, can bear testimony to his uprightness and the integrity of his actions. Virginia, I believe, is the only country in which he has enemies; every where else I never heard his name pronounced but with a mixture of respect, gratitude, and affection. The Americans seem to consider him as their father. Washington, perhaps, is not to be compared to the most celebrated warriors, but he is the model of a republican; he possesses all the qualities and virtues of one.

He spoke to me of M. La Fayette with tenderness. He regarded

---

* Tacitus has given a portrait of Germanicus, in which we find many traits of Washington—*Tanta illi comitas in socios, mansuetudo in hostes, visu que auditu juxta venerabilis, cum magnitudinem, et gravitatem summæ fortunæ retineret, invidiam et adrogantiam effugerat.*

him as his son; and foresaw with a joy mixed with anxiety, the part he was about to play in the revolution preparing in France; he could not predict, with clearness the issue of this revolution. If, on the one side, he knew the ardor of the French in rushing into extremes, he knew on the other, their profound idolatry for their ancient government, and for those monarchs whose inviolability appeared to him a strange idea.

After having passed about three days in the house of this celebrated man, who loaded me with civilities, and gave me much information respecting both the late war and the present situation of the United States, I returned with regret to Alexandria.

JEAN PIERRE BRISSOT was born at the village of Ouarville, France, January 14, 1754. He studied for the legal profession, which he early abandoned for politics and literature, and was thrown into the Bastile for a short time in 1784, on a charge of libel. He afterwards visited Geneva and England, and in 1788 came to America, but intelligence having reached him of the rapid progress liberty was making in France, he returned to his native country the following year. His "Nouveau Voyage dans les Etats-Unis de l'Amerique Septentrionale, fait en 1788," from Vol. 11 of which we translate the recital of his visit to Mount Vernon, was published at Paris in 1791. The work which attracted much attention for its candour and accuracy, was translated and published at London, Dublin and New York, in 1792. 8vo. Brissot added to his name (to distinguish himself from an elder brother), *de Warville*, from his native place, substituting the English *W* for the French dipthong *Ou*. He was accused by Robespierre, and guillotined at Paris, October 31, 1793.

CHARLES JAMES FOX.

1794.

And here, Sir, I cannot help alluding to the President of the United States, General Washington, a character whose conduct has been so different from that, which has been pursued by the ministers of this country. How infinitely wiser must appear the spirit and principles manifested in his late address to Congress, than the policy of modern European courts! Illustrious man, deriving honor less from the splendor of his situation than from the dignity of his mind; before whom all borrowed greatness sinks into insignificance, and all the potentates of Europe (excepting the members of our own royal family) become little and contemptible! He has had no occasion to have recourse to any tricks of policy or arts of alarm; his authority has been sufficiently supported by the same means by which it was acquired, and his conduct has uniformly been characterized by wisdom, moderation, and firmness. Feeling gratitude to France for the assistance received from her in that great contest, which secured the independence of America, he did not choose to give up the system of neutrality. Having once laid down that line of conduct, which both gratitude and policy pointed out as most proper to be pursued, not all the insults and provocation of the French minister, Genet, could turn him from his purpose. Intrusted with the welfare of a great people, he did not allow the misconduct of another, with respect to himself, for one

(44)

moment to withdraw his attention from their interest. He had no fear of the Jacobins, he felt no alarm from their principles, and considered no precaution as necessary in order to stop their progress.

The people over whom he presided he knew to be acquainted with their rights and their duties. He trusted to their own good sense to defeat the effect of those arts, which might be employed to inflame or mislead their minds; and was sensible, that a government could be in no danger, while it retained the attachment and confidence of its subjects; attachment, in this instance, not blindly adopted; confidence not implicitly given, but arising from the conviction of its excellence, and the experience of its blessings. I cannot, indeed, help admiring the wisdom and fortune of this great man. By the phrase 'fortune' I mean not in the smallest degree to derogate from his merit. But, notwithstanding his extraordinary talents and exalted integrity, it must be considered as singularly fortunate, that he should have experienced a lot, which so seldom falls to the portion of humanity, and have passed through such a variety of scenes without stain and without reproach. It must, indeed, create astonishment, that, placed in circumstances so critical, and filling for a series of years a station so conspicuous, his character should never once have been called in question; that he should in no one instance have been accused either of improper insolence, or of mean submission, in his transactions with foreign nations. For him it has been reserved to run the race of glory, without experiencing the smallest interruption to the brilliancy of his career.

Charles James Fox, termed by Burke "the most brilliant and successful debater the world ever saw," was born in London, January 24, 1749, and died at Chiswick, September 13, 1806. He was educated at Eton and Oxford, and was distinguished for ability both at school and college. He entered parliament at the age of nineteen, and during the whole course of our revolutionary war, was a strenuous opponent of the coercive measures adopted by the English government, and a most powerful advocate of the claims of the colonists. Our extract is from some remarks made in parliament January 31, 1794, in allusion to Washington's communications to Congress (Dec. 3, 1793), comprising the reasons for the course he had pursued respecting foreign powers. In the introductory chapter to his " History of the early part of the reign of James the Second," published in 1808, Mr. Fox also says: "A character of virtues so happily tempered by one another, and so wholly unalloyed with any vices, as that of Washington, is hardly to be found in the pages of history."

HENRY WANSEY.

1794.

June 6, (1794,) I had the honor of an interview with the President of the United States, to whom I was introduced by Mr. Dandridge, his secretary. He received me very politely, and after reading my letters, I was asked to breakfast. There was very little of the ceremony of courts, the Americans will not permit this; nor does the disposition of his Excellency lead him to assume it.

I confess, I was struck with awe and veneration, when I recollected that I was now in the presence of one of the greatest men upon earth—the Great Washington—the noble and wise benefactor of the world! as Mirabeau styles him;—the advocate of human nature—the friend of both worlds. Whether we view him as a general in the field, vested with unlimited authority and power, at the head of a victorious army; or in the cabinet, as the President of the United States; or as a private gentleman, cultivating his own farm; he is still the same great man, anxious only to discharge with propriety the duties of his relative situation. His conduct has always been so uniformly manly, honorable, just, patriotic, and disinterested, that his greatest enemies cannot fix on' any one trait of his character that can deserve the least censure. His paternal regard for the army while he commanded it; his earnest and sincere desire to accomplish the glorious object for which they were contending; his endurance of the toils and hazards of war, without ever receiving the least emolument from his country; and his retirement to private life after the peace, plainly evince, that his motives were the most pure and patriotic, that could proceed from a benevolent heart. His letters to congress during the war, now lately published in England, as well as his circular letter and farewell orders to the armies of the United States, at the end of the war, shew him to have been justly ranked among the fine writers of the age. When we look down from this truly great and illustrious character, upon other public servants, we find a glaring contrast; nor can we fix our attention upon any other great men, without discovering in them a vast and mortifying dissimilarity!

The President in his person, is tall and thin, but erect; rather of an engaging than a dignified presence. He appears very thoughtful, is slow in delivering himself, which occasions some to conclude him reserved, but it is rather, I apprehend, the effect of much thinking and reflection, for there is great appearance to me of affability and accommodation. He was at this time in his sixty-third year, being born February 11, 1732, O. S. but he has very little the appearance of age, having been all his life-time so exceeding temperate. There is a certain anxiety visible in his countenance, with marks of extreme sensibility. * * * *

Mrs. Washington herself made tea and coffee for us. On the table were two small plates of sliced tongue, dry toast, bread and butter, etc. but no broiled fish, as is the general custom. Miss Custis, her grand-daughter, a very pleasing young lady, of about sixteen, sat next to her, and her brother George Washington Custis, about two years older than herself. There was but little appearance of form:

one servant only attended, who had no livery; a silver urn for hot water, was the only article of expence on the table. She appears something older than the President, though, I understand, they were both born in the same year; short in stature, rather robust; very plain in her dress, wearing a very plain cap, with her grey hair closely turned up under it. She has routs or levees, (which ever the people chuses to call them) every Wednesday and Saturday at Philadelphia, during the sitting of Congress. But the Anti-federalists object even to these, as tending to give a supereminency, and introductory to the paraphernalia of courts.

HENRY WANSEY, a Wiltshire clothier, who died at Warminster, England, July 19, 1827, at the age of seventy-five, travelled in this country in 1794, and when in Philadelphia took breakfast with Washington, as above mentioned. Mr. Wansey kept a journal of his trip, which was afterwards published at Salisbury, in 1796, with the title, "The Journal of an Excursion to the United States of North America in the summer of 1794," 8vo., from which our extract is made. A second edition appeared in 1798, the title slightly different.

ISAAC WELD.

1796.

On this day, (February 22. 1796,) General Washington terminated his sixty-fourth year; but though not an unhealthy man, he seemed considerably older. The innumerable vexations he has met with in his different public capacities have very sensibly impaired the vigour of his constitution, and given him an aged appearance. There is a very material difference, however, in his looks when seen in private and when he appears in public full drest; in the latter case the hand of art makes up for the ravages of time, and he seems many years younger.

Few persons find themselves for the first time in the presence of General Washington, a man so renowned in the present day for his wisdom and moderation, and whose name will be transmitted with such honour to posterity, without being impressed with a certain degree of veneration and awe; nor do these emotions subside on a closer acquaintance; on the contrary, his person and deportment are such as rather tend to augment them. There is something very austere in his countenance, and in his manners he is uncommonly reserved. I have heard some officers, that served immediately under his command during the American war, say, that they never saw him smile during all the time that they were with him. No man has ever yet been connected with him by the reciprocal and unconstrained ties of friendship; and

(50)

but a few can boast even of having been on an easy and familiar footing with him.

The height of his person is about five feet eleven; his chest is full; and his limbs, though rather slender, well shaped and muscular. His head is small, in which respect he resembles the make of a great number of his countrymen. His eyes are of a light grey colour; and in proportion to the length of his face, his nose is long. Mr. Stewart, the eminent portrait painter, told me, that there are features in his face totally different from what he ever observed in that of any other human being; the sockets for the eyes, for instance, are larger than what he ever met with before, and the upper part of the nose broader. All his features, he observed, were indicative of the strongest and most ungovernable passions, and had he been born in the forests, it was his opinion that he would have been the fiercest man among the savage tribes. In this Mr. Stewart has given proof of his great discernment and intimate knowledge of the human countenance; for although General Washington has been extolled for his great moderation and calmness, during the very trying situations in which he has so often been placed, yet those who have been acquainted with him the longest and most intimately say, that he is by nature a man of a fierce and irritable disposition, but that, like Socrates, his judgment and great self-command have always made him appear a man of a different cast in the eyes of the world. He speaks with great diffidence, and sometimes hesitates for a word; but it is always to find one particularly well adapted to his meaning. His language is manly and expressive. At levee his discourse with strangers turns principally upon the subject of America; and if they have been through any remarkable places, his conversation is free and particularly interesting, as he is intimately acquainted with every part of the country. He is much more open and free in his behaviour at levee than in private, and in the company of ladies, still more so than when solely with men.

General Washington gives no public dinners or other entertainments, except to those who are in diplomatic capacities, and to a few families on terms of intimacy with Mrs. Washington. Strangers with whom he wishes to have some conversation about agriculture, or any such subject, are sometimes invited to tea. This by many is attributed to his saving disposition; but it is more just to ascribe it to his prudence and foresight; for as the salary of the president, as I have before observed, is very small, and totally inadequate by itself to support an expensive style of life, were he to give numerous and splendid entertainments the same might possibly be expected from subsequent presidents, who, if their private fortunes were not considerable, would be unable to live in the same style, and might be exposed to many ill-natured observations, from the relinquishment of what the people had been accustomed to; it is most likely also that General Washington has been actuated by these motives, because in his private capacity at Mount Vernon every stranger meets with a hospitable reception from him.

General Washington's self-moderation is well known to the world already. It is a remarkable circumstance, which redounds to his eternal honour, that while president of the United States he never appointed one of his own relations to any office of trust or emolument, although he has several that are men of abilities, and well qualified to fill the most important stations in the government.

Isaac Weld was born in Dublin, 1774, and died in 1856. He travelled quite extensively in America, and was in Philadelphia, February 22, 1796, Washington's birthday, and writes that the city was unusually gay, every person of consequence in it, Quakers alone excepted, making it a point to visit the General, in its honor. The audience lasted from eleven o'clock in the morning, till three in the afternoon, and a public ball and supper terminated the rejoicings of the day. His travels were published at London in 1799, with the title, "Travels through the States of North America, and the provinces of Upper and Lower Canada during the years 1795, 1796 and 1797," 4to., and from which we quote. A number of two vol. editions were subsequently issued, and it was also translated into French and German.

JOHN MARSHALL.

1799.

REMARKS MADE IN THE HOUSE OF REPRESENTATIVES, DECEMBER 19, 1799, ON PRESENT-ING THE RESOLUTIONS PREPARED BY HENRY LEE, ON THE DEATH OF WASHINGTON.

THE melancholy event which was yesterday announced with doubt, has been rendered but too certain.   Our Washington is no more! The Hero, the Sage, and the Patriot of America—the man on whom in times of danger, every eye was turned, and all hopes were placed,—lives now, only in his own great actions, and in the hearts of an affectionate and afflicted people.

If, sir, it had even not been usual, openly to testify respect for the memory of those whom Heaven had selected as its instruments, for dispensing good to men, yet, such has been the uncommon worth, and such the extraordinary incidents which have marked the life of him whose loss we all deplore, that the whole American nation, impelled by the same feelings, would call with one voice for a public manifestation of that sorrow which is so deep and universal.

More than any other individual, and as much as to one individual was possible, has he contributed to found this our wide spreading empire, and to give to the western world its independence and its freedom.

Having effected the great object for which he was placed at the

(54)

head of our armies, we have seen him converting the sword into the ploughshare, and voluntarily sinking the soldier in the citizen.

When the debility of our federal system had become manifest, and the bonds which connected the parts of this vast continent were dissolving, we have seen him the Chief of those patriots who formed for us a Constitution, which, by preserving the Union, will, I trust, substantiate and perpetuate those blessings which our Revolution had promised to bestow.

In obedience to the general voice of his country, calling on him to preside over a great people, we have seen him once more quit the retirement he loved, and in a season more stormy and tempestuous than war itself, with calm and wise determination, pursue the true interests of the nation and contribute, more than any other could contribute, to the establishment of that system of policy which will, I trust, yet preserve our peace, our honour, and our independence.

Having been twice unanimously chosen the chief magistrate of a free people, we see him at a time, when his re-election with the universal suffrage, could not have been doubted, affording to the world a rare instance of moderation, by withdrawing from his high station to the peaceful walks of private life.

However the public confidence may change, and the public affections fluctuate with respect to others, yet with respect to him they have in war and in peace, in public and in private life, been as steady as his own firm mind, and as constant as his own exalted virtues.

Let us then, Mr. Speaker, pay the last tribute of respect and affection to our departed friend—let the Grand Council of the nation display those sentiments which the nation feels. For which purpose I hold in my hand some resolutions which I take the liberty to offer to the House.

RESOLUTIONS.

"The House of Representatives of the United States, having received intelligence of the death of their highly valued fellow citizen George Washington, general of the armies of the United States; and sharing the universal grief this distressing event must produce, *unanimously resolve:*

1. That this House will wait on the President of the United States, in condolence of this national calamity.

2. That the Speaker's chair be shrouded with black, and that the members and officers of the House wear mourning, during the session.

3. That a joint committee, of both Houses, be appointed to report measures suitable to the occasion, and expressive of the profound sorrow with which Congress is penetrated on the loss of a citizen, first in war, first in peace, and first in the hearts of his countrymen."

SENATE OF THE UNITED STATES.

1799.

ADDRESS OF CONDOLENCE, DECEMBER 23D, 1799, TO THE PRESIDENT OF THE UNITED STATES, ON THE DEATH OF GENERAL GEORGE WASHINGTON. THE ADDRESS WAS REPORTED TO THE SENATE BY MR. DEXTER, FROM THE COMMITTEE APPOINTED FOR THE PURPOSE, DEC. 19TH. THE COMMITTEE WAS COMPOSED OF SAMUEL DEXTER OF MASSACHUSETTS, JAMES ROSS OF PENNSYLVANIA, AND JACOB READ OF SOUTH CAROLINA.

THE Senate of the United States respectfully take leave, Sir, to express to you their deep regret for the loss their country sustains in the death of General George Washington.

This event, so distressing to all our fellow-citizens, must be peculiarly heavy to you, who have long been associated with him in deeds of patriotism. Permit us, sir, to mingle our tears with yours; on this occasion it is manly to weep. To lose such a man, at such a crisis, is no common calamity to the world: our country mourns her father. The Almighty disposer of human events has taken from us our greatest benefactor and ornament. It becomes us to submit with reverence to him, who "maketh darkness his pavilion."

With patriotic pride, we review the life of our Washington, and compare him with those of other countries who have been pre-eminent in fame. Ancient and modern names are diminished before him. Greatness and guilt have too often been allied; but his fame is whiter

8   (57)

than it is brilliant.   The destroyers of nations stood abashed at the majesty of his virtue.   It reproved the intemperance of their ambition, and darkened the splendor of victory.   The scene is closed, and we are no longer anxious least misfortune should sully his glory; he has travelled on to the end of his journey, and carried with him an increasing weight of honor; he has deposited it safely, where misfortune cannot tarnish it, where malice cannot blast it.   Favoured of heaven, he departed without exhibiting the weakness of humanity.   Magnanimous in death, the darkness of the grave could not obscure his brightness.

Such was the man whom we deplore.   Thanks to God! his glory is consummated; Washington yet lives—on earth in his spotless example—his spirit is in Heaven.

Let his countrymen consecrate the memory of the heroic General, the patriotic Statesman, and the virtuous Sage; let them teach their children never to forget that the fruit of his labours and his example, are their inheritance.

JOHN ADAMS.

1799.

Answer to the address of condolence of the Senate of the United States, December 23d, 1799, on the death of General George Washington.

I receive, with the most respectful and affectionate sentiments, in this impressive address, the obliging expressions of your regard for the loss our country has sustained, in the death of her most esteemed, beloved, and admired citizen.

In the multitude of my thoughts and recollections on this melancholy event, you will permit me only to say, that I have seen him in the days of adversity, in some of the scenes of his deepest distress and most trying perplexities; I have also attended him in his highest elevation and most prosperous felicity; with uniform admiration of his wisdom, moderation, and constancy.

Among all our original Associates in that memorable league of the continent in 1774, which first expressed the sovereign will of a free nation in America, he was the only one remaining in the general government. Although, with a constitution more enfeebled than his, at an age when he thought it necessary to prepare for retirement, I feel myself alone, bereaved of my last brother; yet I derive a strong consolation from the unanimous disposition, which appears in all ages and classes to mingle their sorrows with mine, on this common calamity to the world.

(59)

The life of our Washington cannot suffer by a comparison with those of other countries, who have been most celebrated and exalted by fame. The attributes and decorations of royalty, could have only served to eclipse the majesty of those virtues which made him, from being a modest citizen, a more resplendent luminary. Misfortune, had he lived, could hereafter have sullied his glory only with those superficial minds, who, believing that characters and actions are marked by success alone, rarely deserve to enjoy it. Malice could never blast his honour, and envy made him a singular exception to her universal rule.

For himself he had lived enough, to life and to glory. For his fellow-citizens, if their prayers could have been answered, he would have been immortal. For me, his departure is at a most unfortunate moment. Trusting, however, in the wise and righteous dominion of Providence over the passions of men, and the results of their councils and actions, as well as over their lives, nothing remains for me, but humble resignation.

His example is now complete, and it will teach wisdom and virtue to magistrates, citizens, and men, not only in the present age, but in future generations, as long as our history shall be read. If a Trajan found a Pliny, a Marcus Aurelius can never want Biographers, Eulogists, or Historians.

IN an address to the Senate on a previous occasion, when taking the chair as Vice-President of the United States, April 21st, 1789, JOHN ADAMS alluded to Washington in the following terms: "Were I blessed with powers to do justice to his character, it would be impossible to increase the confidence or affection of his country, or make the smallest addition to his glory . . . . May, I, nevertheless, be indulged to inquire, if we look over the catalogue of the first magistrates of nations, whether they have been denominated presidents or consuls, kings or princes, where shall we find one, whose commanding talents and virtues, whose overruling good fortune, have so completely united all hearts and voices in his favor, who enjoyed the esteem and admiration of foreign nations and fellow citizens with equal unanimity? Qualities so uncommon, are no common blessings to the country that possesses them. By those great qualities, and their benign effects, has Providence marked out the head of this nation with a hand, so distinctly visible, as to have been seen by all men, and mistaken by none."

And again, in his inaugural address to both Houses of Congress, as President, March 4th, 1797, Mr. Adams referred to the Presidency of Washington, as "the administration of a citizen, who, by a long course of great actions regulated by prudence, justice, temperance, and fortitude, conducting a people, inspired with the same virtue, and animated with the same ardent patriotism and love of liberty, to independence and peace, to increasing wealth and unexampled prosperity, has merited the gratitude of his fellow-citizens, commanded the highest praises of foreign nations, and secured immortal glory with posterity."

HENRY LEE.

1799.

In obedience to your will,* I rise your humble organ, with the hope of executing a part of the system of public mourning which you have been pleased to adopt, commemorative of the death of the most illustrious and most beloved personage this country has ever produced; and which, while it transmits to posterity your sense of the awful event, faintly represents your knowledge of the consummate excellence you so cordially honour.

Desperate indeed is any attempt on earth to meet correspondently this dispensation of heaven; for, while with pious resignation we submit to the will of an all-gracious Providence, we can never cease lamenting, in our finite view of Omnipotent wisdom, the heart-rending privation for which our nation weeps. When the civilized world shakes to its centre; when every moment gives birth to strange and momentous changes; when our peaceful quarter of the globe, exempt as it happily has been from any share in the slaughter of the human race, may yet be compelled to abandon her pacific policy, and to risk the doleful casualities of war: what limit is there to the extent of our loss?—None within the reach of my words to express; none which your feelings will not disavow.

The founder of our federate republic—our bulwark in war, our

* The two Houses of Congress.

(62)

guide in peace, is no more! Oh that this were but questionable! Hope, the comforter of the wretched, would pour into our agonizing hearts its balmy dew. But, alas! there is no hope for us; our Washington is removed for ever! Possessing the stoutest frame and purest mind, he had passed nearly to his sixty-eighth year, in the enjoyment of high health, when habituated by his care of us to neglect himself, a slight cold disregarded, became inconvenient on Friday, oppressive on Saturday, and defying every medical interposition, before the morning of Sunday, put an end to the best of men. An end did I say?—his fame survives! bounded only by the limits of the earth, and by the extent of the human mind. He survives in our hearts, in the growing knowledge of our children, in the affection of the good, throughout the world; and when our monuments shall be done away; when nations now existing shall be no more; when even our young and far-spreading empire shall have perished, still will our Washington's glory unfaded shine, and die not, until love of virtue cease on earth, or earth itself sinks into chaos.

How, my fellow citizens, shall I single to your grateful hearts his pre-eminent worth! Where shall I begin in opening to your view a character throughout sublime! Shall I speak of his warlike achievements, all springing from obedience to his country's will—all directed to his country's good?

Will you go with me to the banks of the Mongahela, to see your youthful Washington, supporting, in the dismal hour of Indian victory, the ill-fated Braddock; and saving by his judgement and by his valour, the remains of a defeated army, pressed by the conquering savage foe? or, when—oppressed America nobly resolving to risk her all in deſence of her violated rights—he was elevated by the unanimous voice of Congress to the command of her armies? Will you follow him to the high grounds of Boston, where to an undisciplined, courageous, and virtuous yeomanry, his presence gave the stability of system, and infused the invincibility of love of country? or shall I carry you to the painful scenes of Long Island, York Island, and New-Jersey, when, combating superior and gallant armies, aided by powerful fleets, and led by chiefs high in the roll of ſame, he stood the bulwark of our ſafety; undismayed by disaster; unchanged by change of fortune? Or will you view him in the precarious fields of Trenton, where deep gloom unnerving every arm, reigned triumphant through our thinned, worn down, unaided ranks; himself unmoved? Dreadful was the night! It was about this time of winter—the storm raged—the Delaware, rolling furiously with floating ice, forbad the approach of man.   Washington, self-collected, viewed the tremendous scene: his country called; unappalled by surrounding dangers, he passed to the hostile shore; he fought; he conquered.   The morning sun cheered the American world.   Our country rose on the event; and her dauntless Chief pursuing his blow, completed in the lawns of Princeton, what his vast soul had conceived on the shores of Delaware.

Thence to the strong grounds of Morristown he led his small but gallant band; and through an eventful winter, by the high efforts of his genius, whose matchless force was measurable only by the growth of difficulties, he held in check formidable hostile legions, conducted by a chief experienced in the art of war, and ſamed for his valour on the ever-memorable heights of Abraham, where fell Wolfe, Montcalm, and since our much-lamented Montgomery—all covered with glory.

In this fortunate interval, produced by his masterly conduct, our fathers, ourselves, animated by his resistless example, rallied around our country's standard, and continued to follow her beloved Chief through the various and trying scenes to which the destinies of our union led.

Who is there that has forgotten the vales of Brandywine—the fields of Germantown—or the plains of Monmouth? Every where present, wants of every kind obstructing, numerous and valiant armies encountering, himself a host, he assuaged our sufferings, limited our privations, and upheld our tottering Republic. Shall I display to you the spread of the fire of his soul, by rehearsing the praises of the Hero of Saratoga, and his much lov'd compeer of the Carolinas? No! our Washington wears not borrowed glory: To Gates—to Greene—he gave without reserve the applause due to their eminent merit; and long may the Chiefs of Saratoga, and of Eutaws, receive the grateful respect of a grateful people.

Moving in his own orbit, he imparted heat and light to his most distant satellites; and combining the physical and moral force of all within his sphere, with irresistible weight he took his course, commiserating folly, disdaining vice, dismaying treason, and invigorating despondency; until the auspicious hour arrived, when, united with the intrepid forces of a potent and magnanimous ally, he brought to submission the since conquerer of India; thus finishing his long career of military glory with a lustre corresponding to his great name, and in this his last act of war affixing the seal of fate to our nation's birth.

To the horrid din of battle sweet peace succeeded; and our virtuous Chief, mindful only of the common good, in a moment tempting

9

personal aggrandizement, hushed the discontents of growing sedition; and, surrendering his power into the hands from which he had received it, converted his sword into a ploughshare; teaching an admiring world that to be truly great, you must be truly good.

Were I to stop here, the picture would be incomplete, and the task imposed unfinished—Great as was our Washington in war, and as much as did that greatness contribute to produce the American Republic, it is not in war alone his pre-eminence stands conspicuous: His various talents, combining all the capacities of a statesman with those of a soldier, fitted him alike to guide the councils and the armies of our nation.   Scarcely had he rested from his martial toils, while his invaluable parental advice was still sounding in our ears, when he who had been our shield and our sword, was called forth to act a less splendid but more important part.

Possessing a clear and penetrating mind, a strong and sound judgment, calmness and temper for deliberation, with invincible firmness and perseverance in resolutions maturely formed, drawing information from all, acting from himself, with incorruptible integrity and unvarying patriotism: his own superiority and the public confidence alike marked him as the man designed by heaven to lead in the great political as well as military events which have distinguished the era of his life.

The finger of an over-ruling Providence, pointing at Washington, was neither mistaken nor unobserved; when, to realize the vast hopes to which our revolution had given birth, a change of political system became indispensable.

How novel, how grand the spectacle! Independent States stretched over an immense territory, and known only by common difficulty, clinging to their union as the rock of their safety, deciding by frank comparison of their relative condition, to rear on that rock, under the guidance of reason, a common government; through whose commanding protection, liberty and order, with their long train of blessings, should be safe to themselves, and the sure inheritance of their posterity.

This arduous task devolved on citizens selected by the people, from knowledge of their wisdom and confidence in their virtue. In this august assembly of sages and of patriots, Washington of course was found; and, as if acknowledged to be most wise, where all were wise, with one voice he was declared their Chief. How well he merited this rare distinction, how faithful were the labours of himself and his compatriots, the work of their hands and our union, strength and prosperity, the fruits of that work, best attest.

But to have essentially aided in presenting to his country this consummation of her hopes, neither satisfied the claims of his fellow-citizens on his talents, nor those duties which the possession of those talents imposed. Heaven had not infused into his mind such an uncommon share of its etherial spirit to remain unemployed, nor bestowed on him his genius unaccompanied with the corresponding duty of devoting it to the common good. To have framed a constitution, was shewing only, without realizing, the general happiness. This great work remained to be done; and America, steadfast in her preference, with one voice summoned her beloved Washington, unpractised as he was in the duties of civil administration, to execute this last act in the completion of the national felicity. Obedient to her call, he assumed the high office with that self-distrust peculiar to his innate modesty,

the constant attendant of pre-eminent virtue. What was the burst of
joy through our anxious land on this exhilerating event is known to
us all. The aged, the young, the brave, the fair, rivalled each other in
demonstrations of their gratitude; and this high-wrought delightful
scene was heightened in its effect, by the singular contest between the
zeal of the bestowers and the avoidance of the receiver of the honours
bestowed. Commencing his administration,—what heart is not charmed
with the recollection of the pure and wise principles announced by
himself, as the basis of his political life. He best understood the in-
dissoluble union between virtue and happiness, between duty and advantage, between the genuine maxims of an honest and magnanimous
policy, and the solid rewards of public prosperity and individual felicity;
watching with an equal and comprehensive eye over this great assemblage of communities and interests, he laid the foundations of our national policy in the unerring immutable principles of morality based
on religion; exemplifying the pre-eminence of a free government, by
all the attributes which win the affections of its citizens, or command
the respect of the world.

"O fortunatus nimium, sua si bona norint!"

Leading through the complicated difficulties produced by previous obligations and conflicting interests, seconded by succeeding
Houses of Congress enlightened and patriotic, he surmounted all original obstruction, and brightened the path of our national felicity.

The Presidential term expiring, his solicitude to exchange exaltation for humility returned with a force increased with increase of age;
and he had prepared his farewell address to his countrymen, proclaim-

ing his intention, when the united interposition of all around him, enforced by the eventful prospects of the epoch, produced a further sacrifice of inclination to duty. The election of President followed, and Washington, by the unanimous vote of the nation, was called to resume the Chief Magistracy. What a wonderful fixture of confidence! which attracts most our admiration, a people so correct, or a citizen combining an assemblage of talents forbidding rivalry, and stifling even envy itself! Such a nation ought to be happy; such a chief must be for ever revered.

War, long menaced by the Indian tribes, now broke out; and the terrible conflict, deluging Europe with blood, began to shed its baneful influence over our happy land. To the first, outstretching his invincible arm, under the orders of the gallant Wayne, the American Eagle soared triumphant through distant forests. Peace followed victory; and the melioration of the condition of the enemy followed peace—Godlike virtue, which uplifts even the subdued savage!

To the second, he opposed himself. New and delicate was the conjuncture, and great was the stake. Soon did his penetrating mind discern and seize the only course, continuing to us all the felicity enjoyed. He issued his proclamation of neutrality. This index to his whole subsequent conduct was sanctioned by the approbation of both Houses of Congress, and by the approving voice of the people.

To this sublime policy he inviolably adhered, unmoved by foreign intrusion, unshaken by domestic turbulence.

> "Justum et tenacem propositi virum,
> Non civium ardor prava jubentium,
> Non vultus instantis tyranni,
> Mente quatit solida."

Maintaining his pacific system at the expense of no duty, America, faithful to herself, and unstained in her honour, continued to enjoy the delights of peace, while afflicted Europe mourns in every quarter under the accumulated miseries of an unexampled war; miseries in which our happy country must have shared, had not our pre-eminent Washington been as firm in council as he was brave in the field.

Pursuing steadfastly his course, he held safe the public happiness, preventing foreign war, and quelling internal discord, till the revolving period of a third election approached, when he executed his interrupted but inextinguishable desire of returning to the humble walks of private life.

The promulgation of his fixed resolution stopped the anxious wishes of an affectionate people, from adding a third unanimous testimonial of their unabated confidence in the man so long enthroned in their hearts. When before was affection like this exhibited on earth? —Turn over the records of ancient Greece—Review the annals of mighty Rome—Examine the volumes of modern Europe ;—you search in vain.—America and her Washington only afford the dignified exemplification.

The illustrious personage called by the national voice in succession to the arduous office of guiding a free people, had new difficulties to encounter: The amicable effort of settling our difficulties with France, begun by Washington, and pursued by his successor in virtue as in station, proving abortive, America took measures of self-defence.

No sooner was the public mind roused by a prospect of danger, than every eye was turned to the friend of all, though secluded from public view, and grey in public service. The virtuous veteran, following his plough, received the unexpected summons with mingled emotions of indignation at the unmerited ill-treatment of his country, and of a determination once more to risk his all in her defence.

The annunciation of these feelings, in his affecting letter to the President, accepting the command of the army, concludes his official conduct.

First in war, first in peace, and first in the hearts of his countrymen, he was second to none in the humble and endearing scenes of private life: Pious, just, humane, temperate, and sincere; uniform, dignified, and commanding; his example was as edifying to all around him as were the effects of that example lasting.

To his equals he was condescending; to his inferiors kind; and to the dear object of his affections exemplarily tender: Correct throughout, vice shuddered in his presence, and virtue always felt his fostering hand; the purity of his private character gave effulgence to his public virtues.

His last scene comported with the whole tenor of his life: Although in extreme pain, not a sigh, not a groan escaped him; and with undisturbed serenity he closed his well-spent life. Such was the man America has lost!—Such was the man for whom our nation mourns!

Methinks I see his august image, and hear, falling from his venerable lips, these deep-sinking words:

"Cease, sons of America, lamenting our separation: Go on, and confirm by your wisdom the fruits of our joint councils, joint efforts, and common dangers. Reverence religion; diffuse knowledge throughout your land; patronize the arts and sciences; let Liberty and Order be inseparable companions; control party-spirit, the bane of free government; observe good faith to, and cultivate peace with, all nations; shut up every avenue to foreign influence; contract rather than extend national connexion; rely on yourselves only—be American in thought and deed. Thus will you give immortality to that union, which was the constant object of my terrestrial labours: Thus will you preserve undisturbed, to the latest posterity, the felicity of a people to me most dear; and thus will you supply (if my happiness is now aught to you) the only vacancy in the round of pure bliss high Heaven bestows."

HENRY LEE was born in Westmoreland County, Va., January 29th, 1756, and died on Cumberland Island, Georgia, March 25th, 1818. He graduated at the College of New Jersey in 1773, was a Captain of Bland's cavalry in 1776, and joined the main army in September, 1777. In 1778 he was made a major, and joined the Southern army in January, 1781, as lieutenant-colonel. In 1786 he was a delegate to Congress, and in 1792 was made Governor of Virginia. He was much beloved by Washington, and gained honorable distinction in every post he was called to. While a member of Congress in 1799, he delivered the oration which we reprint entire, and in which occurs the celebrated phrase, "First in war, first in peace, and first in the hearts of his countrymen," for the utterance of which he will always be remembered. These words were, however, first used in the resolutions passed by the House of Representatives, December 19th, 1799, on the death of Washington, (p. 56,) which although offered by John Marshall, were really prepared by Mr. Lee. The oration was published with the title, "A funeral oration in honor of the memory of George Washington, late General of the Armies of the United States, prepared and delivered at the request of Congress, at the German Lutheran Church, Philadelphia, on Thursday, the 26th December, 1799, by Major General Henry Lee." 4to, pp. 20, Philadelphia, 1800, with an allegorical plate engraved by Trenchard & Weston. Many editions were printed in 8vo., among which were those of Brooklyn, Boston, London, Portsmouth and Philadelphia.

GOUVERNEUR MORRIS.

1799.

BORN to high destinies, he was fashioned for them by the hand of nature. His form was noble—his port majestic. On his front were enthroned the virtues which exalt, and those which adorn the human character. So dignified his deportment, no man could approach him but with respect—none was great in his presence. You all have seen him, and you all have felt the reverence he inspired; it was such, that to command, seemed in him but the exercise of an ordinary function, while others felt a duty to obey, which (anterior to the injunctions of civil ordinance, or the compulsion of a military code) was imposed by the high behests of nature.

He had every title to command—Heaven, in giving him the higher qualities of the soul, had given also the tumultuous passions which accompany greatness, and frequently tarnish its lustre. With them was his first contest, and his first victory was over himself. So great the empire he had there acquired, that calmness of manner and of conduct distinguished him through life. Yet, those who have seen him strongly moved, will bear witness that his wrath was terrible; they have seen boiling in his bosom, passion almost too mighty for man; yet, when just bursting into act, that strong passion was controlled by his stronger mind.

Having thus a perfect command of himself, he could rely on the

10   (73)

full exertion of his powers, in whatever direction he might order them to act. He was therefore clear, decided and unembarrassed by any consideration of himself. Such consideration did not even dare to intrude on his reflections. Hence it was, that he beheld not only the affairs that were passing around him, but those also in which he was personally engaged, with the coolness of an unconcerned spectator. They were to him as events historically recorded. His judgment was always clear, because his mind was pure. And seldom, if ever, will a sound understanding be met with in the company of a corrupt heart.

In the strength of judgment lay, indeed, one chief excellence of his character. Leaving to feebler minds that splendor of genius, which, while it enlightens others, too often dazzles the possessor; he knew how best to use the rays which genius might emit, and carry into act its best conceptions.

So modest, he wished not to attract attention, but observed in silence, and saw deep into the human heart. Of a thousand propositions he knew to distinguish the best; and to select among a thousand the man most fitted for his purpose. If ever he was deceived in his choice, it was by circumstances of social feeling which did honor to his heart. Should it, therefore, in the review of his conduct, appear that he was merely not infallible, the few errors which fell to his lot, as a man, will claim the affections of his fellow men. Pleased with the rare, but graceful weakness, they will admire that elevation of soul, which, superior to resentment, gave honor and power, with liberal hand, to those by whom he had been offended. Not to conciliate a regard, which, if it be venal, is worth no price; but to draw forth in your service the exercise of talents, which he could duly estimate, in spite of incidents by which a weaker mind could have been thrown from its bias.

In him were the courage of a soldier, the intrepidity of a chief, the fortitude of a hero. He had given to the impulsions of bravery all the calmness of his character, and, if in the moment of danger, his manner was distinguishable from that of common life, it was by superior ease and grace.

To each desire he had taught the lessons of moderation. Prudence became therefore the companion of his life. Never in the public, never in the private hour, did she abandon him even for a moment. And, if in the small circle, where he might safely think aloud, she should have slumbered amid convivial joy, his quick sense of what was just, and decent, and fit, stood ever ready to awaken her at the slightest alarm.

Knowing how to appreciate the world, its gifts and glories, he was truly wise. Wise also in selecting the objects of his pursuit. And wise in adopting just means to compass honorable ends.

Gouverneur Morris was born at Morrisania, New York, January 31st, 1752, and died there, November 6th, 1816. He graduated at King's (now Columbia) College, in 1768, studied law, was admitted to the bar in 1771, and soon attained great reputation. He was a member of the Continental Congress 1777–80, occupied many prominent public positions both at home and abroad, and published a number of political pamphlets, orations, etc. Our extract is from "An oration on the death of General Washington, delivered at the request of the Corporation of the City of New York, December 31, 1799, and published at their request, by Gouverneur Morris." 8vo, pp. 24. New York, 1800. Reprinted in *Washingtoniana*. Lancaster, 1802, and in *Washingtoniana*, Roxbury, Mass., 1865.

JEDIDIAH MORSE.

1799.

General Washington in his person was tall, upright, and well made; in his manners easy and unaffected. His eyes were of a bluish cast, not prominent, indicative of deep thoughtfulness, and when in action, on great occasions remarkably lively. His features strong, manly, and commanding; his temper reserved and serious; his countenance grave, composed, and sensible. There was in his whole appearance an unusual dignity and gracefulness which at once secured for him profound respect, and cordial esteem. He seemed born to command his fellow men. In his official capacity he received applicants for favors, and answered their requests with so much ease, condescension and kindness, as that each retired, believing himself a favorite of his chief. He had an excellent and well cultivated understanding; a correct, discerning, and comprehensive mind; a memory remarkably retentive; energetic passions under perfect control; a judgment sober, deliberate, and sound. He was a man of the strictest honor and honesty, fair and honorable in his dealings; and punctual to his engagements. His disposition was mild, kind, and generous. Candour, sincerity, moderation, and simplicity, were, in common, prominent features in his character; but when an occasion called, he was capable of displaying the most determined bravery, firmness, and independence. He was an affectionate husband, a faithful friend, a humane master,

(76)

and a father to the poor.*   He lived in the unvarying habits of regularity, temperance, and industry.   He steadily rose at the dawn of
day, and retired to rest usually at 9 o'clock in the evening.   The in-
termediate hours all had their proper business assigned them.   In his
allotments for the revolving hours, religion was not forgotten.   Feeling, what he so often publicly acknowledged, his entire dependence
on God, he daily, at stated seasons, retired to his closet, to worship at
his footstool, and to ask his divine blessing.   He was remarkable for
his strict observation of the sabbath, and exemplary in his attendance
on public worship.

Of his faith in the truth and excellence of the holy scriptures, he
gave evidence, not only by his excellent and most exemplary life, but
in his writings; especially when he ascribes the meliorated condition
of mankind, and the increased blessings of society, "*above all, to the*
PURE *and benign light of* REVELATION;" and when he offers to GOD his
earnest prayer, "that he would most graciously be pleased to dispose
us all to do justice, to love mercy, and to demean ourselves with that
charity, humility, and pacific temper of mind, which were the characteristics of the DIVINE AUTHOR OF OUR BLESSED RELIGION; without
an humble imitation of whose example, in these things, we can never
hope to be a happy nation."†   In an address to him, immediately after
he commenced his Presidency over the United States, from a venerable
and respectable body of men, who were in the best situation to know
his religious character, and who, no doubt, expressed what they knew,

---

* Compare John Bell, pp. 12, 13. ED.

† See his Farewell Orders to the Armies of the United States, dated Rocky Hill, near
Princeton, Nov. 2d, 1783.

is the following testimony to his faith in Christianity. "But we derive a presage," say they, "even more flattering, from the piety of your character. Public virtue is the most certain means of public felicity; and religion is the surest basis of virtue. We therefore esteem it a peculiar happiness to behold in our Chief Magistrate, a *steady, uniform,* AVOWED *friend of the Christian religion;* who has commenced his administration in rational and exalted sentiments of piety, and who, in his private conduct, *adorns the doctrines of the Gospel of Christ.*" Grounded on these pure and excellent doctrines, to which his life was so conformable; copying, as he did, with such exemplary strictness and uniformity, the precepts of Christ, we have strong consolation and joy in believing, that ere this, he has heard from his God and Saviour, this enrapturing sentence, *Well done good and faithful servant, enter into the joy of your Lord.*

What a blessing to the world, what an honour to human nature, is a character thus "throughout sublime?" What a bright exemplar for kings, for princes, for rulers of every name, for warriors, for farmers, for Christians, for mankind? Thanks be to God for so rich a gift; praise to his name for bestowing it on our nation, and thus distinguishing it above all others on the globe, and let all the PEOPLE OF COLUMBIA, WITH ONE VOICE, SAY AMEN.

JEDIDIAH MORSE, D.D., was born at Woodstock, Conn., August 23d, 1761, and died at New Haven, June 9th, 1826. He graduated at Yale college in 1783, was licensed to preach in 1785, and installed minister of the First Congregational Church, Charlestown, Mass., in 1789, which he resigned in 1820. The "Biographical Sketch of Gen. George Washington," from which the above extract is made, was published with "A Prayer and Sermon delivered at Charlestown, Dec. 31st, 1799, on the death of George Washington, late President and Commander-in-Chief of the Armies of the United States of America, with an additional sketch of his life, by Rev. Jedidiah Morse." 8vo, pp. 82, Charlestown, 1800. Reprinted in London by J. Bateson, 1800; also in *Washingtoniana*, Baltimore, 1800, the *Memory of Washington*, Newport, R. I., 1800, and *Washington's Political Legacies*, New York, 1800. Dr. Morse had previously given in the first edition of his "American Geography," Elizabeth-Town, N. J., 1789, a brief sketch of the life of Washington, portions of which referring to his habits and daily life at Mount Vernon, will be found on page 30.

SAMUEL STANHOPE SMITH.

1800.

HISTORIANS shall immortalize their page with the name of Washington; and future orators shall quote it with the names of Epaminondas, of Aristides and of Cato, to illuminate their discourse, and to enforce, by great examples, the virtues of a disinterested and heroic patriotism. But his most lasting, and most noble monument shall be the affections of his countrymen, who will transmit their admiration of him as our increasing inheritance to their latest posterity. * * * *

In whom have ever shone with more splendor the talents of war, in creating an army; in successfully maintaining himself in the face of a superior enemy; in inspiring with courage raw troops; in attaching soldiers to order and their country in the midst of extreme hardships, and the injustice of their country itself; in seizing victories by an enterprising bravery, when enterprise was safe for the republic, or in conducting retreats that gained him no less glory than victories; in vanquishing his enemies by a firm undaunted courage, or consuming and wasting them away by a wise and noble patience? Where can we find a conqueror so humble, so disinterested, so devoted solely to his country—so serene, so sublime in adversity—so modest in the midst of triumphs—in dangers so intrepid and calm—and possessing such control over events by his prudence and perseverance. * * * *

In private life he was as aimable, as virtuous, and as great, as he

(80)

appeared sublime on the public theatre of the world. How many conquerors, renowned in history, have been great only while they acted a conspicuous part under the observation of mankind! The soul, in such a situation, perceives an artificial elevation—it 'assumes the sentiments of virtue corresponding to the grandeur of the objects that surround it. In private, it subsides into itself; and, in the ordinary details of life and conduct, the men, who seemed to be raised above others by the splendor of some rare occasion, now sink below them,— they are degraded by their passions,—those who were able to command armies, have lost the power of self-command—and when they are not heroes, they are nothing. Washington was always equal to himself. There was a dignity in the manner in which he performed the smallest things. A majesty surrounded him that seemed to humble those who approached him, at the same time that there was a benignity in his manners that invited their confidence and esteem. His virtues, always elevated and splendid, shone only with a milder light by being placed in the vale of retirement. He was sincere, modest, upright, humane; a friend of religion; the idol of his neighbors as well as of his country; magnificent in his hospitality, but plain in his manners, and simple in his equipage. And the motive of these virtues we are not to seek in a vain affectation of popularity which has often enabled the cunning and the artful to make great sacrifices to public opinion, but in the native impulse and goodness of his heart. His emotions, naturally strong and ardent, as they are, perhaps, in all great men, he had completely subjected to the control of reason, and placed under the guard of such vigilant prudence, that he never suffered himself to be surprised by them. Philosophy and religion in his breast had

11

obtained a noble triumph: and his first title to command over others, was his perfect command of himself. Such a sublime idea had he formed of man, that in him you never detected any of the littlenesses of the passions. His consummate prudence, which was one of his most characteristic qualities, and which never forsook him for a moment, contributed to fix the affections and the confidence of his fellow citizens, which he had acquired by his talents. Eminently distinguished for his conjugal and domestic virtues, the perfect purity of his private morals added not a little to that dignity of character in which he was superior to all men. There is a majesty in virtue, which commands the respect, even of those who do not love it, and which gives to great talents their highest lustre. * * * *

His whole character was consistent. Equally industrious with his plough as with his sword, he esteemed idleness and inutility the greatest disgrace of man, whose powers attain perfection only by constant and vigorous action, and who is placed by providence in so many social relations, only to do good. Every thing round him was marked with a dignified simplicity. While so many affect fastidiously to display their wealth in sumptuous edifices, and splendid equipages, and incur infinitely more expense to be envied and hated, than would be sufficient to make themselves adored, his mansion was as modest as his heart. Strangers from all nations, who visited it, went, not to admire a magnificent pile, but to gratify a noble curiosity in seeing the first man in the world. Palaces, and columns, and porticos, would have shrunk beside him, and scarcely have been seen. Like the imperial palace of Marcus Aurelius, at Rome, the plain and modest walls resembled some august temple, which has no ornament but the deity that inhabits it. You approached it with reverence as the retreat of a hero, the venerable abode of all the virtues. He had no need to seek a false glory by an exterior display of magnificence, who possessed such intrinsic worth and grandeur of soul. Every where he goes without any attendants but his virtues—he travels without pomp; but every one surrounds him, in imagination, with his victories, his triumphs, his glorious toils, his public services. How sublime is this simplicity! How superior to all the fastuous magnificence of luxury! Thus he lived, discharging, without ostentation, all the civil, social, and domestic, offices of life—temperate in his desires—faithful to his duties—retiring from fame, which every where pursued him—living like a beneficent deity in the bosom of his family, its delight, and its glory. * * * *

Under his administration, the United States enjoyed prosperity and happiness at home, and, by the energy of the government, regained in the old world, that importance and reputation which, by its weakness, they had lost. Arduous was his task—innumerable were the difficulties he had to encounter, from the passions, the conflicting interests, the ambition, and the disappointment of men. His own virtue, and the confidence of the nation, supported him. And amidst all the clamors which the violence of faction, or individual chagrin, have raised against the general administration, none have ever dared to impeach the purity of his patriotism, or his incorruptible integrity. * * * *

Behold then this illustrious man, no less sublime as a statesman, than as a warrior? His character is a constellation of all the greatest qualities that dignify or adorn human nature. The virtues and the talents which, in other instances, are divided among many, are combined in him.

Samuel Stanhope Smith, D.D., was born at Pequea, Pa., March 16, 1750, and died at Princeton, N. J., August 21, 1819. He graduated at the College of New Jersey in 1769, and after studying theology was ordained in 1774. In 1779 he became professor of moral philosophy at Princeton, accepted in 1783 the additional office of professor of theology, and in 1786 that of Vice-President of the college. In 1795 he succeeded his father-in-law Dr. John Witherspoon as President, resigning in 1812. Our quotation is from "An oration upon the death of General George Washington, delivered in the State House at Trenton, on the 14th of January, 1800; by the Rev. Samuel Stanhope Smith, D.D., President of the College of New Jersey; and published at the desire of the committee of the citizens, etc., of Trenton, at whose request it was pronounced." Svo, pp. 45. Trenton: 1800. Reprinted 1817. Also reprinted in *Washingtoniana*, Lancaster, 1802, and in *Washingtoniana*, Roxbury, Mass., 1865.

LONDON COURIER.

1800.

THE whole range of history does not present to our view a character upon which we can dwell with such entire and unmixed admiration. The long life of General Washington is not stained by a single blot. He was indeed a man of such rare endowments, and such fortunate temperament, that every action he performed was equally exempted from the charge of vice or weakness. Whatever he said or did, or wrote, was stamped with a striking and peculiar propriety. His qualities were so happily blended, and so nicely harmonized, that the result was a great and perfect whole. The powers of his mind, and the dispositions of his heart, were admirably suited to each other. It was the union of the most consummate prudence with the most perfect moderation. His views, though large and liberal, were never extravagant: his virtues, though comprehensive and beneficent, were discriminating, judicious and practical.

Yet his character, though regular and uniform, possessed none of the littleness which may sometimes belong to these descriptions of men. It formed a majestic pile, the effect of which was not impaired, but improved by order and symmetry. There was nothing in it to dazzle by wildness, and surprise by eccentricity. It was of a higher species of moral beauty. It contained everything great and elevated,

(85)

but it had no false and tinsel ornament. It was not the model cried by the fashion and circumstance: its excellence was adapted to the true and just moral taste, incapable of change from the varying accidents of manners, of opinions and times. General Washington is not the idol of a day, but the hero of ages!

Placed in circumstances of the most trying difficulty at the commencement of the American contest, he accepted that situation which was preëminent in danger and responsibility. His perseverance overcame every obstacle; his moderation conciliated every opposition; his genius supplied every resource; his enlarged view could plan, revise, and improve every branch of civil and military operation. He had the superior courage which can act or forbear to act, as true policy dictates, careless of the reproaches of ignorance either in power or out of power. He knew how to conquer by waiting, in spite of obloquy, for the moment of victory; and he merited true praise by despising undeserved censure. In the most arduous moments of the contest, his prudent firmness proved the salvation of the cause which he supported.

His conduct was, on all occasions, guided by the most pure disinterestedness. Far superior to low and groveling motives, he seemed even to be uninfluenced by that ambition, which has justly been called the instinct of great souls. He acted ever as if his country's welfare, and that alone, was the moving spring. His excellent mind needed not even the stimulus of ambition, or the prospect of fame. Glory was but a secondary consideration. He performed great actions, he persevered in a course of laborious utility, with an equanimity that neither sought distinction, nor was flattered by it. His reward was in the consciousness of his own rectitude, and in the success of his patriotic efforts.

As his elevation to the chief power was the unbiassed choice of his countrymen, his exercise of it was agreeable to the purity of its origin. As he had neither solicited nor usurped dominion, he had neither to contend with the opposition of rivals, nor the revenge of enemies. As his authority was undisputed, so it required no jealous precautions, no rigorous severity. His government was mild and gentle; it was beneficent and liberal; it was wise and just. His prudent administration consolidated and enlarged the dominion of an infant republic. In voluntarily resigning the magistracy which he had filled with such distinguished honor, he enjoyed the unequalled satisfaction of leaving to the state he had contributed to establish, the fruits of his wisdom and the example of his virtues.

It is some consolation, amidst the violence of ambition and the criminal thirst of power, of which so many instances occur around us, to find a character whom it is honorable to admire, and virtuous to imitate. A conqueror, for the freedom of his country! A legislator for its security! A magistrate, for its happiness! His glories were never sullied by those excesses into which the highest qualities are apt to degenerate. With the greatest virtues he was exempt from the corresponding vices. He was a man in whom the elements were so mixed, that "Nature might have stood up to all the world" and owned him as her work. His fame bounded by no country, will be confined to no age. The character of General Washington, which his cotemporaries regret and admire, will be transmitted to posterity; and the memory of his virtues, while patriotism and virtue are held sacred among men, will remain undiminished.

THE preceding character, by an anonymous writer, was originally published in the *Courier*, a London paper of January 24, 1800. It was subsequently reprinted in this country, in *Washingtoniana*, Baltimore, 1800, in the *Memory of Washington*, Newport, R. I., 1800, and in *Washingtoniana*, Roxbury, Mass., 1865; it is also quoted in the "Sketch of the Life of Gen. Washington," appended to *Washingtoniana*, Lancaster, 1802. The first two paragraphs as printed in the *Courier*, and in the reprints as mentioned, were adapted from the first, second and third paragraphs of the character by Isaac Weld, given on page 50. They have, therefore, been omitted from our quotation.

FISHER AMES

1800.

THE best evidence of reputation is a man's whole life. We have now, alas! all Washington's before us. There has scarcely appeared a really great man, whose character has been more admired in his life time, or less correctly understood by his admirers. When it is comprehended, it is no easy task to delineate its excellencies in such a manner, as to give to the portrait both interest and resemblance. For it requires thought and study to understand the true ground of the superiority of his character over many others, whom he resembled in the principles of action, and even in the manner of acting. But perhaps he excels all the great men that ever lived, in the steadiness of his adherence to his maxims of life, and in the uniformity of all his conduct to the same maxims. These maxims, though wise, were yet not so remarkable for their wisdom, as for their authority over his life: for if there were any errors in his judgment, (and he discovered as few as any man) we know of no blemishes in his virtue. He was the patriot without reproach: he loved his country well enough to hold his success in serving it an ample recompense. Thus far self-love and love of country coincided: but when his country needed sacrifices, that no other man could, or perhaps would be willing to make, he did not even hesitate. This was virtue in its most exalted character. More than once he put his fame at hazard, when he had reason to think it

12

would be sacrificed, at least in this age. Two instances cannot be denied. When the army was disbanded; and again, when he stood, like Leonidas, at the pass of Thermopylæ, to defend our independence against France.

It is indeed almost as difficult to draw his character as the portrait of virtue. The reasons are similar. Our ideas of moral excellence are obscure, because they are complex, and we are obliged to resort to illustrations. Washington's example is the happiest to shew what virtue is; and to delineate his character, we naturally expatiate on the beauty of virtue, much must be felt, and much imagined. His preëminence is not so much to be seen in the display of any one virtue, as in the possession of them all, and in the practice of the most difficult. Hereafter, therefore, his character must be studied before it will be striking; and then it will be admitted as a model; a precious one to a free republic.

It is no less difficult to speak of his talents. They were adapted to lead, without dazzling mankind; and to draw forth and employ the talents of others, without being misled by them. In this he was certainly superior, that he neither mistook nor misapplied his own. His great modesty and reserve would have concealed them, if great occasions had not called them forth; and then, as he never spoke from the affectation to shine, nor acted from any sinister motives, it is from their effects only that we are to judge of their greatness and extent. In public trusts, where men, acting conspicuously, are cautious, and in those private concerns, where few conceal or resist their weaknesses, Washington was uniformly great; pursuing right conduct from right maxims. His talents were such as assist a sound judgment, and ripen with it. His prudence was consummate, and seemed to take the direction of his powers and passions; for, as a soldier he was more solicitous to avoid mistakes that might be fatal, than to perform exploits that are brilliant; and, as a statesman, to adhere to just principles, however old, than to pursue novelties; and therefore in both characters, his qualities were singularly adapted to the interest, and were tried in the greatest perils of the country. His habits of enquiry were so far remarkable, that he was never satisfied with investigating, nor desisted from it, so long as he had less than all the light that he could obtain upon a subject; and then he made his decision without bias.

This command over the partialities that so generally stop men short, or turn them aside in their pursuit of truth, is one of the chief causes of his unvaried course of. right conduct in so many difficult scenes, where every human actor must be presumed to err.

If he had strong passions, he had learned to subdue them, and to be moderate and mild. If he had weaknesses, he concealed them, which is rare, and excluded them from the government of his temper and conduct, which is still more rare. If he loved fame, he never made improper compliances for what is called popularity. The fame he enjoyed is of the kind that will last forever; yet it was rather the effect, than the motive, of his conduct. Some future Plutarch will search for a parallel to his character. Epaminondas is perhaps the brightest name of all antiquity. Our Washington resembled him in the purity and ardor of his patriotism; and, like him, he first exalted the glory of his country. There, it is to be hoped, the parallel ends: for, Thebes fell with Epaminondas. But such comparisons cannot be pursued far, without departing from the similitude. For we shall find it as difficult to compare great men as great rivers. Some we admire for the length and rapidity of their current, and the grandeur of their cataracts; others, for the majestic silence and fullness of their streams. We cannot bring them together to measure the difference of their waters. The unambitious life of Washington, declining fame, yet courted by it, seemed like the Ohio, to choose its long way through solitudes, diffusing fertility; or like his own Potomac, widening and deepening his channel, as he approaches the sea, and displaying most the usefulness and serenity of his greatness towards the end of his course. Such a citizen would do honor to any country. The constant veneration and affection of his country will show, that it was worthy of such a citizen.

However his military fame may excite the wonder of mankind, it is chiefly by his civil magistracy that his example will instruct them. Great generals have arisen in all ages of the world, and perhaps most in those of despotism and darkness. In times of violence and convulsion, they rise by the force of the whirlwind, high enough to ride in it and direct the storm. Like meteors, they glare on the black clouds with a splendor, that, while it dazzles and terrifies, makes nothing visible but the darkness. The fame of heroes is indeed growing vulgar: they multiply in every long war: they stand in history, and thicken in their ranks, almost as undistinguished as their own soldiers.

But such a Chief Magistrate as Washington appears like the pole star in a clear sky, to direct the skilful statesman. His presidency will form an epoch, and be distinguished as the age of Washington. Already it assumes its high place in the political region. Like the milky way, it whitens along its allotted portion of the hemisphere. The latest generations of men will survey, through the telescope of history, the space where so many virtues lend their rays, and delight to separate them into groups and distinct virtues. As the best illustration of them, the living monument, to which the first of patriots would have chosen to consign his fame, it is my earnest prayer to Heaven, that our country may subsist, even to that late day, in the plenitude of its liberty and happiness, and mingle its mild glory with Washington's.

FISHER AMES, a leading statesman and orator of his time, was born at Dedham, Mass., April 9th, 1758, and died there July 4th, 1808. He entered college (Harvard), at the early age of twelve, and graduated in 1774; but the poverty of his widowed mother compelled him to teach school for a livelihood until 1781, when he began to practice law, and soon displayed brilliant oratorical powers. He was elected to Congress in 1788, and continued in that body during the whole of Washington's administration, of which he was a zealous defender. He was acknowledged to be the most eloquent debater in the house, and was the author of the address of that body to Washington, on his retirement from the Presidency. Our extract is from "An oration on the sublime virtues of General George Washington, pronounced at the Old South Meeting House in Boston, before his honor the lieutenant governor, the council, and the two branches of the legislature of Massachusetts, at their request, on the 8th of February, 1800, by Fisher Ames." 8vo, pp. 31, Boston, 1800; 8vo, pp. 51, Philadelphia, 1800. Reprinted in the *Memory of Washington*, Newport, R. I., 1800; *Washingtoniana*, Lancaster, 1802; and *Washingtoniana*, Roxbury, Mass., 1865.

BRITISH REGISTER.

1800.

On December 15, at his seat in Virginia, in the 68th year of his age, George Washington, late President of the United States of America; a man superior to all the titles which arrogance or servility have invented for the decoration of hereditary rank. He was one who seemed to have been expressly formed by Providence for the mighty work of establishing the independence of a people, which may one day delight the philanthropist with the view of as great an assemblage of freemen, as Europe now contains of slaves. His firm hand adapted to all circumstances of fortune, equally inaccessible to the flatteries of hope and the suggestions of despair, was kept steady by the grand principles of pure love to his country, and a religious attachment to moral duty. He was one of those truly great men, who can be cool without phlegm, dispassionate without indifference—who, constantly intent upon an important end, are little moved by the vicissitudes and fluctuations in the means which lead to it. In him, even fame, glory, reputation, were subordinate considerations to the successful performance of the high task assigned him; and he could without impatience wait for that reward of public applause and gratitude, which was all he desired for services beyond the power of estimate. In his character were renewed all the qualities we most admire in the noblest names of antiquity. Timoleon, Aristides, Camillus, Fabius, did not

94

surpass him in fortitude, prudence, disinterestedness, and integrity. No one ever more effectually united decisive firmness, with that lenity which flows from true benevolence. No one ever passed through the ordeal of power and influence more free from the remotest suspicion of selfish and ambitious designs. To have passed unsullied through such a career of glory and usefulness, is so high and rare a blessing, that regret for his loss will probably, in those minds which are warmed by a sense of exalted virtue, be sunk in the satisfaction of seeing another illustrious name placed beyond all danger of human infirmity.

THE above admirable obituary, is taken from the *Monthly Magazine or British Register*, for January, 1800. In the March and May Nos. of the same publication, a " Biographical sketch of George Washington, late President of the United States of America," also by an anonymous writer, contains the following. " His character is surrounded with no glare. There is little in it to dazzle. It has nothing to gratify those, who relish only that irregular and monstrous greatness, which fascinates the vulgar of all ranks and in all times. But those whose mental taste is most pure, will always admire in George Washington, the nearest approach to uniform propriety, and perfect blamelessness, which has ever been attained by man, or which is perhaps compatible with the condition of humanity."

LOUIS FONTANES.

1800.

France, unbiassed by those narrow prejudices which exist between nations, and admiring virtue wherever it be found, decrees this tribute of respect to the manes of Washington. At this moment she contributes to the discharge of a debt due by two nations. No government, whatever form it bears, or whatever opinion it holds, can refuse its respect to this great father of liberty. The people who so lately stigmatized Washington as a rebel, regard even the enfranchisement of America, as one of the events consecrated by history and past ages. Such is the veneration excited by great characters. He seems so little to belong to modern times, that he imparts to us the same vivid impressions as the most august examples of antiquity with all that they accomplished. His work is scarcely finished when it at once attracts the veneration which we freely accord to those achievements only that are consecrated by time. The American revolution, the contemporary of our own, is fixed for ever. Washington began it with energy, and finished it with moderation. He knew how to maintain it, pursuing always the prosperity of his country; and this aim alone can justify at the tribunal of the Most High, enterprises so extraordinary. * * * *

Washington had not those fiery and imposing traits which strike every mind: he displayed more order and justice, than force and elevation in his ideas. He possessed above all, in a superior degree,

(96)

that quality which some call vulgar, but which few possess; that quality not less useful to the government of states than to the conduct of life, and which gives more tranquility than emotion to the soul, and more happiness than glory to those who possess it, and to those who feel its effects. It is of good sense that I speak; that good sense which pride has often rejected under ancient rules, but which time must restore to all our laws. Audacity destroys, genius elevates, good sense preserves and perfects. Genius is charged with the glory of empires; but good sense alone assures their safety and repose. * *

Such a character is worthy of the brightest days of antiquity, and we may well doubt whether in all the traits that compose it we can find its parallel in our age. We may here find again one of the lost characters so beautifully delineated by Plutarch, in his Lives of Illustrious Men.

His administration was as mild and firm in internal affairs as it was noble and prudent towards foreign nations. He uniformly respected the usages of other countries, as he would desire the rights of Americans to be respected by them. Thus in all his negotiations, the heroic simplicity of the President of the United States, without elevation or debasement, was brought into communication with the majesty of Kings. He sought not in his administration those conceptions which the age calls great, but which he regarded as vain. His ideas were more sage than bold; he sought not admiration, but he always enjoyed esteem, alike in the field and in the Senate, in the midst of business as in the quiet of retirement.

LOUIS, COUNT DE FONTANES, was born at Niort, France, March 6, 1757, and died in

Paris, March 17, 1821.   He showed an early taste for poetry and letters, and moving to Paris, became one of the editors of the *Memorial,* a literary Journal.   An article in 1797, upon Napoleon, in which his future elevation was predicted, displeasing the Directory, he was banished, and took refuge in England.   The revolution of the 18th Brumaire, however, enabled him to return to France.   The funeral oration in honor of Washington, from which we make the above extract, was delivered at Paris, February 18th, 1800, by direction of Bonaparte, then First Consul.   It was published with the following title: "Eloge Funèbre de Washington; prononcé dans le .Temple de Mars, par Louis Fontanes."   8vo., pp. 29.   Paris, 1800. A Dutch translation was published at Amsterdam, the same year, and a complete English translation, which we use, will be found in *Washingtoniana,* Roxbury, Mass., 1865.   A few days before the delivery of the oration, the First Consul issued the following *Order of the day,* for the Consular Guard, and all the troops of the Republic.   " Washington is no more. That great man fought against tyranny.   He firmly established the liberty of his country. His memory will be ever dear to the French people, as it must be to every friend of freedom in the two worlds, and especially to the French soldiers, who like him and the Americans, bravely fight for liberty and equality.   The First Consul in consequence orders, that for ten days, black crapes shall be suspended to all the standards and flags of the Republic."

ANNUAL REGISTER.

1800.

EXTRACT FROM AN OBITUARY IN THE NEW ANNUAL REGISTER OR GENERAL REPOSITORY
OF HISTORY, POLITICS AND LITERATURE, FOR THE YEAR 1800.   LONDON.

THE American republic has sustained an irreparable loss in the
death of the venerable Washington.   This melancholy event took place
on the 15th of December, 1799, and was occasioned by an inflamma-
tory sore throat, the first symptoms of which appeared only three days
previous to his death.   We have been not inattentive observers of the
career of this illustrious man, from the period of his assuming the
command of the revolutionary army of America; and we do not hesitate to pronounce him the greatest character of modern times; and,
perhaps, with all the embellishments of fabulous and partial historians,
there is scarcely one in the annals of antiquity that will bear a comparison.   In him prudence was united with vigour; wisdom with
patriotism; courage with disinterestedness.   If he had ambition, it
was of the purest kind; exempt from that selfishness with which this
passion is too commonly united; and he built his fame upon the proudest
and most solid basis, that of service to his country, and his love of
human kind.   That rare and valuable quality, improperly called com-
mon-sense, because in reality it is the least common, never appears to
have deserted him, whether in council or the field, in the moment of
depression, or in the still more dangerous crisis, that of his elevation;

(99)

and he is one of the very few of whom it may be asserted, that he scarcely ever said or did a foolish thing. He was one of those who are formed by Providence to be the founders of empires; and, if we look to second causes only, we may venture to affirm, that to the talents of Washington, America is more indebted than to any other circumstance for its liberty and independence. With probably few of the advantages derivable from a regular and classical education, his eloquence was that of the heart, and generally affected the hearts of those to whom it was addressed. Indeed, there are perhaps scarcely to be found more perfect specimens of pure and genuine eloquence than in his answer to the proclamation of General Burgoigne in 1777, and his farewell oration on resigning the presidency of the United States. Without methodical and early instruction in the modern school of tactics, he was enabled to assume the command of a great army, and to contend under infinite disadvantages, with the first generals of Great Britain. Without the regular succession of office, and the discipline of diplomatic science, he was perhaps the first statesman of the present age. He founded a government, he maintained it in external and internal tranquility, and left it in a state of unexampled prosperity.

*   *   *   *

He was chosen a member of the American Congress which met in Philadelphia in 1774; and was soon after appointed to the command of the provincial army. Of his great talents and consummate judgment, that desperate and difficult contest, between the mother country and the colonies, affords the best of proofs; and the character of Washington is written by the historian in every detail that he has given of the incidents of the war. Yet it is remarkable, that such was the humanity of this incomparable man, that he never could afterwards bear to converse on a subject which would have administered to the vanity of almost any other individual. "Sir," said he one day, to a foreign gentleman, "I observe you wish me to speak of the war. It is a conversation I always avoid. I rejoice in the establishment of the liberties of America; but the time of the struggle was a horrid period, in which the best men were compelled to do many things repugnant to their nature." *   *   *   *

At the close of the war he went into retirement; but the disorders arising from paper currency, and an unsettled government, once more called forth his attention. When a new constitution was framed for the United States, he was chosen president. He seems to have accepted it rather from necessity than choice; and afterwards to have relinquished the honour in compliance with his own inclination, when his country seemed to have no further claim or call for his services. In a word, his conduct exhibited to the world the character of a truly *great* and *good* man—epithets so rarely united, that they have almost been supposed incompatible.

DAVID TAPPAN.

1800.

IT was the high destiny of Washington, to be selected in the counsels of Heaven, as its leading agent in the most glorious and beneficent work, which perhaps was ever accomplished in the political world. This peculiar allotment gives him a marked pre-eminence in the annals of human greatness. Though existing or future patriots may possibly rival him in other respects; yet to him was eminently consigned the province of severing the new world from the old, and of erecting the former into an independent, stable, and glorious fabric of liberty and happiness.

The same *uncrring wisdom*, which had appointed him to this work, gradually ripened him for its execution by a nice adjustment of his birth and education, of his bodily and mental constitution, of his early fortunes and pursuits. In these previous steps we recognize the same invisible hand, which by similar arrangements prepared the ancient deliverer and lawgiver of Israel for the great scenes of his public life. In the bodily constitution of our hero were united a vigor, firmness, and dignity, which at once represented and supported the energy and greatness of his mind; and which seemed to designate him for high command and arduous enterprize. His intellectual furniture combined a clear and comprehensive understanding, a correct and cultivated taste, a prompt and retentive memory, a sound and deliberate

(102)

judgment. He conceived and expressed his sentiments with justness, precision, and strength. He formed and executed his plans with circumspection, policy, and vigor. The productions of his pen were uniformly excellent. They furnish an eminent model of chaste and perspicuous, of concise and elegant composition. Their matter and style are ever appropriate to the subject and occasion. They exhibit, in the most unaffected and diversified manner, not only the inexhausted resources of his genius, but the steady and elevated goodness of his heart.

As the greatness of *God*, rightly understood, involves, and indeed is principally formed by infinite *rectitude;* so his departed minister was chiefly ennobled by the majesty of his virtue. His avowed and sublime principles of morality and piety enlarged his understanding, and exalted his affections. They originated some of his great qualities, and imparted direction, vigor, and beauty to all. They supported a constant propriety and dignity both of sentiment and action in his individual, domestic, and public capacities. His unusual command of appetite and passion made the serenity, clearness, and uniformity of his mind resemble those of superior beings. His investigation, discernment, and practical observance of truth, rectitude, and honor were never known to be either obstructed by pleasure, relaxed by indolence, disturbed by resentment, controuled by fear, intercepted by interest, or borne down by ambition. In short, the splendor of his character arose, not so much from the striking predominance of any one virtue, as from the singular union and culture of all, and the wonderful adaptation of his leading moral qualities to his peculiar and arduous situations.

*　*　*　*

Amid the singular discouragements and vicissitudes of a long, fluctuating, and distressing war, his mind, leaning on its own greatness, on the purity of his motives, the rectitude of the cause, and the approbation of his God, seemed to gather strength from surrounding weakness, courage from danger, and hope from despondency. Happy in his conscious integrity, and alive only to his country's interest and honor, he anxiously covered her infirmities and perils even from his own view; he resigned personal character and feeling to her credit and welfare; he enlivened her confidence, and repelled her foes, by needful but feigned appearances of strength, and prospects of victory. While we trace his military career, we admire that uncommon and diversified greatness, which could at once conceal and varnish, endure and surmount, yea finally bend to the public good, so many circumstances of perplexity, alarm, and disgrace. We admire that greatness, which effectually influenced the civil authorities, while it yielded them the most delicate respect and the firmest support; which animated the great mass of the people, and upheld the national Union, without ever stepping over the line of decorum or official propriety. We venerate that controuling genius and virtue, which from raw, shifting, and discordant materials, and amid the most trying and obstinate difficulties, could create and harmonize, encourage and protect the armies of our infant nation; and which, under the visible auspices of an almighty leader, conducted them through a great and terrible wilderness, to the promised land of triumphant freedom, peace, and independence. We reverence that sublime spirit, which, at the close of the war, spurned the allurement of empire, and crushed the embryo of rebellion; and which, after giving its excellent parting advice and benediction to the beloved soldiers and citizens of America, exemplified to the world the precious maxim, that true ambition and glory are compleated in humble and disinterested virtue.

In a word, the character of our hero seemed to border as closely on perfection, as human infirmity would permit. Its multifarious and exquisite texture was admirably fitted to his destination. The God of Washington and of America, appears to have united in him those seemingly incompatible virtues and talents, which had been singly distributed among preceding warriors, because their combined efficiency and example were eminently required, to form a lasting center of union for our nation; to support the interests, and retrieve the honor of our degraded nature; and to instruct mankind in that true heroism, which liberty and christianity alone can inspire.

DAVID TAPPAN, D.D., was born at Manchester, Mass., April 21, 1752, and died August 27, 1803. He graduated at Harvard College in 1771, and after studying divinity was ordained minister of the 3d Church in Newbury, in 1774, and from December 26, 1792 until his death, was Hollis professor of divinity in Harvard. Our extract is from "A discourse delivered before the University of Cambridge, February 21, 1800, in solemn commemoration of General George Washington, by David Tappan, S.T.D., Hollis Professor of Divinity," and published the same year at Cambridge, with an introductory address in Latin by Joseph Willard, L.L.D., President. 8vo, pp. 44. The discourse was reprinted in *Washington's Political Legacies.* New York, 1800. In a note Dr. Tappan says: "The singular trials, virtues, talents, and services of our hero, during the late war, are best seen in his *Official Letters.* These, compared with his conduct, display an unparalleled union of coolness and animation; of caution and vigor; of modesty and decision; of philanthrophy and bravery; of humility and ambition; of comprehensive discernment and patriotic ardor; of prudent, yet heroic patience and enterprise; of fortitude in distress, moderation in victory, and equanimity in all the changes of fortune."

EBENEZER GRANT MARSH.

1800.

To view Washington as a perfect model of military greatness, to rank him with the greatest generals of any age, is no amplification. In him were blended activity, vigilance, great force of judgment, and never failing presence of mind. He could unite information with talents, reflection with experience, and stratagem with glory. Cautious, systematic, and inflexible, his genius was singularly adapted to our revolutionary war. Distinguishing, with precision, the difference between great difficulties and impossibilities, and never discouraged by the former, he often appeared to execute the latter. Indefatigably laborious and active, coolly intrepid in action, he discerned as by intuition, seized with rapidity, and improved with skill, the favorable, and often decisive, moments of battle. Never transported by the enthusiasm of patriotism, never deluded by the ardor of courage, he preferred stratagem to action, and victory to glory. Modest and magnanimous after victory, he became the generous protector of his subdued and captive enemies. Resolute and undejected in misfortunes, he rose superior to distresses, and surmounted difficulties, which no courage, no constancy, but his own, would have resisted. His letters, during his most gloomy prospects, announce a hero, conscious of his danger, but still deriving a well grounded hope from the resources of his own mind. His valor was never unequal to his duty or the occa-

(106)

sion. He attempted great things with means that appeared totally inadequate, and successfully prosecuted what he had boldly resolved. He was never disheartened by difficulties, but had that vigor of mind, which, instead of bending to opposition, rises above it, and seems to have a power of controling even fortune itself. His character combined a cool and penetrating judgment and prompt decision, caution and intrepidity, patience and enterprise, generous tenderness and compassion, with undaunted heroism. He was a never failing resource to those who wanted his assistance. No one could have more happily concentrated the confidence of his troops. Their obedience was less owing to the authority of his post, than to their opinion of his valor; so attached to him were the officers and soldiers, that if a principle of duty and virtue had not secured their obedience to their country, gratitude and respect for their general would have confirmed it. Even when worn out with fatigue they were ever ready to execute his orders, and no danger could intimidate them when they were commanded by Washington. He himself always shared in the toils he was obliged to impose, visited in person the sick and the wounded, and expressed, on every occasion, the greatest regard for a body of men, whose welfare was so closely connected with that of his country. By the strictest rules he labored to inspire them with a sense of duty, and neglected no circumstance which might render them formidable to their enemies. He was eloquent, persuasive, strong, and pathetic, as occasion required. He had arguments and tears at his command. In a word, he was a general formed by heaven for just such a period, country, and cause, as ours. *   *   *   *

In no situation did Washington appear more truly great than at the helm of our federal government. Here he displayed an astonishing extent and precision of political talents, a disinterested integrity, an incorruptible heart, a constant attention to the grand principles of rational liberty, and an invariable attachment to his country. His genius was equal to the most enlarged views, and minute details, of civil policy. A vigorous mind, improved by the experience and study of mankind, dexterity and application in business, a judicious mixture of liberality and economy. Steadiness to pursue his ends, and flexibility to vary his means, marked his administration. He guided the passions of others, because he was master of his own. Had his character and feelings been more fervid, his conduct might not have been so exemplary, nor his glory so exalted and permanent. Patriotic from principle, and temperate from constitution, he neither disdained nor sought elevation; but always retained a humility, which demonstrated, even to political jealousy, that a man, capable of bearing so many honors, fully deserved them. He was provident without timidity, severe in the execution of justice without vigor, moderate when his own interests were the subject of discussion, and inflexibly firm when those of his country were in question. He stood a rock in the midst of the ocean, receiving unmoved the violence of its waves. * * * *

The private character of this great man eminently corresponded with the splendor of his public reputation. The native simplicity of his virtue was a stranger to vanity or affectation. He enjoyed, with moderation, the advantages of his fortune, and the innocent pleasures of society. He was severe to himself, indulgent to the imperfections of others, just and beneficent to all mankind. Sincerity and candor, a true sense of honor, justice, and public liberty, appeared to be the inherent principles of his nature, and the uniform rule of his conduct. The largeness of his heart equalled that of his fortune. Without thinking of his own greatness, without fearing lest others should forget it, he was easy of access, untainted with rancor or jealousy, and ever ready to listen to just complaints. "He appears," indeed, "to have been the complete model of that perfect character, which, under the denomination of a sage or a wise man, the philosophers have been fond of delineating, rather as a fiction of their imagination, than in hope of ever seeing it reduced to practice—so happily were all his virtues tempered together, so justly were they blended, and so powerfully did each prevent the other from exceeding its proper bounds." In a word, cotemporary jealousy, envy, and malignity, were compelled to applaud both his public and private character, and more impartial posterity will read it with admiration.

EBENEZER GRANT MARSH, professor of languages and ecclesiastical history in Yale College, was the son of Dr. John Marsh, minister of Wethersfield, Conn. He graduated at Yale. in 1795, was elected an instructor in the Hebrew language in 1798, and one of the tutors in 1799. In 1802 he was elected professor. He died November 16th, 1803, aged twenty-six years. Our extract, is from "an oration delivered at Wethersfield, February 22d, 1800; on the death of General George Washington, who died December 14th, 1799. By Ebenezer Grant Marsh. Published by request." 8vo, pp. 16. Hartford, 1800.

TIMOTHY DWIGHT.

1800.

General Washington was great, not by means of that brilliancy of mind, often appropriately termed genius, and usually coveted for ourselves, and our children; and almost as usually attended with qualities, which preclude wisdom, and depreciate or forbid worth; but by a constitutional character more happily formed. His mind was indeed inventive and full of resources; but its energy appears to have been originally directed to that which is practical and useful, and not to that which is shewy and specious. His judgment was clear and intuitive beyond that of most who have lived, and seemed instinctively to discern the proper answer to the celebrated Roman question; Cui bono erit? To this his incessant attention, and unwearied observation, which nothing, whether great or minute, escaped, doubtless contributed in a high degree. What he observed he treasured up, and thus added daily to his stock of useful knowledge. Hence, although his early education was in a degree confined, his mind became possessed of extensive, various, and exact information. Perhaps there never was a mind, on which theoretical speculations had less influence, and the decisions of common sense more.

At the same time, no man ever more earnestly or uniformly, sought advice, or regarded it, when given, with more critical attention. The opinion of friends and enemies, of those who abetted, and of

(110)

those who opposed, his own system, he explored, and secured alike. His own opinions, also, he submitted to his proper counsellours, and often to others; with a demand, that they should be sifted, and exposed, without any tenderness to them because they were his; insisting, that they should be considered as opinions merely, and, as such, should be subjected to the freest and most severe investigation.

When any measure of importance was to be acted on, he delayed the formation of his judgment until the last moment; that he might secure to himself, alway, the benefit of every hint, opinion, and circumstance, which might contribute either to confirm, or change, his decision. Hence, probably, it in a great measure arose, that he was so rarely committed; and that his decisions have so rarely produced regret; and have been so clearly justified both by their consequences and the judgment of mankind.

With this preparation, he formed a judgment finally and wholly his own; and although no man was ever more anxious before a measure was adopted, probably no man was ever less anxious afterward. He had done his duty, and left the issue to Providence.

To all this conduct his high independence of mind greatly contributed. By this I intend a spirit, which dares to do its duty, against friends and enemies, and in prosperous and adverse circumstances, alike; and which, when it has done its duty, is regardless of opinions and consequences.

Nor was he less indebted to his peculiar firmness. He not only dared to act in this manner, but uniformly sustained the same tone of thought and feeling, such, as he was at the decision, he ever after continued to be; and all men despaired of operating on him unless through the medium of conviction. The same unchanging spirit supported him through every part of his astonishing trials, during the war; and exhibited him as exactly the same man after a defeat, as after a victory; neither elated nor depressed, but always grave, serene, and prepared for the event.

From other great men he was distinguished by an exemption from favouritism. No man ever so engrossed his attachment, as to be safe, for a moment, from deserved reproof, or censure; nor was any man ever so disrelished by him, as, on that account, to fail of receiving from him whatever applause, or services his merit could claim. Hence his friends feared, and his enemies respected him.

His moderation and self government were such that he was always in his own power, and never in the power of any other person. Whatever passions he felt, they rarely appeared. His conduct, opinions, and life, wore unusually the character of mere intellect. Hence he was never found unguarded, or embarrassed; but was always at full liberty to do that, and that only, which expediency and duty demanded. A striking instance of this trait in his character is seen in the well known fact; that he never exculpated himself from any charge, nor replied to any calumny. His accusers, for such he had, had opportunity to make the most of their accusations; his calumniators, if their consciences permitted, to sleep in peace.

His justice was exact, but tempered with the utmost humanity, which the occasion would suffer. His truth no sober man, who knew him, probably ever doubted. Watchful against his own exposures to error, he was rarely found erring; jealous of doing injustice, if he has done injustice, it is yet, I believe, unrecorded.

His reservedness has been at times censured. To me it appears to have been an important and necessary characteristic of a person situated as he was. In familiar life a communicative disposition is generally pleasing, and often useful; in his high stations it would have been dangerous. One unguarded or ambiguous expression might have produced evils, the remedy of which would have been beyond even his own power. No such expression is recorded of him.

His punctuality was extreme. He rose always with the dawn; he dined at a given minute; he attended every appointment at the moment. Hence his business public and private was always done at the proper time, and always beforehand.

No person appears to have had a higher sense of decorum, and universal propriety. The eye, following his public and private life, traces an unexceptionable propriety, an exact decorum, in every action; in every word; in his demeanour to men of every class; in his public communications; in his convivial entertainments; in his letters; and in his familiar conversation; from which bluntness, flattery, witticism, indelicacy, negligence, passion, and overaction, were alike excluded.

From these things happily combined, always seen, and seen always in their native light, without art, or affectation, it arose, that, wherever he appeared, an instinctive awe and veneration attended him on the part of all men. Every man, however great in his own opinion, or in reality, shrunk in his presence, and became conscious of an inferiority, which he never felt before. Whilst he encouraged every man, particularly every stranger, and peculiarly every diffident man, and raised him to self-possession, no sober person, however secure

15

he might think himself of his esteem, ever presumed to draw too near him.

With respect to his religious character there have been different opinions. No one will be surprised at this, who reflects, that this is a subject, about which, in all circumstances not involving inspired testimony, doubts may and will exist. The evidence concerning it must of course arise from an induction of particulars. Some will induce more of these particulars, and others fewer; some will rest on one class, or collection, others on another; and some will give more, and others less, weight to those which are induced; according to their several modes, and standards, of judging. The question in this, and all other cases, must be finally determined before another tribunal, than that of human judgment; and to that tribunal it must ultimately be left. For my own part, I have considered his numerous and uniform public and most solemn declarations of his high veneration for religion, his exemplary and edifying attention to public worship, and his constancy in secret devotion, as proofs, sufficient to satisfy every person, willing to be satisfied. I shall only add, that if he was not a Christian, he was more like one, than any man of the same description, whose life has been hitherto recorded.

As a warrior, his merit has, I believe, been fully and readily acknowledged; yet I have doubted whether it has always been justly estimated. His military greatness lay not principally in desperate sallies of courage; in the daring and brilliant exploits of a partisan: These would have ill suited his station, and most probably have ruined his cause and country. It consisted in the formation of extensive and masterly plans; effectual preparations, the cautious prevention of great evils, and the watchful seizure of every advantage; in combining heterogeneous materials into one military body, producing a system of military and political measures, concentering universal confidence, and diffusing an influence next to magical; in comprehending a great scheme of war, pursuing a regular system of acquiring strength for his country, and wearing out the strength of his enemies. To his conduct, both military and political, may, with exact propriety, be applied the observation, which has been often made concerning his courage; that in the most hazardous situations no man ever saw his countenance change.

TIMOTHY DWIGHT, D.D., was born at Northampton, Mass., May 14, 1752, and died at New Haven, Conn., January 11, 1817. He graduated at Yale College in 1769, was licensed to preach and acted as chaplain in the revolutionary army from Sept. 1777, to Oct. 1778, doing much to heighten the enthusiasm of the soldiers by his popular patriotic songs. From Sept. 1795, until his death, he was President of Yale College. Dr. Dwight had great industry and research, was a sound and impressive preacher, and an able writer. Our extract is from "A discourse delivered at New Haven, Feb. 22, 1800, on the character of George Washington, Esq., at the request of the citizens, by Timothy Dwight, D.D., President of Yale College." 8vo, pp. 39. New Haven, 1800.

WILLIAM LINN.

1800.

When God in his adorable providence intends to accomplish some glorious work upon earth, he provides and prepares his instruments among the children of men. Who does not see that Moses, by the manner in which he was preserved, the instruction which he received, and the habits of life to which he was inured, was fitted to lead the people of Israel? Who, that Cyrus, had we not been expressly informed, was "guided by the Lord?" The intention is frequently hidden from the persons themselves, and may not be obvious to others; though they will sometimes discern presages of future greatness. Washington was endued from his youth with a military spirit. When a stripling, like David, he encountered the enemies of his country. His first destination was to enter as a midshipman in a British vessel of war. This was happily prevented, that so, instead of the admiral, he might become the general. He gave such early and uncommon indications of heroism as occasioned public mention of him by an eminent divine, in a discourse delivered soon after Braddock's defeat. The subject was *religion and patriotism.* "As a remarkable instance," said he, "I may point out to the public that heroic youth Colonel Washington, whom I cannot but hope Providence has hitherto preserved in so signal a manner, for some important

(116)

service to his country."*   We will not call these words prophetic, but they have been repeatedly quoted as a testimony of the budding honors of the American hero. * * * *

Learning to estimate justly all human glory, and matured by experience; accustomed to lofty conceptions, and moving always in the important spheres of life; impressed with a sense that he derived all from God, and that all should be devoted to his service; his deportment was noble, equally removed from the supercilious and the vain.   Some men have been great at one time, and despicable at another; some men have performed a single great action, and never rose to the like again; but to him great actions seemed common. Some men have appeared great at the head of armies, or when surrounded by the trappings of power, and little when stripped of these, and alone; some men have withstood the storms of adversity, and been melted by the sunshine of prosperity; some men have possessed splendid public talents, and disgraced these by sordid private vices; but it is difficult to determine when and where Washington shone the brightest.   It can only be said, that he was *uniformly* great. * * * *

Incomparable man!   He devoted his time, his talents and his labors to our service; and he hath left his advice and his example to us, and to all generations!

---

* The discourse referred to, was delivered August 17, 1755, in Hanover County, Va., and published at Philadelphia the same year, with the title, " Religion and Patriotism the constituents of a good soldier," in a note to which, p. 9, the words quoted, occur.   The author, Samuel Davies, D.D., was born in New Castle County, Del., November 3, 1723, and was officiating at the time in that part of Virginia.   In 1759, he succeeded Jonathan Edwards as president of the College of New Jersey, and died at Princeton, February 4, 1761.—ED.

There was in him that assemblage of qualities which constitutes real greatness; and these qualities were remarkably adapted to the conspicuous part which he was called to perform.   He was not tinsel, but gold; not a pebble, but a diamond; not a meteor, but a sun. Were he compared with the sages and the heroes of antiquity, he would gain by the comparison; or rather, he would be found to be free from the blemishes, and to unite the excellencies of them all. Like Fabius he was prudent; like Hannibal he was unappalled by difficulties·; like Cyrus he conciliated affection; like Cimon he was frugal; like Scipio he was chaste; like Philopemen he was humble; and like Pompey he was successful.   If we compare him with characters in the sacred records, he combined the exploits of Moses and Joshua, not only by conducting us safely across the Red Sea and through the wilderness, but by bringing us into the promised land. Like David he conquered an insulting Goliah, and rose to the highest honors from an humble station; like Hezekiah he ruled; and like Josiah at his death, there is a mourning "as the mourning of Hada-drimmon in the valley of Megiddon."   Nor is the mourning confined to us, but extends to all the wise and the good who ever heard of his name.   The generals whom he opposed will wrap their hilts in black, and stern Cornwallis drop a tear.   *   *   *   *

In the eighteenth century have flourished a number of the most eminent philosophers, historians, orators, poets, patriots, and states-men; the close of it has been eventful and astonishing beyond all precedent.   In the end of the fifteenth century, Columbus discovered this new world; in the end of the eighteenth, Washington arose to give Columbia independence and rank among the nations.   To the lustre of so many names, and to a period of such wonderful events, he joins his blaze. Memorable æra! The age of great men, the age of extraordinary revolutions, the age of Washington.

WILLIAM LINN, D.D., an eloquent Presbyterian divine, was born at Shippensburg, Pa., in 1752, and died at Albany, N. Y., January, 1808. He graduated at the College of New Jersey, in 1772, and after serving some time as chaplain in the Revolutionary Army, was pastor of a church near Shippensburg; in 1787 he became pastor of the Presbyterian Church in Elizabethtown, N. J., and shortly afterwards, settled as a collegiate pastor in the Dutch Reformed Church in New York City, where he resided twenty years. Our extract is from a "Funeral Eulogy on the death of George Washington, delivered Feb. 22, 1800, before the New York State Society of Cincinnati, by Rev. William Linn, D.D." Svo, pp. 44. New York, 1800. Reprinted in *Washingtoniana*, Lancaster, 1802.

MASON L. WEEMS.

1800.

IT is hardly exaggeration to say that Washington was pious as
Numa; just as Aristides; temperate as Epictetus; patriotic as Regu-
lus; in giving public trusts, impartial as Severus; in victory, modest
as Scipio; prudent as Fabius; rapid as Marcellus; undaunted as Hannibal; as Cincinnatus disinterested; to liberty firm as Cato; and respectful of the laws as Socrates. Or, to speak in plainer terms; he
was religious without superstition; just without rigour; charitable
without profusion; hospitable without making others pay for it; generous but with his own money; rich without covetousness; frugal
without meanness; humane without weakness; brave without rashness; successful without vanity; victorious without pride; a lover of
his country, but no hater of French or English; a staunch friend of
government but respectful of those who pointed out its defects with
decency; true to his word without evasion or perfidy; firm in adversity; moderate in prosperity; glorious and honoured in life; peaceful
and happy in death.

Thus singularly virtuous was the man, whom Heaven was pleased
to select as his honored instrument to establish this great WESTERN
REPUBLIC. And if every thing be duly considered, I trust it will appear Washington was raised up of God as a forerunner to some mighty
event. In 1774, when a dark gloom hung over the spirits of our

(120)

Fathers; a gloom occasioned by the alarm of a mighty nation coming forward with her armies and fleets, (shading the ocean) to strike at our dearest liberties; then it was, *that, the spirit of God came mightily on Washington*, and raised him up as an Ensign of Hope to our trembling countrymen. And when we consider how wonderfully this man was enabled to inspire *confidence;* insomuch that thirteen little Colonies, which, a few years before, had been thrown into a panic by a handful of French Indians, now headed by Washington, were resolved, to oppose one of the most formidable powers in Europe.—When we consider, how wonderfully he inspired *union;* insomuch that all the souls of thirteen Colonies, so widely distant in their situation, Religion, Customs and Interests, clave to him even as one man, beyond all conjecture of reason, and all suspicion of Lord North—when we consider how miraculously, this man was preserved to us, during our long and critical struggle, notwithstanding the attempts (one or two of which have come to light) that were made to take him from us— when we consider, how wonderfully he kept up the spirit, and the union, of these states, during the long contest of eight years, notwithstanding the many horrors and distresses of war, the great want of luxuries for the rich, and of necessaries and pay for the soldiers—and, after the establishment of Heaven-born freedom in our land; how wonderfully, his parental influence led the people of these states to adopt one grand system of pure Republican policy, happily uniting civil liberty with effective government—when, I say, all this is considered, who but must feel a sweet flutter of hope that great events are connected with us, and that God has sent on his servant Washington, as a Day-Star to some mighty Revolution, big with blessings to man-

16

kind, which will ere long dawn on the land where Washington was born?

MASON L. WEEMS, an eccentric clergyman and writer, was born at Dumfries, Va., and died at Beaufort, S. C., May 23d, 1825. He studied theology in London, was Rector for several years of Mount Vernon Parish, and subsequently became a book-agent for Mathew Carey of Philadelphia, traveling in that capacity extensively over the Southern States. His Life of Washington with a dedication to Mrs. Washington, published at Georgetown [1800], under the title " A History of the Life and Death, Virtues and Exploits of General George Washington, etc.," 8vo, is a curious compound of enthusiasm, exhortation and patriotism, presented in the most original manner and in the quaintest language. Other editions subsequently appeared in Philadelphia and Elizabeth-Town, N. J. Our quotation taken from the second edition, Philadelphia [1800], is what may be termed his summing up of the character of Washington as set forth in the text, under the heads of Piety, Patriotism, Industry, Benevolence and Justice. The sixth edition published at Philadelphia in 1808, under the title "The Life of George Washington with curious anecdotes equally honourable to himself and exemplary to his young countrymen," 12mo, and in which the *hatchet story* first appears, is quite a different production from the preceding editions, being almost entirely rewritten. This is the book as it is printed and in circulation at the present day, and of which so many editions have been issued.

J. M. WILLIAMS.

1800.

GENERAL WASHINGTON was in his person about six feet in height, his eyes were grey, but full of animation; his visage was serene, and the temper of his thoughtful mind did not seem disposed to the frequent indulgence of mirth; his limbs were well proportioned and muscular, and his deportment carried an air of majesty and solemnity in it, that was altogether awful to folly; though no man did more for the interests of human nature in general, yet few men have unbosomed themselves with more circumspection than he did, to any particular individual; but this habit of reserve has been the characteristic of the wisest persons that ever lived, when possessed of similar authority—it has been asserted that he was never seen to smile, during the revolutionary war; in the more unrestrained moments of private intercourse, he expressed himself with perspicuity and diffidence, but seldom used more words than were necessary for the elucidation of his opinion: the lineaments of his face implied that he was an older man than he really was; but the weight of care, that must necessarily have pressed upon the reflection of a man, engaged in such a continuity of vast enterprize and deep responsibility, could not fail to antedate in some degree, the works of time.

The graces of General Washington's person, were not unfrequently instrumental in the promotion of his views; the advantages

(123)

resulting from natural grace, in polished and even in savage life, are wonderfully convictive; and this effect will not be amazing, when it is known, that the most penetrating analyzers of man, and his attributes, have determined that all action is graceful, in proportion as the impulses are innocent; nothing that is vicious or abominable can be charming; nor does it breathe or exist in any emotions arising from vanity or folly: grace is the sublimity of beauty; it is a quality analagous to the most exquisite tenderness of affection; that modest, yet gay illustration of action, which accompanies pure love: gracefulness is an expression of dignified pleasure; but that high order of pleasure is not ease, it is something more.

As a didactic writer, he can scarcely be esteemed too much; his sentiments have a force and fascination to restore reason, invigorate patriotism, and awaken piety; his public letters and documents should be engraved upon the tablet of the nation, as examples of profound sagacity, genuine integrity, and unaffected humility: they should be eternally regarded, in a political interpretation, as "eyes to the blind": his simplicity of style proves him to have been guided by a fine taste; when a writer is verbose or glittering, his argument is weakened, and none but the unwise can admire him.

It was the peculiar honor of General Washington, not only to deserve, but to enjoy the approbation of all men of probity in either hemispheres; those persons who had been his opponents in Britain, from an attachment to their sovereign and the prevailing councils of the hour, became his friends at the conclusion of a peace, from contemplating the moderation of his deportment, and the moral energies of his mind; and some of the more distinguished, considered it as a reflected merit, to be in the habits of correspondence and the inter-change of civilities, with such an embellished and admirable personage.

He had the urbanity of a gentleman, without the littleness of pride; and in the very plenitude of his authority, would sheathe a denial so kindly, that the sting of disappointment was absorbed in the beauty of the declaration: he embraced the delegation to rule, as a great man should; not to indulge the luxury of the senses, or the insatiate aims of ambition, but for the blessed purpose of disseminating love and protection to all: he stood as a preëminent supporter in society; like a Tuscan column, with sober magnificence; plain, strong, attractive and erect: with Atlantean properties, equal to more than the weight he had sustained: at once the vital principle and the ornament of that constitution he had sanctioned, and his fame will be co-eternal with the existence of freedom.

We have never contemplated the character of a magistrate more inflexible to wrong, nor of a man so active and so spotless, in any record, either ancient or modern: he did more for imitation, and less for repentance, than any contemporary: had he derived his ideas of legislation and forbearance from the statutes of the golden age, he could not have done more to enforce innocency and mutual truth; and he confessedly lived to make mankind better, if it is in the virtue of an individual to correct our frailty.

Having followed this august statesman to the sepulchre, it now devolves upon the grateful and the provident of his countrymen, to hang it round with symbols of regard, and inscribe it with the texts of his policy: let them inform a future age, that he shunned no public question, nor omitted any duty; in the cherishing hope that other men may copy the impressive example: and the insinuation of hope makes our delusion our joy; but, in simplicity, yet force, of language; in clearness of understanding and depth of judgment: in his disdain of any commutation with falsehood: in his contempt of trivial expedients, and his ability to make that spirit governing: in his appropriation of direct remedies for national evils, and in his majesty of character altogether, we have seriously to apprehend that he will be never equalled; he had all the decision of *Cato*, without his coarseness—he had raised himself, by progressive excellence, above the tooth of envy, and the desperation of malice: and was not assailable by any mortal hand:

> . . . . Nec Jovis ira, nec ignes,
> Nec poterit ferrum, nec edax abolere vetustas.
>
> Ovid, Metam. Lib. 15.

The character as above delineated, is extracted from a " Biographical outline of General George Washington," by J. M. Williams, printed in *Washington's Political Legacies* Boston, 1800, and also in *Legacies of Washington*, Trenton, 1800. The biographical outline is a simple statement of facts suited for the purpose of the publications mentioned. Of the author we have no particulars, but our extracts indicate the scholar and thinker.

MALLET DU PAN.

1800.

IT may be made a question whether Washington, as a General and Statesman, equalled in genius Prince Eugene, Frederick II, or Chatham? But how is it possible with propriety to compare men who were placed in situations no wise analogous?

Were we allowed to venture an opinion on this subject, we would observe, that if Washington was inferior to some other illustrious men in extent and boldness of mind, he surpassed them by the union of qualities and talents the most rarely found together, and by a character almost faultless.

Constitution, soul, and intellect, were in him in constant harmony, and perfectly adapted to his public career. It might be said, that Providence had created him for the part he has sustained, for the people he governed, and for the circumstances in which his country stood. At Athens, his lot would have been that of Aristides or Phocion; in a a Republic well constituted and long established, his services would not have been called forth; in a corrupt Republic, he would have chosen a private station as *the post of honour*.

In his military and political life, wisdom was the prominent feature of his character. It is given to few men to possess that admirable moral temperature which marked all the actions of Washington. His courage and his talents for war would have been insufficient, and per-

(127)

haps hurtful, without the patience, coolness, and equality of spirits, which he displayed in bad as well as good fortune.

At the head of the Republic he preserved the same uprightness and the same spirit of conduct by which he had been guided in battle. He was indebted to the excellence of his judgment, as well as to the ascendency of his public and private virtues, for the permanence of the reputation he enjoyed. His speeches, letters, actions, were always marked with the same reason, and that strong good sense which is the highest gift of Nature to a public man, and his highest merit; that good sense which alone resists the agitations of the soul, and corrects the wanderings of the understanding.

The habitual moderation of Washington; his firmness, which was ever calm and well-timed; his prudence, which neither difficulty nor passion, neither hope nor fear, could shake; his superiority to all artifice and intrigue; and his artless politics, dictated by a just estimation of times, men, and things; have never degenerated for a moment. Placed at the head of an infant Republic, he acquired all the dignity usually bestowed on high offices by the force of custom and of ages; and he preserved it as if he had ruled America for a century: his administration was better supported by respect and confidence, than by laws or armies.

He has not been charged with a vice or a weakness. No one has raised a doubt of his integrity or his disinterestedness. Free from ambition, he never would have sought superior rank, or have been anxious to make a figure: he was led to them by his services, the general esteem he attracted, and by circumstances. In him superiority was pardoned; the jealousy of his equals vanished before the admirable simplicity of his manners, the purity of his morals, and the rectitude of his conduct. In short, neither a vain love of glory, nor the desire of distinction, nor any personal view, ever gave a bias to his patriotism, which was the principle of all his thoughts, and the spring of all his actions.

If the title, so much abused, of *a great man*, ought to be reserved for one whose successes never injured justice or honour, and in whom great virtues united with great talents, who shall refuse it to Washington? * * * *

General Washington has carried with him to the tomb the general esteem of Europe. His conduct had compelled even his enemies to respect him. It was reserved for the French Republicans alone to differ from the rest of the world, and to insult, as basely as grossly, the President of the United States. It is true, that he had very wisely forseen, and so early as the year 1789, the horrible career of a Revolution, which set out with overthrowing all public order; which, forming crime into theory, made patriotism to consist in assassination, and liberty in the impunity of every outrage against the freedom of the citizens.

The national gratitude of America has honoured the memory of Washington by public testimonies of grief, and by solemnizing the funeral of her illustrious Chief in the most distinguished manner.

Washington has quitted life without the slightest diminution of his glory, tranquility, and happiness. He died on fields cultivated by himself, in the bosom of his country, of his family, of his friends; and the veneration of America accompanied him to the grave.

17

Jacques Mallet du Pan was born at Geneva, Switzerland, in 1749, and died at Richmond, England, May 10th, 1800. He went to Paris in 1784, and became editor of the political division of a journal called the *Mercure de France,* which was quite successful. In the Revolution he defended the royal cause, and, in 1792, was compelled to suspend the publication of the journal. He then went to London, and in 1798, was installed as editor of the *Mercure Brittanique,* which was ranked among the ablest political papers of the time. The character preceding was written shortly after the death of Washington, for the *Mercure Brittanique,* and quoted in an " Account of George Washington," published in the *European Magazine* for March and April, 1800, the introduction to which is as follows: " Time which moderates the virulence of parties, has at length in its revolution brought on that period in which the life of this great man may be viewed free from those prejudices, both for and against him, which have been heretofore entertained. Death has put the seal to his fame, and his character and conduct will now be admitted to have been deserving of every tribute of praise which have been bestowed upon them. His coolness in danger, his firmness in distress, his moderation in the hour of victory, his resignation of power, and his meritorious deportment in private life, have established a name which will go down to posterity with those who have deserved well of their country—with those who are entitled to be considered the benefactors of mankind."

JOHN CORRY.

1800.

Washington was tall, erect, and well made, but thin. His eyes were light blue, his nose rather long, and his countenance expressive of extreme sensibility. His demeanor was dignified and modest. "There was a mild serenity in his deportment; he was slow and moderate in his resentments; and if he had faults, he must have been sensible of them, and was very successful in concealing them from the world." He was affable, generous, and conscientious. His valuable library, and a correspondence with eminent men, furnished him with a rich fund of knowledge; and the productions of his pen are perspicuous and sensible. He was an affectionate husband, a disinterested friend, a benign master, and a benefactor to the indigent. He practised the social virtues not merely because they were enjoined by religion, but from his innate love of rectitude.

The similarity between his public virtues and those of Alfred the Great is admirable. These extraordinary men were both celebrated for their love of justice, their fortitude, patriotism, and piety. When Alfred exchanged the military garb for that of the peasant, he suffered a greater reverse of fortune than ever befel Washington ; and when in disguise he explored the camp of the Danes, and lulled suspicion by the melody of his harp, he evinced a more enterprising genius than the American. The capture of the Hessians at Trenton, however,

(131)

reminds us of the achievement of Alfred; who, by surprising the Danish camp, revived the hopes of his countrymen. Washington founded a republic; he was instrumental to the establishment of its polity, and retired "with all his blushing honours thick upon him"; obedient to the will of his country, he resumed the command of her armies, and died as he had lived, a true patriot. Alfred, by the subju-gation of his country's enemies, secured her liberties and peace; he was "her voice in council, in the field her sword." As a legislator, he immortalized his name by the institution of a trial by jury; as a magistrate, he presided with unparalled wisdom; the sceptre of power was consecrated by his hand; and he was beloved, revered, nay, almost deified, by his countrymen. Washington, in some instances, seems to have been undecided: Alfred was energetic and determined in every emergency. Though their virtues were homogeneal, Alfred claims the palm for ardour and brilliancy of genius: Washington ex-celled him in discretion; he weighed the consequences of every step, and his prudence triumphed over opposition. In short, Alfred the Great was like the rising sun, which breaking through a dark cloud, illumines and beautifies the creation. His superior mind shone with an effulgence that dissipated the gloom of superstition and ignorance which surrounded him, and, like the Vicegerent of Heaven, he pro-moted the happiness of the human species. Washington the Great was like the declining sun that adorns the face of nature with the mildest radiance; his actions, though not so brilliant as those of Alfred, were more imitable; and the virtuous American will be es-teemed by posterity as worthy to stand in the same rank with the more illustrious Englishman.   *   *   *   *

Perhaps the only instance in which the public conduct of Washington was censurable, was his condemnation of the unfortunate André. It must be owned that he was a slave-holder, and his exemplary kindness to his dependents cannot reconcile us to that inconsistency in a man who was so strenuous and successful an asserter of liberty.

But these errors of the American hero were concealed by the dazzling lustre of his virtues. Our admiration is excited when we contemplate the series of his actions.

When we behold him at the head of the army, then President of the Senate, and afterwards breathing the pure air of his fields in the shade of his retirement, we confess that the venerable philosopher has attained what may be called the *sublime* of human nature. Just as Aristides, we behold him set his seal to that solemn engagement by which he emancipates those slaves who were deprived of their liberties by the avarice of his ancestors; and, actuated by the purest beneficence, he endows seminaries for the promotion of knowledge.

In his comprehensive mind were united the disinterestedness of Cincinnatus, the munificence of Cyrus the Great, and the piety of Marcus Aurelius. We may say of him as Augustus did of Cicero, "he was an honest man, and loved his country.".

THE "Sketch of the life of the late General Washington," by JOHN CORRY, printed in the *British Magazine*, February to June, 1800, possesses much interest as being the first of any importance, prepared in England. This production is, however, almost entirely different from the Life as published in London the same year, in a 12mo volume, and from which we extract the above parallel between Washington and Alfred the Great. This Life has been frequently published in this country, with variations in the title and alterations of the text, but, however changed in substance or form, the opening paragraph has been always retained, thus serving as a means of identification. This paragraph is as follows: "In the history of man, we contemplate with particular satisfaction those legislators and heroes whose wisdom and valour have conributed to the happiness of the human species. We trace the luminous progress of those excellent beings with secret complacency; our emulation is roused, while we behold them steadily pursue the path of rectitude in defiance of every obstruction; we rejoice that we are of the same species, and thus self-love becomes the handmaid of virtue." From the preface to the edition, 12mo, printed by Joseph Charless at Philadelphia in 1801, we make the following quotation: "The virtues of Washington require no adventitious embellishment; like the sun, they are visible by their own lustre. Yet, if on some occasions the author has been led by enthusiasm to panygeric, those effusions of a heart enamoured of virtue were involuntary, for he is convinced that the achievements of his hero, are"

"Above all Greek, above all Roman fame."

ANONYMOUS.

In no one thing has the world been so much deceived, as in the article of what is commonly called *Great Men.* Most of them, upon a nearer, and closer inspection, have been found to be either great hypocrites, or great robbers!—Not so the man whose character is now attempted to be delineated.—Whether in public or in private, he was still the same; and in that humble, but useful and honourable employment, a Farmer, he pointed the way to Fortune, as, in his public capacities, he had pointed the way to Fame; eminently proving, in his own person, the difference between a system of method and economy, and a course of idleness and dissipation.

By his regular and economical conduct, Mr. Washington became one of the extensive and opulent Farmers on the continent. He had about 10,000 acres of land attached to his seat of Mount Vernon, where he combined theory with practice, and, by successive improvements, rendered his grounds highly productive. Including his household servants, and those who worked upon the farm, he daily maintained about one thousand persons, all of whom moved and acted according to the rules of a strict, but beneficent system. Like a well-regulated clock, the whole machine moved in perfect time and order.—The effects were, that he was completely independent, and died possessed of a great property.

It does not appear that Mr. Washington's education was either classical or extensive; a knowledge of the English language, with a portion of geography and mathematics, seem to have been the whole of his juvenile improvements. Altho' his grammatical instructions could not be very accurate, he notwithstanding, attained, by dint of study and observation, a proficiency in the writing of English, smooth, uniform, and even dignified—he wrote in a style that has extorted the approbation of the most fastidious critics. He is an eminent proof, that a man may become an able General without having read Cæsar in the original, and an able politician without having studied either the Greek or Roman authors.

With a tall, majestic person, and a manly countenance, he had a strong but well-governed mind—his perceptions were not quick, but, when once he did take a position, it was generally well chosen, and firmly adhered to—Neither wit nor vivacity brightened his features; it was a face of care, of thought, and of caution; all was calmness and deliberation—Washington's great forte was prudence, or discretion; it covered him like a shield in the hour of danger, and it was his sure guide in the day of prosperity; by this single talent, he acquired all his wealth, and obtained all his celebrity.—Whilst he fulfiled all the relative duties, he was obedient to every temperate rule, and every moral principle; and knowing its vast importance both to individual and national happiness, he paid a proper respect to the observances of Religion.

THE Character of Washington given above, will be found quoted at the end of " Biographical Memoirs of the Illustrious General George Washington, Late President of the United States of America, and Commander in Chief of their Armies during the Revolutionary War," New Haven, Sidney's Press, 1809, 16mo. The Biography, is one of the numerous versions of the Life by John Corry (see page 133), and the character, stated to be by a *Scotch Traveller*, of whom we have no information, was written in all probability shortly after the death of Washington. It will also be found in a " Life of George Washington, Late President etc.," published by Isaiah Thomas, Jun., Boston: 1815; 16mo. The following obituary, the substance of which originally appeared in the *True American*, Philadelphia, Dec. 19, 1799, forms part of the contents of these volumes, which in this respect are the same. "On Saturday the 14th inst. died at his seat in Virginia, General George Washington, Commander in Chief of the Armies, and late President of the Congress, of the United States of America—mature in years, covered with glory, and rich in the affections of a free people, and the admiration of the whole civilized world. When men of common character are swept from the theatre of life, they die without the tribute of public concern, as they had lived without a claim to public esteem—But when Personages of great and exalted worth, are summoned from this sublunary scene, their death calls forth a burst of general regret, and invigorates the flame of public gratitude—In obedience therefore to the voice of their Country, the Poet, the Orator, and the Historian, will combine to do justice to the character of this illustrious Patriot: whilst the ingenious labours of the Sculptor, the Statuary, and the Painter, will unite in perpetuating the virtues of THE MAN OF THE AGE.

ANONYMOUS.

The following eulogy is said to have been written in monumental
form in two columns, by an unknown English gentleman, and pasted
by him on the back of one of the Sharpless crayon portraits of Washington, made in 1796. The portrait was owned by John R. Smith of
Philadelphia, and was in his possession in 1804, as stated by Benson
J. Lossing, in his "Mount Vernon and its Associations," published in
1859, from which volume this admirable tribute is transcribed.

WASHINGTON,

The Defender of his Country,

The Founder of Liberty,

The Friend of Man.

History and Tradition are explored in vain

For a Parallel to his Character.

In the Annals of Modern Greatness,

He stands alone,

And the noblest Names of Antiquity

Lose their Lustre in his Presence.

Born the *Benefactor of Mankind*,

He was signally endowed with all the Qualities

Appropriate to his *Illustrious Career*.

(138)

Nature made him *Great*,
And, Heaven directed,
He made *himself Virtuous*.

Called by his Country to the *Defence* of her *Soil*
And the *vindication* of her Liberties,
He led to the Field
Her Patriot Armies;
And displaying in rapid and brilliant succession,
The united Powers
Of *Consummate Prudence*
And Heroic Valour,
He triumphed in Arms
Over the most powerful Nation
Of Modern Europe;
His Sword giving *Freedom to America*,
His Counsels breathing *Peace to the world*.

After a short repose
From the *tumultuous Vicissitudes*
Of a Sanguinary War,
The astounding Energies of
WASHINGTON
Were again destined to a *New Course*
Of *Glory and Usefulness*.
The Civic Wreath
Was spontaneously placed

By the *Gratitude* of the *Nation*,
On the brow of the Deliverer of *his* Country.
He was twice *solemnly invested*
With the Powers of *Supreme Magistracy*,
By the *Unanimous Voice* of
A Free People;
And in his Exalted and Arduous station,
His *Wisdom* in the *Cabinet*
Transcended the *Glories of the Field.*

The *Destinies* of *Washington*
Were now complete.
Having passed the Meridian of a *Devoted Life*,
Having founded on the Pillars
Of National Independence
The Splendid Fabric
Of a *Great Republic*,
And having firmly established
The Empire of the West,
He solemnly deposited on the *Altar of his Country*,
His *Laurels* and his *Sword*,
And retired to the *Shades*
Of Private Life.
A *Spectacle* so *New* and *so Sublime*,
Was contemplated by *Mankind*
With the *Profoundest admiration;*
And the name of Washington,

Adding new *Lustre* to *Humanity*,
Resounded
To the remotest regions of the Earth.

Magnanimous in Youth,
Glorious through Life,
Great in Death,
His highest Ambition
The *Happiness* of *Mankind,*
His *noblest victory*
The *Conquest* of *Himself.*
Bequeathing to America
The *Inheritance* of his *Fame,*
And building his *Monument*
In the *Hearts of his Countrymen,*
He Lived,
The *Ornament* of the 18th Century;
He Died,
Lamented by a Mourning World.

JOHN MARSHALL.

1804–7.

GENERAL WASHINGTON was rather above the common size, his frame was robust, and his constitution vigorous, capable of enduring great fatigue, and requiring a considerable degree of exercise for the preservation of his health. His exterior created in the beholder the idea of strength united with manly gracefulness.

His manners were rather reserved than free, though they partook nothing of that dryness and sternness which accompany reserve when carried to an extreme; and on all proper occasions, he could relax sufficiently to show how highly he was gratified by the charms of conversation, and the pleasures of society. His person and whole deportment exhibited an unaffected and indescribable dignity, unmingled with haughtiness, of which all who approached him were sensible; and the attachment of those who possessed his friendship and enjoyed his intimacy, was ardent but always respectful.

His temper was humane, benevolent, and conciliatory; but there was a quickness in his sensibility to any thing apparently offensive, which experience had taught him to watch and to correct.

In the management of his private affairs he exhibited an exact yet liberal economy. His funds were not prodigally wasted on capricious and ill examined schemes, nor refused to beneficial though costly improvements. They remained therefore competent to that

(142)

expensive establishment which his reputation, added to a hospitable temper, had in some measure imposed upon him; and to those donations which real distress has a right to claim from opulence.

He made no pretensions to that vivacity which fascinates, or to that wit which dazzles and frequently imposes on the understanding. More solid than brilliant, judgment rather than genius constituted the most prominent feature of his character.

As a military man, he was brave, enterprising, and cautious. That malignity which has sought to strip him of all the higher qualities of a general, has conceded to him personal courage, and a firmness of resolution which neither dangers nor difficulties could shake. But candour will allow him other great and valuable endowments. If his military course does not abound with splendid achievements, it exhibits a series of judicious measures adapted to circumstances, which probably saved his country.

Placed, without having studied the theory, or been taught in the school of experience, the practice of war, at the head of an undisciplined, ill organized multitude which was unused to the restraints and unacquainted with the ordinary duties of a camp, without the aid of officers possessing those lights which the commander in chief was yet to acquire, it would have been a miracle indeed had his conduct been absolutely faultless. But, possessing an energetic and distinguishing mind, on which the lessons of experience were never lost, his errors, if he committed any, were quickly repaired; and those measures which the state of things rendered most advisable were seldom if ever neglected. Inferior to his adversary in the numbers, in the equipment, and in the discipline of his troops, it is evidence of real merit that no great and decisive advantages were ever obtained over him, and that the opportunity to strike an important blow never passed away unused. He has been termed the American Fabius; but those who compare his actions with his means will perceive at least as much of Marcellus as of Fabius in his character.   He could not have been more enterprising without endangering the cause he defended, nor have put more to hazard without incurring justly the imputation of rashness.   Not relying upon those chances which sometimes give a favourable issue to attempts apparently desperate, his conduct was regulated by calculations made upon the capacities of his army, and the real situation of his country.   When called a second time to command the armies of the United States, a change of circumstances had taken place, and he meditated a corresponding change of conduct.   In modelling the army of 1798, he sought for men distinguished for their boldness of execution, not less than for their prudence in counsel, and contemplated a system of continued attack.   "The enemy," said the general in his private letters," must never be permitted to gain foothold on our shores."

In his civil administration, as in his military career, were exhibited ample and repeated proofs of that practical good sense, of that sound judgment which is perhaps the most rare, and is certainly the most valuable quality of the human mind.   Devoting himself to the duties of his station, and pursuing no object distinct from the public good, he was accustomed to contemplate at a distance those critical situations in which the United States might probably be placed; and to digest, before the occasion required action, the line of conduct which it would be proper to observe.   Taught to distrust first impressions, he sought to acquire all the information which was obtainable, and to hear, without prejudice, all the reasons which could be urged for or against a particular measure. His own judgment was suspended until it became necessary to determine, and his decisions, thus maturely made, were seldom if ever to be shaken. His conduct therefore was systematic, and the great objects of his administration were steadily pursued.

Respecting, as the first magistrate in a free government must ever do, the real and deliberate sentiments of the people, their gusts of passion passed over without ruffling the smooth surface of his mind. Trusting to the reflecting good sense of the nation for approbation and support, he had the magnanimity to pursue its real interests in opposition to its temporary prejudices; and, though far from being regardless of popular favour, he could never stoop to retain by deserving to lose it. In more instances than one, we find him committing his whole popularity to hazard, and pursuing steadily, in opposition to a torrent which would have overwhelmed a man of ordinary firmness, that course which had been dictated by a sense of duty.

In speculation he was a real republican, devoted to the constitution of his country, and to that system of equal political rights on which it is founded. But between a balanced republic and a democracy, the difference is like that between order and chaos. Real liberty, he thought, was to be preserved only by preserving the authority of the laws, and maintaining the energy of government. Scarcely did society present two characters which, in his opinion, less resembled each other than a patriot and a demagogue.

No man has ever appeared upon the theatre of public action

19

whose integrity was more incorruptible, or whose principles were more perfectly free from the contamination of those selfish and unworthy passions which find their nourishment in the conflicts of party. Having no views which required concealment, his real and avowed motives were the same; and his whole correspondence does not furnish a single case from which even an enemy would infer that he was capable, under any circumstances, of stooping to the employment of duplicity. No truth can be uttered with more confidence than that his ends were always upright, and his means always pure. He exhibits the rare example of a politician to whom wiles were absolutely unknown, and whose professions to foreign governments and to his own countrymen were always sincere. In him was fully exemplified the real distinction which forever exists between wisdom and cunning, and the importance as well as truth of the maxim that "honesty is the best policy."

If Washington possessed ambition, that passion was, in his bosom, so regulated by principles, or controlled by circumstances, that it was neither vicious nor turbulent. Intrigue was never employed as the means of its gratification, nor was personal aggrandizement its object. The various high and important stations to which he was called by the public voice were unsought by himself; and in consenting to fill them, he seems rather to have yielded to a general conviction that the interests of his country would be thereby promoted, than to his particular inclination.

Neither the extraordinary partiality of the American people, the extravagant praises which were bestowed upon him, nor the inveterate opposition and malignant calumnies which he experienced, had any visible influence upon his conduct. The cause is to be looked for in the texture of his mind.

In him, that innate and unassuming modesty which adulation would have offended, which the voluntary plaudits of millions could not betray into indiscretion, and which never obtruded upon others his claims to superior consideration, was happily blended with a high and correct sense of personal dignity, and with a just consciousness of that respect which is due to station. Without exertion, he could maintain the happy medium between that arrogance which wounds, and that facility which allows the office to be degraded in the person who fills it.

It is impossible to contemplate the great events which have occurred in the United States under the auspices of Washington, without ascribing them, in some measure, to him. If we ask the causes of the prosperous issue of a war, against the successful termination of which there were so many probabilities? of the good which was produced, and the ill which was avoided during an administration fated to contend with the strongest prejudices that a combination of circumstances and of passions could produce? of the constant favour of the great mass of his fellow citizens, and of the confidence which, to the last moment of his life, they reposed in him? the answer, so far as these causes may be found in his character, will furnish a lesson well meriting the attention of those who are candidates for political fame.

Endowed by nature with a sound judgment, and an accurate discriminating mind, he feared not that laborious attention which made him perfectly master of those subjects, in all their relations, on which he was to decide: and this essential quality was guided by an unvarying sense of moral right, which would tolerate the employment only of

those means that would bear the most rigid examination; by a fairness
of intention which neither sought nor required disguise: <u>and by a
purity of virtue which was not only untainted, but unsuspected.</u>

JOHN MARSHALL was born at Germantown, Fauquier County, Va., September 24th,
1755, and died at Philadelphia, July 6th, 1835. He entered with ardor into the revolutionary
struggle; was a lieutenant in 1776, a captain in May, 1777, and fought at Brandywine, Germantown, and Monmouth. He was a member of Congress in 1799, and offered the resolutions on the death of Washington, prepared by Henry Lee, in the beautiful address given on
page 54. After serving in various prominent public positions, he was made Chief Justice of
the United States, January 31st, 1801, which office he filled with distinguished reputation and
unsullied dignity, until his death. His "Life of George Washington, Commander in Chief,
etc. etc.," 5 vols., 8vo. London and Philadelphia, 1804-7,—the first volume, however, being
devoted to a history of the American Colonies—was the first important and is the best biography of Washington. Our quotation is the conclusion of the last volume. Judge Story referring to this work in his sketch of the author, in the "National Portrait Gallery," says,
"The Life of Washington is indeed entitled to a very high rank, as it was prepared from a
diligent perusal of the original papers of that great man, which were submitted to the liberal
use of his biographer. It does not affect to deal with mere private and personal anecdotes,
to amuse the idle or the vicious. Its object is to expound the character and public services
of Washington, and to give a faithful outline of his principles and measures." A French
edition in five vols. was published in 1807, and an edition in two vols. without the introduction or Colonial history, at Philadelphia, in 1832.

AARON BANCROFT.

1807.

General Washington was exactly six feet in height, he appeared taller, as his shoulders rose a little higher than the true proportion. His eyes were of a grey, and his hair of a brown colour. His limbs were well formed, and indicated strength. His complexion was light, and his countenance serene and thoughtful. His manners were graceful, manly and dignified. His general appearance never failed to engage the respect and esteem of all who approached him.

Possessing strong natural passions, and having the nicest feelings of honour, he was in early life prone keenly to resent practices which carried the intention of abuse or insult; but the reflections of maturer age gave him the most perfect government of himself. He possessed a faculty above all other men to hide the weaknesses inseparable from human nature; and he bore with meekness and equanimity his distinguished honours.

Reserved, but not haughty, in his disposition, he was accessible to all in concerns of business, but he opened himself only to his confidential friends; and no art or address could draw from him an opinion, which he thought prudent to conceal.

He was not so much distinguished for brilliancy of genius as for solidity of judgment, and consummate prudence of conduct.* He was

---

* Compare John Marshall, page 143.—Ed.

(149)

not so eminent for any one quality of greatness and worth, as for the union of those great, aimable and good qualities, which are very rarely combined in the same character.

His maxims were formed upon the result of mature reflection, or extensive experience; they were the invariable rules of his practice; and on all important instances, he seemed to have an intuitive view of what the occasion rendered fit and proper. He pursued his purposes with a resolution, which, one solitary moment excepted, never failed him.*

Alive to social pleasures, he delighted to enter into familiar conversation with his acquaintance, and was somtimes sportive in his letters to his friends; but he never lost sight of the dignity of his character, nor deviated from the decorous and appropriate behaviour becoming his station in society.

He commanded from all the most respectful attention, and no man in his company ever fell into light or lewd conversation. His stile of living corresponded with his wealth; but his extensive establishment was managed with the strictest economy, and he ever reserved ample funds liberally to promote schemes of private benevolence, and works of publick utility. Punctual himself to every engagement, he exacted from others a strict fulfilment of contracts, but to the necessitous he was diffusive in his charities, and he greatly assisted the poorer classes of people in his vicinity, by furnishing them with means successfully to prosecute plans of industry.

In domestick and private life, he blended the authority of the master with the care and kindness of the guardian and friend. Solici-

* On York Island, in 1776.

tous for the welfare of his slaves, while at Mount Vernon, he every morning rode round his estates to examine their condition; for the sick, physicians were provided, and to the weak and infirm every necessary comfort was administered. The servitude of the negroes lay with weight upon his mind; he often made it the subject of conversation, and revolved several plans for their general emancipation; but could devise none, which promised success, in consistency with humanity to them, and safety to the state.

The address presented to him at Alexandria, on the commencement of his presidency, fully shows how much he was endeared to his neighbors, and the affection and esteem, in which his friends held his private character.*

His industry was unremitted, and his method so exact, that all the complicated business of his military command, and civil administration, was managed without confusion, and without hurry.

Not feeling the lust of power, and ambitious only for honourable fame, he devoted himself to his country upon the most disinterested principles; and his actions wore not the semblance but the reality of virtue: The purity of his motives was accredited, and absolute confidence placed in his patriotism.

While filling a publick station, the performance of his duty took the place of pleasure, emolument and every private consideration. During the more critical years of the war, a smile was scarcely seen upon his countenance, he gave himself no moments of relaxation; but his whole mind was engrossed to execute successfully his trust.

As a military commander, he struggled with innumerable em-

---

* For this address, see Marshall's Life of Washington, Vol. V, p. 155.—ED.

barrassments, arising from the short inlistment of his men, and from the want of provisions, clothing, arms and ammunition; and an opinion of his achievements should be formed in view of these inadequate means.

The first years of his civil administration were attended with the extraordinary fact, that while a great proportion of his countrymen reprobated his measures, they universally venerated his character, and relied implicitly on his integrity. Although his opponents eventually deemed it expedient to vilify his character, that they might diminish his political influence; yet the moment that he retired from publick life, they returned to their expressions of veneration and esteem; and after his death, used every endeavour to secure to their party the influence of his name.

He was as eminent for piety, as for patriotism. His publick and private conduct evince, that he impressively felt a sense of the superintendence of God and of the dependence of man. In his addresses while at the head of the army, and of the national government, he gratefully noticed the signal blessings of Providence, and fervently commended his country to divine benediction. In private, he was known to have been habitually devout.

In principle and practice he was a *Christian.* The support of an Episcopal church, in the vicinity of Mount Vernon, rested principally upon him, and here, when on his estate, he with constancy attended publick worship. In his address to the American people, at the close of the war, mentioning the favourable period of the world at which the independence of his country was established, and enumerating the causes which unitedly had ameliorated the condition of human society, he, above science, philosophy, commerce, and all other considerations, ranked "*the pure and benign light of Revelation.*" Supplicating Heaven that his fellow citizens might cultivate the disposition, and practise the virtues, which exalt a community, he presented the following petition to his God, "That he would most graciously be pleased to dispose us all to do justice, to love mercy, and to demean ourselves with that charity, humility and pacifick temper of mind, which were the characteristicks of the *Divine Author of our blessed religion;* without an humble imitation of whose example, in these things, we can never hope to be an happy nation."

During the war, he not unfrequently rode ten or twelve miles from camp to attend publick worship; and he never omitted this attendance, when opportunity presented.

In the establishment of his presidential houschold, he reserved to himself the Sabbath, free from the interruptions of private visits, or publick business; and throughout the eight years of his civil administration, he gave to the institutions of christianity the influence of his example.

He was as fortunate as great and good.

Under his auspices, a civil war was conducted with mildness, and a revolution with order. Raised himself above the influence of popular passions, he happily directed these passions to the most useful purposes. Uniting the talents of the soldier with the qualifications of the states-man,* and pursuing, unmoved by difficulties, the noblest end by the

---

* Compare John Bell, page 12. The earliest expression of this idea, however, is to be found on the first medal issued in honor of Washington—struck at Paris in 1778 by direction of Voltaire, and known as the *Voltaire Medal*—the legend of which is: "Washington réunit par un rare assemblage les talens du guerrier et les vertus du sage."—ED.

20

purest means, he had the supreme satisfaction of beholding the complete success of his great military and civil services, in the independence and happiness of his country.

Aaron Bancroft, D.D., a Unitarian minister, was born at Reading, Mass., November 10th, 1755, and graduated at Harvard College in 1778. He was a volunteer at Lexington and Bunker Hill, and although his studies were much interrupted by the Revolution, became one of the most accomplished scholars of the country. After spending some time in teaching, he studied theology, was licensed to preach, and spent three years as a missionary in Yarmouth, N. S. He afterwards (1786), settled in Worcester, Mass., where he died August 19th, 1839. His " Essay on the Life of George Washington, Commander in Chief of the American Army, through the Revolutionary War; and the first President of the United States," from which we make the above extract, was published at Worcester, in 1807. 8vo. It was reprinted in London by Stockdale in 1808, and several American editions have appeared. Dr. Bancroft also delivered, " An Eulogy on the character of the late Gen. George Washington, before the inhabitants of the town of Worcester, Commonwealth of Massachusetts, on Saturday, the 22d of February, 1800." 8vo, pp. 21, Worcester, 1800. From this we make the following quotation : " In other countries, individuals have been illustrious as Heroes and Statesmen. The talents which immortalized their respective names were united in our American Alfred ; and he was free from the vices and weaknesses, which were the shades of their characters. In him were combined the most excellent qualities of man ; and in his life appeared an assemblage of the noblest virtues of humanity. ' His life was one stream of light,' and the shadow of night rests not upon it. The picture of man in him was perfect, and there is no blot to tarnish its brightness. His character we must all contemplate with supreme delight : In it we view the dignity of our nature ; and the glory of our race. As an American character, we may all exult in it, as the ornament of our nation and the honor of our age. As the Patriot, whose exalted talents and pre-eminent endowments were devoted to our country, we feel the obligations of public gratitude—we are melted to emotions of tenderness—we are disposed to express every mark of admiration and respect."

DAVID RAMSAY.

1807.

THE person of George Washington was uncommonly tall. Mountain air, abundant exercise in the open country, the wholesome toils of the chase, and the delightful scenes of rural life, expanded his limbs to an unusual, but graceful and well-proportioned size. His exterior suggested to every beholder the idea of strength, united with manly gracefulness. His form was noble, and his port majestic. No man could approach him but with respect. His frame was robust, his constitution vigorous, and he was capable of enduring great fatigue. His passions were naturally strong; with them was his first contest, and over them his first victory. Before he undertook to command others, he had thoroughly learned to command himself. The powers of his mind were more solid than brilliant. Judgment was his forte.* To vivacity, wit, and the sallies of a lively imagination, he made no pretensions. His faculties resembled those of Aristotle, Bacon, Locke, and Newton; but were very unlike those of Voltaire. Possessed of a large proportion of common sense, directed by a sound practical judgment, he was better fitted for the exalted stations to which he was called, than many others, who, to a greater brilliancy of parts, frequently add the eccentricities of genius.

---

* Compare John Marshall, page 143.—ED.

(155)

Truth and utility were his objects. He steadily pursued, and generally attained them. With this view he thought much, and closely examined every subject on which he was to decide, in all its relations. Neither passion, party spirit, pride, prejudice, ambition, nor interest, influenced his deliberations. In making up his mind on great occasions, many of which occurred in which the fate of the army or nation seemed involved, he sought for information from all quarters, revolved the subject by night and by day,* and examined it in every point of view. Guided by these lights, and influenced by an honest and good heart, he was imperceptibly led to decisions which were wise and judicious. Perhaps no man ever lived who was so often called upon to form a judgment in cases of real difficulty, and who so often formed a right one. Engaged in the busy scenes of life, he knew human nature, and the most proper methods of accomplishing proposed objects. Of a thousand propositions he knew to distinguish the best, and to select among a thousand the individual most fitted for his purpose.

As a military man, he possessed personal courage, and a firmness which neither danger nor difficulties could shake. His perseverance overcame every obstacle; his moderation conciliated all opposition; his genius supplied every resource. He knew how to conquer by delay, and deserved true praise by despising unmerited censure. Inferior to his adversary in the numbers, the equipment, and discipline of

---

* In a letter to Gen. Knox, written after the termination of the revolutionary war, Washington observed—"Strange as it may seem, it is nevertheless true, that it was not until lately I could get the better of my usual custom of ruminating as soon as I awoke in the morning, on the business of the ensuing day; and of my surprise at finding, after revolving many things in my mind, that I was no longer a public man, or had any thing to do with public transactions."

his troops, no great advantage was ever obtained over him, and no opportunity to strike an important blow was ever neglected.* In the most ardent moments of the contest, his prudent firmness proved the salvation of his country.

The whole range of history does not present a character on which we can dwell with such entire unmixed admiration. His qualities were so happily blended, and so nicely harmonized, that the result was a great and perfect whole.†

The integrity of Washington was incorruptible. His principles were free from the contamination of selfish and unworthy passions. His real and avowed motives were the same. His ends were always upright, and his means pure. He was a statesman without guile, and his professions, both to his fellow-citizens and to foreign nations, were always sincere. No circumstances ever induced him to use duplicity. He was an example of the distinction which exists between wisdom and cunning; and his manly, open conduct, was an illustration of the soundness of the maxim—"that honesty is the best policy."

The learning of Washington was of a particular kind. He over-stepped the tedious forms of the schools, and by the force of a correct taste and sound judgment, seized on the great ends of learning, with-out the assistance of those means which have been contrived to prepare less active minds for public business. By a careful study of the English language; by reading good models of fine writing, and above all, by the aid of a vigorous mind, he made himself master of a pure, elegant, and classical style. His composition was all nerve; full of correct and

---

* John Marshall, page 143.—ED.

† London Courier, page 85.—ED.

manly ideas, which were expressed in precise and forcible language. His answers to the innumerable addresses which on all public occasions poured in upon him, were promptly made, handsomely expressed, and always contained something appropriate. His letters to Congress; his addresses to that body on the acceptance and resignation of his commission; his general orders as Commander in Chief; his speeches and messages as President; and above all, his two farewell addresses to the people of the United States, will remain lasting monuments of the goodness of his heart, of the wisdom of his head, and of the eloquence of his pen.

The powers of his mind were in some respects peculiar. He was a great, practical, self-taught genius; with a head to devise, and a hand to execute, projects of the first magnitude and greatest utility.

There are few men of any kind, and still fewer of those the world calls great, who have not some of their virtues eclipsed by corresponding vices. But this was not the case with General Washington. He had religion without austerity, dignity without pride, modesty without diffidence, courage without rashness, politeness without affectation, affability without familiarity. His private character, as well as his public one, will bear the strictest scrutiny. He was punctual in all his engagements; upright and honest in his dealings; temperate in his enjoyments; liberal and hospitable to an eminent degree; a lover of order; systematical and methodical in all his arrangements. He was the friend of morality and religion; steadily attended on public worship; encouraged and strengthened the hands of the clergy. In all his public acts, he made the most respectful mention of Providence; and, in a word, carried the spirit of piety with him both in his private life and public administration. *   *   *   *

He also possessed equanimity in an eminent degree. One even tenour marked the greatness of his mind, in all the variety of scenes through which he passed. In the most trying situations he never despaired, nor was he ever depressed. He was the same when retreating through Jersey from before a victorious enemy with the remains of his broken army, as when marching in triumph into Yorktown, over its demolished fortifications. The honours and applause he received from his grateful countrymen, would have made almost any other man giddy; but on him they had no mischievous effect. He exacted none of those attentions; but when forced upon him, he received them as favours, with the politeness of a well-bred man. He was great in deserving them, but much greater in not being elated with them.

The patriotism of Washington was of the most ardent kind, and without alloy. He was very different from those noisy patriots, who, with love of country in their mouths, and hell in their hearts, lay their schemes for aggrandizing themselves at every hazard; but he was one of those who love their country in sincerity, and who hold themselves bound to consecrate all their talents to its service. Numerous were the difficulties with which he had to contend—Great were the dangers he had to encounter—Various were the toils and services in which he had to share; but to all difficulties and dangers he rose superior. To all toils and services he cheerfully submitted for his country's good.

* * * *

Rulers of the world! Learn from Washington wherein true glory consists—Restrain your ambition—Consider your power as an obligation to do good—Let the world have peace, and prepare for yourselves, the enjoyment of that ecstatic pleasure which will result from devoting all your energies to the advancement of human happiness.

Citizens of the United States! while with grateful hearts you recollect the virtues of your Washington, carry your thoughts one step farther. On a review of his life, and of all the circumstances of the times in which he lived, you must be convinced, that a kind Providence in its beneficence raised him, and endowed him with extraordinary virtues, to be to you an instrument of great good. None but such a man could have carried you successfully through the revolutionary times which tried men's souls, and ended in the establishment of your independence. None but such a man could have braced up your government after it had become so contemptible, from the imbecility of the federal system. None but such a man could have saved your country from being plunged into war, either with the greatest naval power in Europe, or with that which is most formidable by land, in consequence of your animosity against the one, and your partiality in favour of the other.

Youths of the United States! Learn from Washington what may be done by an industrious improvement of your talents, and the cultivation of your moral powers. Without any extraordinary advantages from birth, fortune, patronage, or even of education, he, by virtue and industry, attained the highest seat in the temple of fame. You cannot all be commanders of armies, or chief magistrates; but you may all resemble him in the virtues of private and domestic life, in which he excelled, and in which he most delighted. Equally industrious with his plough as his sword, he esteemed idleness and inutility as the greatest disgrace of man, whose powers attain perfection only by constant and vigorous action.* Washington, in private life, was as aimable as virtuous; and as great as he appeared sublime, on the public theatre of the world. He lived in the discharge of all the civil, social, and domestic offices of life. He was temperate in his desires, and faithful to his duties. For more than forty years of happy wedded love, his high example strengthened the tone of public manners. He had more real enjoyment in the bosom of his family, than in the pride of military command, or in the pomp of sovereign power.

On the whole, his life affords the brightest model for imitation, not only to warriors and statesmen, but to private citizens; for his character was a constellation of all the talents and virtues which dignify or adorn human nature.

> "He was a man, take him for all in all,
> We ne'er shall look upon his like again."

DAVID RAMSAY, M.D., was born in Lancaster County, Pa., April 2d, 1749, and died at Charleston, S. C., May 8th, 1815. He graduated at the College of New Jersey in 1765, studied medicine in Philadelphia, and removed to Charleston in 1773, where he soon acquired celebrity as a physician and labored zealously with his pen in the cause of his country. Dr. Ramsay was a leading member of the South Carolina legislature, and served in the army as a surgeon. He was an accomplished scholar, and an unselfish patriot. His " Life of George Washington " from which we quote, was published in 1807. 8vo, New York and London. A number of 12mo editions have been published, Boston, 1811, Baltimore, 1814 and 1825, Ithaca, N. Y., 1840, and at Hartford; also in French, Paris, 1809 and 1819, 8vo; in Spanish, Paris, 1809, and at Barcelona, 1842, 2 vols., 8vo.

---

* Samuel Stanhope Smith, page 82.—ED.

21

JOHN JAY.

1811.

There have been in the world but two systems or schools of policy, the one founded on the great principles of wisdom and rectitude, the other on cunning, and its various artifices. To the first of these belonged Washington, and all the other worthies of every other country who ascended to the Temple of Honor through the Temple of Virtue. The doctrines, maxims, and precepts of this school have been explained and inculcated by the ablest writers, ancient and modern. In all civilized countries they are known, though often neglected; and in free States have always been publicly commended and taught; they crossed the Atlantic with our forefathers, and in our days particularly, have not only engaged the time and attention of students, but have been constantly and eloquently displayed by able men in our senates and assemblies. What reason can there be that Washington did not understand those subjects? If it be asked what these subjects comprehend or relate to, the answer is this—they relate to the nature and duties of man, to his propensities and passions, his virtues and vices, his habits and prejudices, his real and relative wants and enjoyments, his capacities for social and national happiness, and the means by which, according to time, place, and other existing circumstances, it is in a greater or less degree to be procured, preserved, and increased. From a profound investigation of these subjects, enlightened by

(162)

experience, result all that knowledge and those maxims and precepts of sound policy, which enable legislators and rulers to manage and govern public affairs wisely and justly.

By what other means than the practical use of this knowledge, could Washington have been able to lead and govern an army hastily collected from various parts, and who brought with them to the field all the license and all the habits which they had indulged at home? Could he, by the force of orders and proclamations, have constrained them to render to him that obedience, confidence, and warm attachment which he so soon acquired, and which throughout all vicissitudes and distresses, continued constant and undiminished to the last? By what other means could he have been able to frustrate the designs of dark cabals, and the unceasing intrigues of envious competitors, and the arts of the opposing enemy? By what other means could he have been able, in so masterly a manner, to meet and manage all those perplexing embarrassments which the revolutionary substitution of a new government,—which the want of that power in congress which they had not, and of that promptitude which no deliberative body can have,—which the frequent destitution and constant uncertainty of essential supplies,—which the incompetency of individuals on whom much depended, the perfidy of others, and the mismanagement of many, could not fail to engender? We know, and history will inform posterity, that, from the first of his military career, he had to meet, and encounter, and surmount a rapid succession of formidable difficulties, even down to the time when his country was enabled, by the success of their arms, to obtain the honourable peace which terminated the war. His high and appointed course being then finished, he disdained the intimations of lawless ambition to prolong it. He disbanded the army under circumstances which required no common degree of policy or virtue; and with universal admiration and plaudits, descended, joyfully and serenely, into the shades of retirement. They who ascribe all this to the guidance and protection of Providence do well, but let them recollect that Providence seldom interposes in human affairs, but through the agency of human means.

When at a subsequent and alarming period, the nation found that their affairs had gone into confusion, and that clouds portending danger and distress were rising over them, in every quarter, they instituted under his auspices a more efficient government, and unanimously committed the administration of it to him. Would they have done this without the highest confidence in his political talents and wisdom? Certainly not—no novice in navigation was ever unanimously called upon to take the helm or command of a ship on the point of running aground among the breakers. This universal confidence would have proved universal mistake, had it not been justified by the event. The unanimous opinion entertained and declared by a whole people in favor of any fellow-citizen is rarely erroneous, especially in times of alarm and calamity.

To delineate the course, and enumerate the measures which he took to arrive at success, would be to write a volume. The firmness and policy with which he overcame the obstacles placed in his way by the derangement of national affairs, by the devices of domestic demagogues and of foreign agents, as well as by the deleterious influences of the French revolution, need not be particularized. Our records, and histories, and memories, render it unnecessary. It is sufficient to say, and it can be said with truth, that his administration raised the nation out of confusion into order, out of degradation and distress into reputation and prosperity; it found us withering—it left us flourishing.

JOHN JAY, first Chief Justice of the United States, of whom it has been said that, "In lofty disinterestedness, in unyielding integrity, in superiority to the illusions of passion, no one of the great men of the Revolution approached so near to Washington," was born in New York City, December 12, 1745, and died at Bedford, Westchester County, N. Y., May 17, 1829. Our extract is from a letter to Richard Peters, Esq., dated Bedford, March 29th, 1811, written in support of his conviction that Washington was the author of the *Farewell Address*, and furnishing some direct evidence to that effect, which had come to his personal knowledge. The letter is printed in "The Life of John Jay with selections from his correspondence and miscellaneous papers. By his son William Jay." New York, 1833. 2 vols., 8vo. In an address to the New York State legislature as Governor, January 28, 1800, John Jay alluding to the death of Washington, said, "His memory will be cherished by the wise and good of every nation; and truth, triumphing over her adversaries, will transmit his character to posterity in all its genuine lustre. His excellent example and excellent admonitions still remain with us, and happy will that people be whose leaders imitate the one and observe the other."

CHARLES PHILLIPS.

No matter what may be the birth-place of such a man as Washington. No climate can claim, no country can appropriate him—the boon of Providence to the human race—his fame is eternity, and his residence creation! Though it was the defeat of our arms, and the disgrace of our policy, I almost bless the convulsion in which he had his origin; if the heavens thundered and the earth rocked, yet when the storm passed, how pure was the climate that it cleared—how bright in the brow of the firmament was the planet it revealed to us! In the production of Washington it does really appear as if nature was endeavoring to improve upon herself, and that all the virtues of the ancient world were but so many studies preparatory to the patriot of the new. Individual instances, no doubt there were, splendid exemplifications of some single qualification—Cæsar was merciful—Scipio was continent—Hannibal was patient—but it was reserved for Washington to blend them all in one, and like the lovely *chef d'œuvre* of the Grecian artist, to exhibit in one glow of associated beauty, the pride of every model, and the perfection of every master.

As a general, he marshalled the peasant into a veteran, and supplied by discipline the absence of experience. As a statesman, he enlarged the policy of the cabinet into the most comprehensive system of general advantage; and such was the wisdom of his views, and the philosophy of his councils, that to the soldier and the statesman he

(166)

almost added the character of the sage.* A conqueror, he was untainted with the crime of blood—a revolutionist, he was free from any stain of treason; for aggression commenced the contest, and a country called him to the command. Liberty unsheathed his sword—necessity stained—victory returned it. If he had paused here, history might doubt what station to assign him—whether at the head of her citizens, or her soldiers,—her heroes or her patriots. But the last glorious act crowned his career, and banishes hesitation. Who like Washington, after having freed a country, resigned her crown, and retired to a cottage rather than reign in a capital! Immortal man! He took from the battle its crime, and from the conquest its chains—he left the victorious the glory of his self-denial, and turned upon the vanquished only the retribution of his mercy.

CHARLES PHILLIPS, a native of Sligo, Ireland, was born in 1787, and died in 1859. He was admitted to the University of Dublin in 1802, and entered the middle Temple in 1807; was called to the Irish bar in 1811, and to the English bar in 1821. Mr. Phillips was made a Commissioner of the Court of Insolvent Debtors in 1846, the duties of which he discharged with great credit until his death. Our extract is from " A Tribute to the memory of the late General Washington, President of the United States of America, by Charles Phillips." 8vo., pp. 12. London, n. d. The tribute was pronounced about the year 1813 at a dinner near Killarney, Ireland, in prefacing a toast, *The Memory of Washington.*

* See note, p. 153.—ED.

THOMAS JEFFERSON.

1814.

I THINK I knew General Washington intimately and thoroughly; and were I called on to delineate his character, it should be in terms like these. His mind was great and powerful, without being of the very first order; his penetration strong, though not so acute as that of a Newton, Bacon or Locke; and, as far as he saw, no judgment was ever sounder. _It was slow in operation, being little aided by invention or imagination, but sure in conclusion. Hence the common remark of his officers, of the advantage he derived from councils of war, where, hearing all suggestions, he selected whatever was best; and certainly no General ever planned his battles more judiciously. But if deranged during the course of the action, if any member of his plan was dislocated by sudden circumstances, he was slow in re-adjustment. The consequence was, that he often failed in the field, and rarely against an enemy in station, as at Boston and York. He was incapable of fear, meeting personal dangers with the calmest unconcern.

Perhaps the strongest feature in his character was prudence, never acting until every circumstance, every consideration, was maturely weighed; refraining, if he saw a doubt, but, when, once decided, going through with his purpose whatever obstacles opposed. His integrity was most pure, his justice the most inflexible I have ever known, no motives of interest or consanguinity, of friendship or hatred, being able

(168)

to bias his decision.   He was, indeed, in every sense of the words, a
wise, a good, and a great man.   His temper was naturally irritable
and high-toned; but reflection and resolution had obtained a firm and
habitual ascendency over it.   If ever, however, it broke its bonds, he
was most tremendous in his wrath.

In his expenses he was honorable, but exact; liberal in contributions to whatever promised utility; but frowning and unyielding on
all visionary projects, and all unworthy calls on his charity.   His
heart was not warm in its affections; but he exactly calculated every
man's value, and gave him a solid esteem proportioned to it.   His
person, you know, was fine, his stature exactly what one would wish,
his deportment easy, erect and noble; the best horseman of his age,
and the most graceful figure that could be seen on horseback.   Although in the circle of his friends, where he might be unreserved with
safety, he took a free share in conversation, his colloquial talents were
not above mediocrity, possessing neither copiousness of ideas, nor
fluency of words.

In public when called on for a sudden opinion, he was unready,
short and embarrassed.   Yet he wrote readily, rather diffusely, in an
easy and correct style.   This he had acquired by conversation with
the world, for his education was merely reading, writing and common
arithmetic, to which he added surveying at a later day.   His time was
employed in action chiefly, reading little, and that only in agriculture
and English history.   His correspondence became necessarily extensive, and, with journalizing his agricultural proceedings, occupied
most of his leisure hours within doors.   On the whole, his character
was, in its mass, perfect, in nothing bad, in few points indifferent; and

22

it may be truly said, that never did nature and fortune combine more perfectly to make a man great, and to place him in the same constellation with whatever worthies have merited from man an everlasting remembrance. For his was the singular destiny and merit, of leading the armies of his country successfully through an arduous war for the establishment of its independence; of conducting its councils through the birth of a government, new in its form and principles, until it had settled down into a quiet and orderly train; and of scrupulously obeying the laws through the whole of his career, civil and military, of which the history of the world furnishes no other example. I felt on his death, with my countrymen, that "verily a great man hath fallen this day in Israel."

THOMAS JEFFERSON, Secretary of State under Washington, and third President of the United States (1801-9), was born at Shadwell, afterwards called Monticello, Va., April 2d, 1743, and died there July 4th, 1826. As the author of the Declaration of Independence and the founder of the Democratic party, Jefferson has probably exerted a greater influence on the institutions of the United States, than any other American, except Washington. The just and carefully drawn character above given, is taken from a letter to Dr. Walter Jones, an eminent physician of Virginia, dated Monticello, January 2d, 1814, printed in Vol. VI, of "The Writings of Thomas Jefferson," Washington, D. C., 1853-5. 9 vols., 8vo.

FRANCOIS MARBOIS.

1816.

When the war broke out in America, it was soon recognized that Washington was the man the best fitted to command the armies of the new republic; and if the title of great man should be awarded to those who, in difficult situations, perform the highest duties most beneficially to their country, and most in accord with the rules of wisdom, no character of ancient history, none of modern times, has been more worthy than he of this noble name.

In private life, the correctness of his principles and his conduct earned the affection of all those with whom he lived; and they valued more than any other of their experiences, the good fortune of having been admitted to an intimate acquaintance with a man so justly illustrious.

He possessed also, in the highest degree, the qualities which make up the character of a statesman: vigilance and foresight in the ordinary course of affairs; a steadfastness under adversity that could not be shaken; moderation in success; and perseverance in the execution of his designs.

Clothed with the authority conferred by talents and virtue on exalted characters, the most powerful leader that ever commanded the armies of a republic, he was never carried away by the intoxication of power, the strongest and most consuming passion that can possess the

(171)

human heart, the passion to which so many madmen have sacrificed life and even honor. The public welfare was constantly the end of his efforts; they were crowned with success; and his renown, so great while he lived, and increasing from day to day, has no other foundation than his virtues.

Above all things else, he desired to be numbered with the founders of the independence of the colonies. The universal verdict assigns him the first place among them.

He cared nothing for the popular applause which flattery showers on vanity. One day, after a great victory while listening to harangues and felicitations, he seemed to give them the attention rarely refused by the most modest men to evidences of public admiration. With one hand he received the addresses that were presented to him, and placed them in his breast. In the other he held replies prepared in advance; but he attached so little importance to them, or he was so preoccupied with serious matters, that he read from beginning to end to a deputation of magistrates, the one which he had intended for the generals.

This man, deaf to the empty sound of plaudits, had, from early youth, contracted the habit of sacrificing everything to duty, and of departing in nothing from the rules of justice.

It was never necessary to remind him of a promise. He said: "When I arouse an expectation, I am signing a contract."

His troops had unlimited confidence in him, and he obtained from them more by a kindly word than others could by benefits and gifts.

It might have been expected that having acquired so much glory and power by his military talents, he would retain a belligerent disposition, even in peaceful times.

Those who would have liked to engage him in the war which arose between France and England, publicly claimed that the independence of the United States was concerned in the contest; but he resisted them steadily; and if he consented to make some preparations for war, it was always with the intention of better assuring peace.

When, after a public life so full of usefulness, he retired to his home to live as a simple citizen, he felt that he was only pursuing his accustomed course, in obedience to reason, to age, and to nature.

FRANCOIS MARBOIS, Marquis of Barbé Marbois, was born at Metz, January 31, 1745, and died January 14, 1837. He was appointed in 1779 to the post of Secretary of the French legation to the United States, during our Revolution, and was the principal agent in the most important operations of the embassy. His "Complot D'Arnold et de Sir Henry Clinton contre Les Etats-Unis D'Amérique et contre Le Général Washington—Septembre, 1780," from which we quote, was published at Paris in 1816. 12 mo. A translation by Robert Walsh was printed in the *American Register* for 1817. This, however, does not include the above, which we translate from a note at the end of the volume, omitted by Mr. Walsh.

ELKANAH WATSON.

I HAD feasted my imagination for several days in the near prospect of a visit to Mount Vernon, the seat of Washington. No pilgrim ever approached Mecca with deeper enthusiasm. I arrived there, in the afternoon of January 23d, '85. I was the bearer of the letter from Gen. Green, with another from Col. Fitzgerald, one of the former aids of Washington, and also the books from Granville Sharp. Although assured, that these credentials would secure me a respectful reception, I trembled with awe as I came into the presence of this great man. I found him at table, with Mrs. Washington and his private family, and was received in the native dignity and with that urbanity so peculiarly combined in the character of a soldier and eminent private gentleman. He soon put me at ease, by unbending in a free and affable conversation.

The cautious reserve, which wisdom and policy dictated, whilst engaged in rearing the glorious fabric of our independence, was evidently the result of consummate prudence, and not characteristic of his nature. Although I had frequently seen him in the progress of the Revolution, and had corresponded with him from France in '81 and '82, this was the first occasion on which I had contemplated him in his private relations. I observed a peculiarity in his smile, which seemed to illuminate his eye; his whole countenance beamed with

(174)

intelligence, while it commanded confidence and respect. The gentleman who had accompanied me from Alexandria, left in the evening, and I remained alone in the enjoyment of the society of Washington, for two of the richest days of my life. I saw him reaping the reward of his illustrious deeds, in the quiet shade of his beloved retirement. He was at the matured age of fifty-three. Alexander and Cæsar both died before they reached that period of life, and both had immortalized their names. How much stronger and nobler the claims of Washington to immortality! In the impulses of mad and selfish ambition, they acquired fame by wading to the conquest of the world through seas of blood. Washington, on the contrary, was parsimonious of the blood of his countrymen, and stood forth, the pure and virtuous champion of their rights, and formed for them, (not himself,) a mighty Empire.

To have communed with such a man in the bosom of his family, I shall always regard as one of the highest privileges, and most cherished incidents of my life. I found him kind and benignant in the domestic circle, revered and beloved by all around him; agreeably social, without ostentation; delighting in anecdote and adventures, without assumption; his domestic arrangements harmonious and systematic. His servants seemed to watch his eye, and to anticipate his every wish; hence a look was equivalent to a command. His servant Billy, the faithful companion of his military career, was always at his side. Smiling content animated and beamed on every countenance in his presence.

The first evening I spent under the wing of his hospitality, we sat a full hour at table by ourselves, without the least interruption, after the family had retired. I was extremely oppressed by a severe cold and excessive coughing, contracted by the exposure of a harsh winter journey. He pressed me to use some remedies, but I declined doing so. As usual after retiring, my coughing increased. When some time had elapsed, the door of my room was gently opened, and on drawing my bed-curtains, to my utter astonishment, I beheld Washington himself, standing at my bed-side, with a bowl of hot tea in his hand. I was mortified and distressed beyond expression. This little incident, occurring in common life, with an ordinary man, would not have been noticed; but as a trait of the benevolence and private virtue of Washington, deserves to be recorded.

ELKANAH WATSON was born at Plymouth, Mass., January 22, 1758, and died at Port Kent, New York, December 5, 1842. In August 1779 he was bearer of dispatches to Franklin at Paris, and afterwards opened a commercial house at Nantes, in which enterprise however, after a short period of prosperity, he failed. He then visited England, Holland and Flanders, and returned to the United States in 1784, settling in Pittsfield, Mass., in 1807 and devoting himself to agriculture. In 1816 he went to Albany and organized the first Agricultural Society in the State of New York, and in 1828 moved to Port Kent on Lake Champlain. His Journals recording his observations of men and incidents, as the events occurred to which they relate, were revised by him in 1821, and published at New York in 1856, by his son Winslow, under the title, " Men and Times of the Revolution or Memoirs of Elkanah Watson," 8vo., from which we quote.

COUNT DE SÉGUR.

1824.

ONE of my most earnest wishes was to see Washington, the hero of America. He was then encamped at a short distance from us, and the Count de Rochambeau was kind enough to introduce me to him. Too often reality disappoints the expectations our imagination had raised, and admiration diminishes by a too near view of the object upon which it had been bestowed; but, on seeing General Washington, I found a perfect similarity between the impression produced upon me by his aspect, and the idea I had formed of him.

His exterior disclosed, as it were, the history of his life: simplicity, grandeur, dignity, calmness, goodness, firmness, the attributes of his character, were also stamped upon his features, and in all his person. His stature was noble and elevated; the expression of his features mild and benevolent; his smile graceful and pleasing; his manners simple, without familiarity.

He did not display the luxury of a monarchical general; every thing announced in him the hero of a republic; he inspired with, rather than commanded respect, and the expression of all those that surrounded his person manifested the existence in their breasts of feelings of sincere affection, and of that entire confidence in the chief upon whom they seemed exclusively to found all their hopes of safety. His quarters, at a little distance from the camp, offered the image of the

23   (177)

order and regularity displayed in the whole tenor of his life, his manner, and conduct.

I had expected to find, in this popular camp, soldiers ill equipped
officers without instruction, republicans destitute of that urbanity so
common in our old civilized countries.   I recollected the first moment
of their revolution, when husbandmen, and artizans, who had never
held a gun, had hastened, without order, and in the name of their
country, to go and fight the British phalanxes, offering only to the
view of their astonished enemies an assemblage of rough and unpol-
ished beings, whose only military insignia consisted of a cap, upon
which the word *liberty* was written.

It will, therefore, be easily imagined how much I was surprised
at finding an army well disciplined, in which every thing offered the
aspect of order, reason, information, and experience.   The manners
and language of the generals, their aids-de-camp, and the other officers
were noble and appropriate, and were heightened by that natural benevolence which appears to me as much preferable to politeness, as a
mild countenance is preferable to a mask upon which the utmost
labour has been bestowed to render its features graceful.

The personal dignity of each individual, the noble pride with
which all were inspired by the love of liberty, and a sentiment of
equality, had been no slight obstacles to the elevation of a chief, who
was to rise above them without exciting their jealousy, and to subject
their independent spirit to the rules of discipline without promoting
discontent.

Any other man but Washington would have failed in the attempt;
but such were his genius and his wisdom, that, in the midst of the

storms of a revolution, he commanded, during seven years, the army of a free nation, without exciting the alarms of his countrymen, or the suspicions of the Congress.

Under every circumstance he united in his favor the suffrages of rich and poor, magistrate and warriors; in short, Washington is, perhaps, the only man who ever conducted and terminated a civil war without having drawn upon himself any deserved censure.* As it was known to all that he entirely disregarded his own private interest, and consulted solely the general welfare, he enjoyed, during his life, those unanimous homages which the greatest men generally fail to receive from their contemporaries, and which they must only expect from posterity. It might have been said that envy, seeing him so highly established in public estimation, had become discouraged, and cast away her shafts in despair of their ever being able to reach him.

Washington, when I saw him, was forty-nine years of age. He endeavored modestly to avoid the marks of admiration and respect which were so anxiously offered to him, and yet no man ever knew better how to receive and to acknowledge them. He listened, with an obliging attention, to all those who addressed him, and the expression of his countenance had conveyed his answer before he spoke.

Inspired with the purest and most disinterested love for his country, he refused to receive the salary assigned to him as general-

---

* This point is more forcibly expressed by the Marquis de Chastellux, page 27. William Ellery Channing, also in his *Essay on the Life and Character of Napoleon Bonaparte (Discourses, Reviews, &c., 1830)* says: "To Washington belonged the proud distinction of being the leader in a revolution, without awakening one doubt or solicitude as to the spotless purity of his purpose."—ED.

in-chief, and it was almost in spite of him that the state undertook to defray the cost of his table.   That table was, every day, prepared for thirty guests, and the dinner, which, according to the custom of the English and of the Americans, lasted several hours, was concluded by numerous toasts.   Those most generally given were—"The independence of the United States"—"The King and Queen of France"—"Success to the Allied Armies."   After these came private toasts, or, as they were called in America, "sentiments."   In general, after the table had been cleared, and nothing was left but bottles and cheese, the company still remained seated round it until night.   Temperance was, however, one of Washington's virtues; and, in thus protracting the duration of his repast, he had only one object in view; the pleasure of conversation, which afforded a diversion from his cares, and repose from his fatigues.

General Washington received me with great kindness.   He spoke to me of the gratitude which his country would ever retain for the King of France and for his generous assistance; highly extolled the wisdom and skill of General Count de Rochambeau, expressing himself honored by having deserved and obtained his friendship; warmly commended the bravery and discipline of our army; and concluded by speaking to me, in very obliging and handsome terms, of my father whose long services and numerous wounds were becoming ornaments, he said, to a minister of war.

Louis Phillipe, Count de Ségur, son of Marshal Ségur, minister of war under Louis XVI, was born at Paris, December 10th, 1753, and died there August 27th, 1832.   He entered the army in 1767, and being appointed lieutenant-colonel to the regiment de Soissonnais then in America, embarked May 19th, 1782, on board the frigate *La Gloire* for the

United States, but in consequence of an accident to the vessel, and through conflicting orders did not leave France until July 15th. After an eventful voyage, being also intercepted by an English Squadron in Delaware Bay, and obliged to make a landing by boats, he succeeded in joining his regiment in camp at Crampond, nine miles from Peekskill, on the Hudson, September 26th. He shortly afterwards dined with Washington at his headquarters at Verplanck's Point, and returned to France with his regiment, sailing from Boston, December 24th, of the same year. Our extract is from his "Memoirs and Recollections," written in 1824, and of which a translation was published at Boston in 1825. 8vo. The Count represented France at the Court of St. Petersburg in 1789, as mentioned by PAUL JONES in a letter to Washington, dated Amsterdam, December 20th of that year, which, being pertinent to our subject we transcribe. "Sir,—I avail myself of the departure of the Philadelphia packet, Captain Earle, to transmit to your excellency a letter I received for you on leaving Russia in August last, from my friend, the Count de Ségur, minister of France at St. Petersburg. That gentleman and myself have frequently conversed on subjects that regard America: and the most pleasing reflection of all has been, the happy establishment of the new constitution, and that you are so deservedly placed at the head of the government by the unanimous voice of America. Your name alone, Sir, has established in Europe a confidence that was for some time before entirely wanting in American concerns; and I am assured, that the happy effects of your administration are still more sensibly felt throughout the United States. This is more glorious for you than all the laurels that your sword so nobly won in the support of the rights of human nature. In war your fame is immortal as the hero of liberty! In peace you are her patron, and the firmest supporter of her rights! Your greatest admirers, and even your best friends, have now but one wish left for you,—that you may long enjoy health and your present happiness."

CHATEAUBRIAND.

1828.

IF we compare Washington and Buonaparte, man to man, the genius of the former seems of a less elevated order than that of the latter. Washington belongs not, like Buonaparte, to that race of the Alexanders and Cæsars, who surpass the ordinary stature of mankind· Nothing astonishing attaches to his person; he is not placed on a vast theatre; he is not pitted against the ablest captains and the mightiest monarchs of his time; he traverses no seas; he hurries not from Memphis to Vienna and from Cadiz to Moscow: he defends himself with a handful of citizens on a soil without recollections and without celebrity, in the narrow circle of the domestic hearths. He fights none of those battles which renew the triumphs of Arbela and Pharsalia; he overturns no thrones to re-compose others with their ruins; he places not his foot on the necks of kings; he sends not word to them in the vestibules of his palaces,

Qu'ils se font trop attendre, et qu' Attila s'ennuie.

Something of stillness envelopes the actions of Washington; he acts deliberately: you would say that he feels himself to be the representative of the liberty of future ages, and that he is afraid of compromising it. It is not his own destinies but those of his country with which this hero of a new kind is charged; he allows not himself to hazard what does not belong to him. But what light bursts forth from this

(182)

profound obscurity! Search the unknown forests where glistened the sword of Washington, what will you find there? graves? no! a world! Washington has left the United States for a trophy of his field of battle.

Buonaparte has not any one characteristic of this grave American: he fights on an old soil, surrounded with glory and celebrity; he wishes to create nothing but his own renown; he takes upon himself nothing but his own aggrandizement. He seems to be aware that his mission will be short, that the torrent which falls from such a height will speedily be exhausted: he hastens to enjoy and to abuse his glory, as men do a fugitive youth. Like the gods of Homer, he wants to reach the end of the world in four steps: he appears on every shore, he hastily inscribes his name in the annals of every nation; he throws crowns as he runs to his family and his soldiers; he is in a hurry in his monuments, in his laws, in his victories. Stooping over the world, with one hand he overthrows kings, and with the other strikes down the revolutionary giant; but in crushing anarchy he stifles liberty, and finally loses his own in the field of his last battle.

Each is rewarded according to his works: Washington raises his nation to independence: a retired magistrate he sinks quietly to rest beneath his paternal roof, amid the regrets of his countrymen and the veneration of all nations.

Buonaparte robbed a nation of its independence: a fallen emperor, he is hurried into an exile where the fears of the world deem him not safely enough imprisoned in the custody of the ocean. So long as, feeble and chained upon a rock, he struggles with death, Europe dares not lay down its arms. He expires: this intelligence, published at the gate of the palace before which the conqueror had caused so many funerals to be proclaimed, neither stops nor astonishes the passenger: what had the citizens to deplore?

The republic of Washington subsists, whereas the empire of Buonaparte is destroyed: he died between the first and second voyage of a Frenchman, who found a grateful nation where he had fought for a few oppressed colonists.

Washington and Buonaparte sprang from the bosom of a republic: both born of liberty, the one was faithful to it, the other betrayed it. Their lot in futurity will be as different as their choice.

The name of Washington will spread with liberty from age to age; it will mark the commencement of a new era for mankind.

The name of Buonaparte also will be repeated by future generations; but it will not be accompanied with any benediction, and will frequently serve for authority to oppressors, great or small.

Washington was completely the representative of the wants, the ideas, the knowledge, and the opinions of his time; he seconded instead of thwarting the movement of mind; he aimed at that which it was his duty to aim at: hence the coherence and the perpetuity of his work. This man, who appears not very striking, because he is natural and in his just proportions, blended his existence with that of his country; his glory is the common patrimony of growing civilization: his renown towers like one of those sanctuaries, whence flows an inexhaustible spring for the people.

FRANCOIS AUGUSTE, VICOMTE DE CHATEAUBRIAND, the celebrated French author, was born at St. Malo, September 4, 1768, and died, July 4, 1848. He received his early education in the college at Rennes. Impelled by a desire to travel, he sailed for the United States, May 6, 1791, and landing at Baltimore, proceeded to Philadelphia, where he dined with

Washington. After traveling quite extensively through the country, and noticing particularly the habits and customs of the Indians, he returned to France the following year. His "Travels in America and Italy," were translated and published in two vols., 8vo, at London, in 1828, from volume first of which, we extract the above parallel between Washington and Buonaparte. Chateaubriand in referring to his visit to Washington, says, "Such was my interview with the man who gave liberty to a whole world. Washington sunk into the tomb before any little celebrity had attached to my name. I passed before him as the most unknown of beings; he was in all his glory, I in the depth of my obscurity. My name probably dwelt not a whole day in his memory. Happy, however, that his looks were cast upon me! I have felt myself warmed for it all the rest of my life. There is a virtue in the looks of a great man."

WILLIAM SULLIVAN.

1833.

The following are recollections of Washington, derived from repeated opportunities of seeing him during the three last years of his public life. He was over six feet in stature; of strong, bony, muscular frame, without fullness of covering, well-formed and straight. He was a man of most extraordinary strength. In his own house, his action was calm, deliberate, and dignified, without pretension to gracefulness, or peculiar manner, but merely natural, and such as one would think it should be in such a man. When walking in the street, his movement had not the soldierly air which might be expected. His habitual motions had been formed, long before he took command of the American Armies, in the wars of the interior and in the surveying of wilderness lands, employments in which grace and elegance were not likely to be acquired. At the age of sixty-five, time had done nothing towards bending him out of his natural erectness. His deportment was invariably grave; it was sobriety that stopped short of sadness. His presence inspired a veneration, and a feeling of awe, rarely experienced in the presence of any man. His mode of speaking was slow and deliberate, not as though he was in search of fine words, but that he might utter those only adapted to his purpose.

It was the usage for all persons in good society, to attend Mrs. Washington's levee every Friday evening. He was always present.

(186)

The young ladies used to throng around him, and engage him in conversation. There were some of the well-remembered *belles* of that day, who imagined themselves to be favorites with him. As these were the only opportunities which they had of conversing with him, they were disposed to use them. One would think, that a gentleman and gallant soldier, if he could ever laugh, or dress his countenance in smiles, would do so when surrounded by young and admiring beauties. But this was never so; the countenance of Washington never softened; nor changed its habitual gravity. One who had lived always in his family, said, that his manner in public life, and in the seclusion of most retired life, was always the same. Being asked whether Washington *could* laugh; this person said, that this was a rare occurrence, but that one instance was remembered, when he laughed most heartily at her narration of an incident in which she was a party concerned; and in which he applauded her agency.

WILLIAM SULLIVAN was born at Saco, Maine, November 30, 1774, and died at Boston, Mass. September 3, 1839. He graduated at Harvard College in 1792, was admitted to the bar in 1795, and practiced for many years with great reputation in Boston. He published a number of addresses, was an elegant scholar and a persuasive orator. Our extract is from a letter dated March 30, 1833, one of a series published at Boston, in 1834, under the title of "Familiar letters on the public men of the Revolution," 8vo, written in vindication of the Federal party. An enlarged edition, title "The public men of the Revolution," with a biographical sketch of the author by his son, John T. S. Sullivan, was published at Philadelphia in 1847.

JAMES K. PAULDING.

1835.

In analyzing the character of Washington, there is nothing that strikes me as more admirable than its beautiful symmetry. In this respect it is consummate. His different qualities were so nicely balanced, so rarely associated, of such harmonious affinities, that no one seemed to interfere with another, or predominate over the whole. The natural ardour of his disposition was steadily restrained by a power of self-command which it dared not disobey. His caution never degenerated into timidity, nor his courage into imprudence or temerity. His memory was accompanied by a sound, unerring judgment, which turned its acquisitions to the best advantage; his industry and economy of time neither rendered him dull or unsocial; his dignity never was vitiated by pride or harshness, and his unconquerable firmness was free from obstinacy, or self-willed arrogance. He was gigantic, but at the same time he was well-proportioned and beautiful. It was this symmetry of parts that diminished the apparent magnitude of the whole; as in those fine specimens of Grecian architecture, where the size of the temple seems lessened by its perfection. There are plenty of men who become distinguished by the predominance of one single faculty, or the exercise of a solitary virtue; but few, very few, present to our contemplation such a combination of virtues unalloyed by a single vice; such a succession of actions, both public and private, in which even his enemies can find nothing to blame.

(188)

Assuredly he stands almost alone in the world. He occupies a region where there are, unhappily for mankind, but few inhabitants. The Grecian biographer could easily find parallels for Alexander and Cæsar, but were he living now, he would meet with great difficulty in selecting one for Washington. There seems to be an elevation of moral excellence, which, though possible to attain to, few ever approach. As in ascending the lofty peaks of the Andes, we at length arrive at a line where vegetation ceases, and the principle of life seems extinct; so in the gradations of human character, there is an elevation which is never attained by mortal man. A few have approached it, and none nearer than Washington.

He is eminently conspicuous as one of the great benefactors of the human race, for he not only gave liberty to millions, but his name now stands, and will for ever stand, a noble example to high and low. He is a great work of the Almighty artist, which none can study without receiving purer ideas and more lofty conceptions of the grace and beauty of the human character. He is one that all may copy at different distances, and whom none can contemplate without receiving lasting and salutary impressions of the sterling value, the inexpressible beauty of piety, integrity, courage, and patriotism, associated with a clear, vigorous, and well-poised intellect.

Pure, and widely disseminated as is the fame of this great and good man, it is yet in its infancy. It is every day taking deeper root in the hearts of his countrymen, and the estimation of strangers, and spreading its branches wider and wider, to the air and skies. He is already become the saint of liberty, which has gathered new honours by being associated with his name; and when men aspire to free nations, they must take him for a model. It is, then, not without ample reason that the suffrages of mankind have combined to place Washington at the head of his race. If we estimate him by the examples recorded in history, he stands without a parallel in the virtues he exhibited, and the vast, unprecedented consequences resulting from their exercise. The whole world was the theatre of his actions, and all mankind are destined to partake sooner or later in their results. He is a hero of a new species: he had no model; will he have any imitators? Time, which bears the thousands and thousands of common cut-throats to the ocean of oblivion, only adds new lustre to his fame, new force to his example, and new strength to the reverential affection of all good men. What a glorious fame is his, to be acquired without guilt, and enjoyed without envy; to be cherished by millions living, hundreds of millions yet unborn! Let the children of my country prove themselves worthy of his virtues, his labours, and his sacrifices, by reverencing his name and imitating his piety, integrity, industry, fortitude, patience, forbearance, and patriotism. So shall they become fitted to enjoy the blessings of freedom and the bounties of heaven.

JAMES KIRKE PAULDING was born in Dutchess County, New York, August 22d, 1779, and died at Hyde Parke, New York, April 5th, 1860. He went in early life to New York City, and becoming acquainted with Washington Irving, began with him in 1807, a humorous and satirical magazine entitled "Salmagundi." He wrote many novels and tales which became very popular, was an elegant essayist, and excelled in humorous satire. The " Life of Washington," from which we quote, was published at New York, in 1835. 2 vols., 16mo. It is stated that five thousand copies of this work were purchased for the public schools in the United States. An edition was published in Aberdeen, Scotland, in 1836.

CYRUS R. EDMONDS.

1835.

General Washington died in his sixty-seventh year. His constitution had always been robust, and although it had recently suffered in some degree from the labours and vexations of political life, yet it is evident from the amount of business which he daily accomplished, that it retained to the last much of its pristine vigour. His person was fine, his stature and bearing erect, easy, and dignified, and he is said by one of his most intimate friends to have been "The best horseman of his age, and the most graceful figure that could be seen on horseback." *

It is not an easy task to delineate his character with minuteness and accuracy. It was marked by few prominent and distinguishing features. Though as a whole it exhibited a singular instance of greatness, it possessed but few individual elements in which it far surpassed the higher class of men. Its imposing effect is more dependent upon the nice balance and exact symmetry of parts, than upon the commanding stature of any of his faculties, if estimated singly. Yet there was in him, as was remarked of Sir Thomas More, whom, in some respects, he strongly resembled, a certain original homeliness, and even roughness, which relieves the insipidity of a character in which the physical passions and the moral powers are seen in such perfect equipoise.

* Thomas Jefferson, page 169.—Ed.

It is obvious to remark that the greatness of Washington did not consist in any extraordinary development of the intellectual faculties. He was not pre-eminently an intellectual man. Though he possessed that acuteness of perception which seems gradually to unravel an intricate subject, and to pierce as far into futurity as is permitted to men —yet his mind was slow in its operations, and thus resembles an optical instrument, which is difficult of adjustment, but which, when regulated by care, brings into distinct view the most minute and distant objects. Thus his conversation rarely developed the exercise of a discursive intellect, or of a brilliant imagination, though it always indicated a sound understanding; and the temperate movements of a well regulated mind.

As little did his greatness depend upon his literary acquirements. For such pursuits he had through life but little leisure, and apparently no very marked predilection. His composition was nervous and correct, warmed occasionally by a zealous interest in his subject, and doubtless formed by the perusal of excellent models, but generally diffuse, and partaking of all the characteristics of his conversation, and his public addresses. There is indeed a deep interest attaching to all his written remains; but it will be generally found to terminate upon the comprehensive views which they exhibit, and upon the patriotic, moral, and religious sentiments by which they are occasionally elevated into perfect sublimity. They indicate but little originality or fancy. He was naturally averse to speculation, and seems to have estimated everything according to its practical tendency. At the same time it is proper to distinguish between his system of opinions, and those of a contemporary school of pseudo-philosophers in France, who pretended to tread in his footsteps, but whose notions, professedly based upon expediency, tended to supersede every moral duty, and to emancipate mankind from the tender bonds of their primary and instinctive emotions. As little is he to be confounded with some other apostles of liberty, who, while they offer a feigned homage to virtue, subordinate its sanctions to short-sighted considerations of utility.

Nor is the greatness of Washington to be attributed in any degree to that good fortune to which so many military commanders have owed their fame and success. His whole life was one of constant difficulty and frequent disappointment. An attentive reader of his history cannot fail to be struck with the rare exceptions of success which crowned his best efforts; and will only feel surprise that, amidst such a succession of distressing failures, his confidence in the justice of his cause, and his overwhelming sense of duty, preserved him from abandoning in despair the great designs which he had formed.

The elements of his greatness are chiefly to be discovered in the moral features of his character. In this point of view it is as easy to account for his superiority to many men of equal celebrity, as it is for the greater and more enduring benefits which he has conferred upon mankind. There have been many whose commanding powers of mind, stimulated by personal ambition or some less worthy passion, have placed them in a position to influence the destinies of nations. In reviewing their history the mind is captivated by their talents, awed by the vastness of their designs, sympathises in their elation, and participates for a moment in the glory of their success. But history knows of but one, raised by his virtues to a position of supreme command, who identified himself with his people in all but the prosperity

25

he achieved for them, and bequeathed to them the blessings of peace and freedom, without injury to a single nation upon the face of the globe. In all other instances the elevation of the individual has cast upon succeeding generations a long and gloomy shadow of public adversity or political subserviency; but the greatness of Washington stands as under a vertical luminary, while the whole nation, of whom he was the centre, far and near, partake its genial warmth and rejoice in its reflected beams.

CYRUS READ EDMONDS was born at Exeter, England, September 14, 1809, and died near London, August 4, 1868. His father the Rev. Thomas Clarke Edmonds, M.A., was Pastor of a Baptist Church at Exeter, but removed soon after the birth of his son, to Cambridge, where he succeeded the celebrated divine, Robert Hall. Mr. Edmonds assisted his father in conducting a large school at Cambridge, having been privately educated by University tutors, —non-conformists being unable at the time to enter the University—and subsequently engaged in literary work in London. He afterwards lived for some twelve years at Leicester, as Head Master of the Leicester Proprietary Grammar School. Our extract is from his "Life and Times of General Washington," London, 1835-6. 2 vols., 18mo. The work is written with ability and impartiality, and the character of Washington, a small portion only of which we transcribe, carefully and judiciously considered.

JAMES GRAHAME.

1836.

THE nomination of a commander-in-chief of the American forces was the next, and not the least important, measure which demanded from the congress the united exercise of its wisdom and authority. Its choice (and never was choice more happily directed) fell upon George Washington.* * * * *

Nature and fortune had singularly combined to adapt and to designate this individual for the distinguished situations which he now and afterwards attained, and the arduous duties they involved. A long struggle to defend the frontiers of Virginia against continual incursions of the French and Indians,—the command of a clumsy, ill-organized provincial militia, prouder of being free citizens than effective soldiers, and among whom he had to introduce and establish the restraints of discipline,—obliged with minute labor and constant activity to superintend and give impulsion to every department of the service over which he presided, to execute as well as order, to negotiate, conciliate,

---

* "The congress at Philadelphia, who had assumed the title of *Representatives of the united colonies of North America*, appointed as commander-in-chief Washington, a member from Virginia, who had previously distinguished himself. He was one of those virtuous citizens, to whom the world refuses the credit of genius, because they are not gifted with a destructive restlessness, nor devoured with the ambition of domineering over mankind; but who really deserve the name of great, better than many others, because their number is rare." —FELIX BODIN: *Resumé de L'Histoire D'Angleterre. Bruxelles, 1824.*—ED.

(195)

project, command, and endure;—there could not have been a better
preparatory education for the office of commander-in chief of the mot-
ley, ardent, and untrained levies that constituted at present the army
of America.   His previous functions and exertions, arduous rather than
splendid, excited respect without envy, and, combined with the influence
of his character and manners, qualified him to exercise command and
prepared his countrymen to brook his ascendency.   The language and
deportment of this truly great man were in general remarkably exempt
from every strain of irregular vehemence and every symptom of inde-
liberate thought; disclosing an even tenor of steadfast propriety, an
austere but graceful simplicity, sound considerate sense and prudence,
the gravity of a profound understanding and habitual reflection, and
the tranquil grandeur of an elevated soul.   Of this moral superiority,
as of all human virtue, part was the fruit of wise discipline and resolute
self-control; for Washington was naturally passionate and irritable, and
had increased the vigor and authority of every better quality of his
mind by the conquest and subjection of those rebellious elements of
its composition.   Calm, modest, and reserved, yet dignified, intrepid,
inflexibly firm, and persevering; indefatigably industrious and methodical; just, yet merciful and humane; frugal and calculating, yet disinterested; circumspect, yet enterprising; serious, virtuous, consistent,
temperate, and sincere,—his moral portraiture displays a blended
variety of excellence, in which it is difficult to assign a predominant
lustre to any particular grace, except perhaps a grave majestic compos-
ure.   Ever superior to fortune, he enjoyed her smiles with moderation, endured her frowns with serenity, and showed himself alike in
victory forbearing, and in defeat undaunted.   No danger or difficulty

could disturb his equanimity, and no disaster paralyze his energy or
dishearten his confidence.   The same adverse vicissitude that would
have drained an ordinary breast of all its spirit served but to call forth
new streams of vigor from Washington's generous soul.   His countenance and general aspect corresponded with the impression produced
by his character.   Fixed, firm, collected, and resolved, yet consider-
ately kind, it seemed composed for dignity and high exploit. A sound
believer in the divine doctrines of Christianity, he was punctual and
devout in discharging every public and private office of Christian piety.
Perhaps there never was another man who trod with more unsullied
honor the highest ways of glory, or whose personal character and conduct exercised an influence so powerful and so beneficial on the destiny
of a great nation.

JAMES GRAHAME was born at Glasgow, Scotland, December 21, 1790, and died in
London, July 3, 1842. In 1812 he was admitted an advocate at the Scottish bar, and after
fourteen years practice, settled on account of ill health in the South of England, and commenced his "History of the United States of America, from the plantation of the British
Colonies till their assumption of National Independence," from which we make the extract.
The first two volumes appeared in 1827, and a new edition, 4 vols., 8vo, in 1836, bringing
the history to the year 1776. Republished in Philadelphia in 1845, with a memoir of the
author by Josiah Quincy.

EDWARD C. M'GUIRE.

1836.

THE mental and moral constitution of Washington was of the most excellent kind. He possessed faculties and affections in such peculiar combination, as to place him almost alone in that respect.

His mind was of the very best order. The structure thereof was plain, but on a scale of unusual strength and greatness. Its basis seems to have been *strong common sense.* To this was superadded a discernment clear and penetrating; a memory of great tenacity; and a judgment as sound as man ever possessed. Imagination had but little place in his mind. His materials of thought were first truths, together with such facts and events in life as were worthy of attention. These he carefully marked and compared with one another, noting their relations with a cool and enlightened comprehension; viewing them in all their aspects and bearings, weighing them in the balances of the mind, till conducted to the safest and soundest conclusions of reason.

He was alike happy in his moral constitution. Here the elements were mixed up in the finest and most admirable proportions. They were in perfect harmony with the higher powers of the mind. The equipose was rare and excellent. From hence, in a great degree, arose the force and effectiveness of his intellectual efforts. The action of his mind encountered no hindrance from the waywardness of his affections, or the turbulence of passion. These never cast obstacles in the way

(198)

of his judgment, or embarrassed its decisions by a conflict between inclination and conviction. With feelings unusually healthy, his understanding, ordinarily, had free and unimpeded course. Unbiassed by mere emotions of the breast, he always regarded objects presented to his consideration, with a steady eye and serene contemplation. No delusive vapour ascending from a selfish bosom, shut out from his mind the bright rays of truth. His perceptions were clear, because in him were united a sound head, with an honest and single heart.

The moral qualities in him were mingled and held together in a combination so admirable, that they all tended with the utmost harmony to the formation of a character so remarkable. He united in himself affections, dispositions and tempers, which are never looked for in the same person, being regarded in the light of antagonistic and contending qualities. They are often found to exist separately, but not unitedly, proving in their ordinary operation, destructive of each other. But in him they appeared to exist in a concord, as complete, as it was marvellous. Each filled with energy its own assigned sphere, whilst the whole were promptly combined, when the union was necessary for the effectuation of great and important objects.

The unequivocal developments of his character, exhibit him as possessed at the same time of such opposite qualities as courage and caution; of ardour and self-possession; of decision and moderation; of self-esteem and humility. He had modesty without diffidence; benevolence without ostentation; humanity without weakness. In him frugality was unattended by parsimony; temperance by austerity; the love of praise, by the fear of censure. He was dignified, yet condescending; had gravity without moroseness; seriousness without gloom. Quick in discerning defects in men, he was yet kind to all; alive to offence and insult, he was tolerant and ready to forgive.   He was of incorruptible integrity; had the highest and purest sense of justice; his truthfulness was rigid; and his faithfulness to principles and engagements unwavering.   He loved peace, yet was ready for war, when duty called. He was patriotic without ambition; industrious without covetousness. He was affectionate to his family and kindred; kind to his neighbors; obliging to his friends; courteous to associates; compassionate to servants, and merciful to animals.   When the severity of the trials to which his patience was often exposed, is considered, the wonder is, not that he should have been sometimes carried away by them, but that he should have so frequently resisted them with success. Under many and great provocations, he was usually calm, calling to his aid that self-command, of which experience had taught him the necessity, and conscience the propriety.   Few persons so constituted as he was in this respect, have done themselves, or others, so little injury thereby.

EDWARD CHARLES M'GUIRE, D.D., was born at Winchester, Va., July 14, 1793, and died at Fredericksburgh, October 8, 1858, where for forty-five years he was Rector of St. Georges P. E. Church.   He was the eldest son of Major William M'Guire of the Virginia line of the Revolutionary Army, and married a daughter of Robert Lewis, one of the nephews of Washington.   His "Religious Opinions and Character of Washington," from which we quote, was published at New York in 1836.   12mo.

JARED SPARKS.

1837.

Tʜᴇ person of Washington was commanding, graceful, and fitly proportioned; his stature six feet, his chest broad and full, his limbs long and somewhat slender, but well shaped and muscular. His features were regular and symmetrical, his eyes of a light blue color, and his whole countenance, in its quiet state, was grave, placid, and benignant. When alone, or not engaged in conversation, he appeared sedate and thoughtful; but, when his attention was excited, his eye kindled quickly and his face beamed with animation and intelligence. He was not fluent in speech, but what he said was apposite, and listened to with the more interest as being known to come from the heart. He seldom attempted sallies of wit or humor, but no man received more pleasure from an exhibition of them by others; and, although contented in seclusion, he sought his chief happiness in society, and participated with delight in all its rational and innocent amusements. Without austerity on the one hand, or an appearance of condescending familiarity on the other, he was affable, courteous, and cheerful; but it has often been remarked, that there was a dignity in his person and manner, not easy to be defined, which impressed every one that saw him for the first time with an instinctive deference and awe. This may have arisen in part from a conviction of his superiority, as well as from the effect produced by his external form and de- deportment.

26   (201)

The character of his mind was unfolded in the public and private acts of his life; and the proofs of his greatness are seen almost as much in the one as the other. The same qualities, which raised him to the ascendency he possessed over the will of a nation as the commander of armies and chief magistrate, caused him to be loved and respected as an individual. Wisdom, judgment, prudence, and firmness were his predominant traits. No man ever saw more clearly the relative importance of things and actions, or divested himself more entirely of the bias of personal interest, partiality, and prejudice, in discriminating between the true and the false, the right and the wrong, in all questions and subjects that were presented to him. He deliberated slowly, but decided surely; and, when his decision was once formed, he seldom reversed it, and never relaxed from the execution of a measure till it was completed. Courage, physical and moral, was a part of his nature; and, whether in battle or in the midst of popular excitement, he was fearless of danger and regardless of consequences to himself.

His ambition was of that noble kind, which aims to excel in whatever it undertakes, and to acquire a power over the hearts of men by promoting their happiness and winning their affections. Sensitive to the approbation of others and solicitous to deserve it, he made no concessions to gain their applause, either by flattering their vanity or yielding to their caprices. Cautious without timidity, bold without rashness, cool in counsel, deliberate but firm in action, clear in foresight, patient under reverses, steady, persevering, and self-possessed, he met and conquered every obstacle that obstructed his path to honor, renown, and success. More confident in the uprightness of his intentions, than in his resources, he sought knowledge and advice from other men. He chose his counsellors with unerring sagacity; and his quick perception of the soundness of an opinion, and of the strong points in an argument, enabled him to draw to his aid the best fruits of their talents, and the light of their collected wisdom.

His moral qualities were in perfect harmony with those of his intellect. Duty was the ruling principle of his conduct; and the rare endowments of his understanding were not more constantly tasked to devise the best methods of effecting an object, than they were to guard the sanctity of conscience. No instance can be adduced, in which he was actuated by a sinister motive, or endeavored to attain an end by unworthy means. Truth, integrity, and justice were deeply rooted in his mind; and nothing could rouse his indignation so soon, or so utterly destroy his confidence, as the discovery of the want of these virtues in any one whom he had trusted. Weaknesses, follies, indiscretions, he could forgive; but subterfuge and dishonesty he never forgot, rarely pardoned. He was candid and sincere, true to his friends, and faithful to all, neither practising dissimulation, descending to artifice, nor holding out expectations which he did not intend should be realized. His passions were strong, and sometimes they broke out with vehemence, but he had the power of checking them in an instant: Perhaps self-control was the most remarkable trait of his character. It was in part the effect of discipline; yet he seems by nature to have possessed this power to a degree, which has been denied to other men.

A Christian in faith and practice, he was habitually devout. His reverence for religion is seen in his example, his public communications, and his private writings. He uniformly ascribed his successes to the beneficent agency of the Supreme Being. Charitable and humane, he was liberal to the poor, and kind to those in distress. As a husband, son, and brother, he was tender and affectionate. Without vanity, ostentation, or pride, he never spoke of himself or his actions, unless required by circumstances which concerned the public interests. As he was free from envy, so he had the good fortune to escape the envy of others, by standing on an elevation which none could hope to attain. If he had one passion more strong than another, it was love of his country. The purity and ardor of his patriotism were commensurate with the greatness of its object. Love of country in him was invested with the sacred obligation of a duty; and from the faithful discharge of this duty he never swerved for a moment, either in thought or deed, through the whole period of his eventful career.

Such are some of the traits in the character of Washington, which have acquired for him the love and veneration of mankind. If they are not marked with the brilliancy, extravagance, and eccentricity, which in other men have excited the astonishment of the world, so neither are they tarnished by the follies nor disgraced by the crimes of those men. It is the happy combination of rare talents and qualities, the harmonious union of the intellectual and moral powers, rather than the dazzling splendor of any one trait, which constitute the grandeur of his character. If the title of great man ought to be reserved for him, who cannot be charged with an indiscretion or a vice, who spent his life in establishing the independence, the glory, and durable prosperity of his country, who succeeded in all that he undertook, and whose successes were never won at the expense of honor justice, integrity, or by the sacrifice of a single principle, this title will not be denied to Washington.*

JARED SPARKS was born at Willington, Conn., May 10, 1789, and died at Cambridge, Mass., March 4, 1866. He graduated at Harvard College in 1815, studied theology at Cambridge, and also became one of the conductors of the *North American Review*, of which he was sole proprietor and editor in 1823–30. He was chaplain of the House of Representatives in 1821; McLean professor of history at Harvard in 1839–49, and president in 1849–52, when he resigned on account of ill health. Mr. Sparks published a number of extremely important historical and biographical works, "which show thorough research, candid judgment, dispassionate criticism, and accuracy and simplicity of style." The "Writings of George Washington with a life of the author," 12 vols., 8vo, Boston, 1834–7, cost him nine years of labor, including researches in 1828 in the archives of London and Paris, then opened for the first time for historical purposes. Vol. I, which contains the Life of Washington, and from which we quote, was published (with Vol. XII) in 1837, and was issued for separate sale in 1839, '53, '54 and 1855. An abridgment by the author was published in 1843—2 vols., 12mo.

---

* Compare Mallet du Pan, page 129.—ED.

LORD BROUGHAM.

How grateful the relief which the friend of mankind, the lover of virtue, experiences when, turning from the contemplation of such a character, (Napoleon,) his eye rests upon the greatest man of our own or of any age; the only one upon whom an epithet so thoughtlessly lavished by men, to foster the crimes of their worst enemies, may be innocently and justly bestowed! In Washington we truly behold a marvellous contrast to almost every one of the endowments and the vices which we have been contemplating; and which are so well fitted to excite a mingled admiration, and sorrow, and abhorrence. With none of that brilliant genius which dazzles ordinary minds; with not even any remarkable quickness of apprehension; with knowledge less than almost all persons in the middle ranks, and many well educated of the humbler classes possess; this eminent person is presented to our observation clothed in attributes as modest, as unpretending, as little calculated to strike or astonish, as if he had passed unknown through some secluded region of private life. But he had a judgment sure and sound; a steadiness of mind which never suffered any passion, or even any feeling to ruffle its calm; a strength of understanding which worked rather than forced its way through all obstacles,— removing or avoiding rather than overleaping them. If profound sagacity, unshaken steadiness of purpose, the entire subjugation of all the passions which carry havoc through ordinary minds, and oftentimes lay waste the fairest prospects of greatness,—nay, the discipline

(206)

of those feelings which are wont to lull or to seduce genius, and to mar
and to cloud over the aspect of virtue herself,—joined with, or rather
leading to the most absolute self-denial, the most habitual and exclu-
sive devotion to principle,—if these things can constitute a great
character, without either quickness of apprehension, or resources of
information, or inventive powers, or any brilliant quality that might
dazzle the vulgar,—then surely Washington was the greatest man
that ever lived in this world uninspired by Divine wisdom, and unsus-
tained by supernatural virtue.

Nor could the human fancy create a combination of qualities,
even to the very wants and defects of the subject, more perfectly fitted
for the scenes in which it was his lot to bear the chief part; whether
we regard the war which he conducted, the political constitution over
which he afterwards presided, or the tempestuous times through
which he had finally to guide the bark himself had launched. Averse
as his pure mind and temperate disposition naturally was from the
atrocities of the French Revolution, he yet never leant against the
cause of liberty, but clung to it even when degraded by the excesses
of its savage votaries. Towards France, while he reprobated her
aggressions upon other states, and bravely resisted her pretensions to
control his own, he yet never ceased to feel the gratitude which her
aid to the American cause had planted eternally in every American
bosom; and for the freedom of a nation which had followed the noble
example of his countrymen in breaking the chains of a thousand
years, he united with those countrymen in cherishing a natural sympathy and regard. Towards England, whom he had only known as a
tyrant, he never, even, in the worst times of French turbulence at

home, and injury to foreign states, could unbend from the attitude of distrust and defiance into which the conduct of her sovereign and his Parliament, not unsupported by her people, had forced him, and in which the war had left him. Nor was there ever among all the complacent self-delusions with which the fond conceits of national vanity are apt to intoxicate us, one more utterly fantastical than the notion wherewith the politicians of the Pitt school were wont to flatter themselves and beguile their followers,—that simply because the Great American would not yield either to the bravadoes of the Republican envoy, or the fierce democracy of Jefferson, he therefore had become weary of republics, and a friend to monarchy and to England. In truth his devotion to liberty, and his intimate persuasion that it can only be enjoyed under the republican scheme, constantly gained strength to the end of his glorious life; and his steady resolution to hold the balance even between contending extremes at home, as well as to expel any advance from abroad incompatible with perfect independence, was not more dictated by the natural justice of his disposition, and the habitual sobriety of his views, than it sprang from a profound conviction that a commonwealth is most effectually served by the commanding prudence which checks all excesses, and guarantees it against the peril that chiefly besets popular governments.

His courage, whether in battle or in council, was as perfect as might be expected from this pure and steady temper of soul. A perfect just man, with a thoroughly firm resolution never to be misled by others, any more than to be by others overawed; never to be seduced or betrayed, or hurried away by his own weaknesses or self-delusions, any more than by other men's arts; nor ever to be dis-

heartened by the most complicated difficulties, any more than to be
spoilt on the giddy heights of fortune—such was this great man—
great, pre-eminently great, whether we regard him sustaining alone
the whole weight of campaigns all but desperate, or gloriously termin-
ating a just warfare by his resources and his courage—presiding over
the jarring elements of his political council, alike deaf to the storms of
all extremes*—or directing the formation of a new government for a
great people, the first time that so vast an experiment had ever been
tried by man—or finally retiring from the supreme power to which his
virtue had raised him over the nation he had created, and whose destinies he had guided as long as his aid was required—retiring with the
veneration of all parties, of all nations, of all mankind, in order that
the rights of men might be conserved, and that his example never
might be appealed to by vulgar tyrants. This is the consummate glory
of Washington; a triumphant warrior where the most sanguine had a
right to despair; a successful ruler in all the difficulties of a course
wholly untried; but a warrior, whose sword only left its sheath when
the first law of our nature commanded it to be drawn; and a ruler who,
having tasted of supreme power, gently and unostentatiously desired
that the cup might pass from him, nor would suffer more to wet his

---

* " The success of America was owing, next to the errors of her adversaries, to the conduct and character of General Washington. In him were united the purity of the most disinterested patriotism with all the energy of the most stirring ambition; the utmost reluctance
to engage in the contest, with the firmest will never to abandon it when begun; the most
intrepid devotion of his life and his fame in hazardous attacks, with the calmest judgment in
all matters political and military. The dissensions of Congress, the envy of rivals, the apathy
of his troops, the calumnies of his enemies, neither excited him to rashness, nor stopped him
in his career."—LORD JOHN RUSSEL: *Memorials and Correspondence of Charles James Fox,*
Vol. I, 1853.—ED.

27

lips than the most solemn and sacred duty to his Country and his God required!

To his latest breath did this great patriot maintain the noble character of a Captain the patron of Peace, and a Statesman the friend of Justice. Dying he bequeathed to his heirs the sword which he had worn in the War of Liberty, and charged them "Never to take it from the scabbard but in self-defence, or in defence of their country and her freedom; and commanding them, that when it should thus be drawn, they should never sheath it nor ever give it up, but prefer falling with it in their hands to the relinquishment thereof"—words, the majesty and simple eloquence of which are not surpassed in the oratory of Athens and Rome.

It will be the duty of the Historian and the Sage in all ages to let no occasion pass of commemorating this illustrious man; and until ‚time shall be no more will a test of the progress which our race has made in wisdom and in virtue be derived from the veneration paid to ˙the immortal name of Washington!

HENRY, LORD BROUGHAM, was born in Edinburgh, September 19, 1778, and died at Cannes, France, May 7, 1868. He studied law at Edinburgh, and in company with Jeffrey, Horner, and Sydney Smith, helped to start the *Edinburgh Review*, to which he contributed for a quarter of a century. He was called to the English bar in 1808, entered parliament in 1810, was raised to the peerage in 1830, and was Lord High Chancellor for four years, 1830 –34. Conspicuous in public affairs during the greater portion of his life, the vigor of his intellect, his energy, his eloquence, and his attachment to and services in the cause of freedom, progress and humanity, have caused him to be classed as one of the most illustrious and extraordinary men of his age and country. Of his numerous writings, the "Sketches of the Statesmen of the time of George III," 3 vols., 8vo, London, 1839, are considered the best. Our quotation is the conclusion of the sketch entitled, Napoleon-Washington, in Vol. II, portions of which, originally appeared in the *Edinburgh Review*, October, 1838.

COUNT DUMAS.

1839.

General Washington, accompanied by the Marquis de la Fayette, repaired in person to the French headquarters. We had been im-
patient to see the hero of liberty. His dignified address, his simplicity
of manners, and mild gravity, surpassed our expectation, and won every
heart. After having conferred with Count Rochambeau, as he was
leaving us to return to his headquarters near West Point, I received
the welcome order to accompany him as far as Providence. We arrived
there at night; the whole of the population had assembled from the
suburbs, we were surrounded by a crowd of children carrying torches,
reiterating the acclamations of the citizens; all were eager to approach
the person of him whom they called their father, and pressed so closely
around us that they hindered us from proceeding. General Washington
was much affected, stopped a few moments, and pressing my hand,
said, "We may be beaten by the English; it is the chance of war; but
behold an army which they can never conquer." *   *   *   *

As soon as General Washington was informed of the expedition
of Arnold, and of the danger which threatened Virginia, he proposed
to Count de Rochambeau to carry immediate succors thither, and to
attack the traitor in the post where he had entrenched himself. It was
on occasion of the discussions which the two commanders-in-chief had
on this subject that I was despatched by General Rochambeau to Gen-

eral Washington, whose head-quarters were then at New Windsor, on the right bank of the Hudson, three leagues above West Point. He had with him only the Marquis de la Fayette and their respective aids-de-camp. His army was in barracks or cantonments five or six leagues further off, on the road to Philadelphia. The garrison of West Point consisted of 2000 continental troops.

I here interrupt the succinct narrative of the most remarkable events of the winter of 1781, to recall the impressions which I received during the short stay that I made in the family of the deliverer of America. The brilliant actions of great men cannot fail to be recalled by history; the anecdotes of their private life are equally worthy of being preserved because they often make us better acquainted with the principal traits of their character. The General gave me a most cordial reception. He appeared to be highly satisfied with the despatches which I delivered to him, in the presence of M. de la Fayette, Colonel Hamilton, his aid-de-camp, and Colonel Humphries, who performed the duties of chief of the staff. He withdrew to confer with them. Being invited to dinner, which was remarkably plain, I had leisure to admire the perfect harmony of his noble and fine countenance, with the simplicity of his language and the justice and depth of his observations. He generally sat long at table, and animated the conversation by unaffected cheerfulness. Much was said of the treachery of Arnold, of the firmness and moderation with which the General had just suppressed the insubordination of the troops of the State of Pennsylvania, and lastly of the situation of Virginia, of the marches and counter-marches of Lord Cornwallis. I was particularly struck with the marks of affection which the General showed to his pupil, his adopted son, the Marquis de la Fayette. Seated opposite to him, he looked at him with pleasure, and listened to him with manifest interest. One of the company, (if I remember rightly, it was, I think, Colonel Hamilton, who was afterwards so unfortunately and so prematurely snatched from the hopes of his country,) related the manner in which the General had received a despatch from Sir Henry Clinton, addressed to Mr. Washington. Taking it from the hands of the flag of truce, and seeing the direction, "This letter," said he, "is directed to a planter of the State of Virginia. I shall have it delivered to him, after the end of the war; till that time it shall not be opened." A second despatch was addressed to his Excellency General Washington.

On the following day General Washington was to go to West Point, and allowed me to accompany him. Count de Charlus, who had just arrived to pay his respects to the General, and to spend some days with his friend M. de la Fayette, was likewise of the party. By rather difficult paths, we passed the mountain, at the other side of which is the plateau, surrounded by steep eminences, where block houses had been built and strong batteries had been erected, to bar the course of the river by the aid of the bend, caused by the projection of the promontory. After having visited the forts and reviewed the garrison, as the day was declining, and we were going to mount our horses, the General perceived that M. de la Fayette, in consequence of his old wound, was very much fatigued. "It will be better," said he, "to return by water; the tide will assist us in ascending against the stream." A boat was soon manned with good rowers, and we embarked. The cold became excessive; we had to make our way between the large flakes of ice which the river brought down. A heavy snow and the obscurity of the night soon rendered the danger more imminent, and the management of the boat, which filled with water, became increasingly difficult. We coasted the rocks which lined the right bank of the Hudson, between West Point and New Windsor, at the foot of which it is impossible to land. General Washington, perceiving that the master of the boat was very much alarmed, took the helm, saying, "courage, my friends; I am going to conduct you, since it is my duty to hold the helm." After having with much difficulty made our way against the stream and the ice, we landed, and had to walk a league before we reached the head-quarters.

MATHIEU, COUNT DUMAS, was born at Montpelier, France, November 23, 1753, and died at Paris, October 16, 1837. He entered the army in 1773, and served as aid-de-camp to Rochambeau, in America, 1780, '81. His "Memoirs," written in 1836, were translated and published at London, in 1839, and reprinted at Philadelphia, the same year, 2 vols., 12mo. from Vol. I. of which, our extracts are made. The first paragraph as quoted, evidently refers to Washington's visit of March 6, 1781, to Rochambeau, at Newport, R. I., but errs in stating that he was accompanied by the Marquis de la Fayette, that officer being in Virginia at the time, having left headquarters on February 20th. The remainder of the quotation points to a period somewhere between January 1st, 1781, the date of the mutiny of the Pennsylvania troops, and Feb. 20th; the error and chronological discrepancy, may be accounted for, by the lapse of time between the occurrences and the writing of the "Memoirs,"—fifty-five years. The visit to Newport is also recorded by CLAUDE BLANCHARD, Commissary of the French army, in his Journal (entry of March 5, (?) 1781), as follows, "This day General Washington, who was expected, arrived about two o'clock. He first went to the Duc de Bourgogne (the flag-ship), where all the generals were. He then landed; all the troops were under arms; I was presented to him. His face is handsome, noble and mild. He is tall (at least, five feet, eight inches). In the evening, I was at supper with him. I mark, as a fortunate day, that in which I have been able to behold a man so truly great." COUNT DE FERSEN, one of the aids-de-camp to Rochambeau, and who came to America with the Count Dumas in the same vessel, *Le Jason*, attended the French Commander on his first interview with Washington at Hartford, Conn. Sept. 22, 1780; referring to it in a letter to his father, dated Newport,

16th Octo. 1780, (*Magazine of American History*, May 1879), he says, " I was about fifteen days ago at Hartford, forty leagues distant from here, with M. de Rochambeau. We were only six, the Admiral, his chief of Engineers, his son, the Vicomte de Rochambeau, and two aids-de-camp, of whom I was one. He had an interview there with General Washington. M. de Rochambeau sent me in advance to announce his arrival, and I had time to see this man, illustrious, if not unique in our century. His handsome and majestic, while at the same time mild and open countenance perfectly reflects his moral qualities; he looks the hero; he is very cold; speaks little, but is courteous and frank. A shade of sadness over-shadows his countenance, which is not unbecoming, and gives him an interesting air."

JOHN QUINCY ADAMS.

1839.

THE first element of its longevity (the Constitution of the United States), was undoubtedly to be found in itself—but we may, without superstition or fanaticism, believe that a superintending Providence had adapted to the character and principles of this institution, those of the man by whom it was to be first administered. To fill a throne was neither his ambition nor his vocation. He had no descendants to whom a throne could have been transmitted, had it existed. He was placed by the unanimous voice of his country, at the head of that government which they had substituted for a throne, and his eye looking to futurity, was intent upon securing to after ages, not a throne for a seat to his own descendants, but an immovable seat upon which the descendants of his country might sit in peace, and freedom, and happiness, if so it please Heaven, to the end of time.

That to the accomplishment of this task he looked forward with a searching eye, and even an over-anxious heart, will not be surprising to any who understands his character, or is capable of comprehending the magnitude and difficulty of the ask itself.

There are incidental to the character of man two qualities, both developed by his intercourse with his fellow-creatures, and both belonging to the immortal part of his nature; of elements apparently so opposed and inconsistent with each other, as to be irreconcilable to-

(216)

gether; but yet indispensable in their union to constitute the highest excellence of the human character. They are the spirit of command, and the spirit of meekness. They have been exemplified in the purity of ideal perfection, once only in the history of mankind, and that was in the mortal life of the Saviour of the world. It would seem to have been exhibited on earth by his supernatural character, as a model to teach mortal man to what sublime elevation his nature is capable of ascending. They had been displayed, though not in the same perfection by the preceding legislator of the children of Israel;—

> "That Shepherd, who first taught the chosen seed
> In the beginning, how the heavens and earth
> Rose out of Chaos;"

but so little were they known, or conceived of in the antiquity of profane history, that in the poems of Homer, that unrivalled delineator of human character in the heroic ages, there is no attempt to introduce them in the person of any one of his performers, human or divine. In the poem of his Roman imitator and rival, a feeble exemplification of them is shadowed forth in the inconsistent composition of the pious Æneas; but history, ancient or modern, had never exhibited in the real life of man, an example in which those two properties were so happily blended together, as they were in the person of George Washington. These properties belong rather to the moral than to the intellectual nature of man. They are not unfrequently found in minds little cultivated by science, but they require for the exercise of that mutual control which guards them from degenerating into arrogance or weakness, the guidance of a sound judgment, and the regulation of a profound sense of responsibility to a higher Power. It was this

28

adaptation of the character of Washington to that of the institution over the composition of which he had presided, as he was now called to preside over its administration, which constituted one of the most favorable omens of its eventual stability and success.

JOHN QUINCY ADAMS, Sixth President of the United States, (1825–9) and son of President John Adams, was born at Braintree, now Quincy, Mass., July 11th, 1767, and died in the Capitol, Washington, D. C., February 23d, 1848. Our extract is from "The Jubilee of the Constitution, a Discourse delivered at the request of The New York Historical Society, in the City of New York, on Tuesday, the 30th of April, 1839; being the Fiftieth Anniversary of the inauguration of George Washington as President of the United States, on Thursday, the 30th of April, 1789. By John Quincy Adams." 8vo, pp. 120. New York: 1839. On a subsequent occasion, the presentation of the sword carried by Washington during the Revolutionary war, to the people of the United States, by Samuel T. Washington, a grand-nephew—House of Representatives, Feb. 7, 1843—Mr. Adams said: "Washington, the warrior and the legislator! In War, contending by the wager of battle for the independence of his country, and for the freedom of the human race; ever manifesting, amidst its horrors, by precept and example, his reverence for the laws of Peace, and for the tenderest sympathies of humanity: in Peace, soothing the ferocious spirit of discord, among his own countrymen, into harmony and union, and giving to that very sword now presented to his country a charm more potent than that attributed in ancient times to the lyre of Orpheus."

GEORGE COMBE.

1839.

I visited the studio of Mr. Rembrandt Peale. He is the son of the earliest portrait painter that America can boast of, and his father seems to have been an enthusiast in the art (as this gentleman is himself), for he named two of his sons Rembrandt and Titian, and educated both as painters. Mr. Rembrandt Peale was personally acquainted with General Washington, and painted a large equestrian portrait of him, which he preserves in his studio. The charger is white: The picture appeared to me to possess much merit as a work of art; and the likeness has been pronounced to be faithful. Washington's head, as here delineated, is obviously large; and the anterior lobe of the brain is large in all directions; the organ of Benevolence is seen to rise, but the moral organs disappear under the hair. The temperament is bilious-sanguine; the action of the muscles of the mouth strongly express Sensitiveness and Firmness, and the eyes bespeak these qualities combined with Cautiousness. The general expression of the countenance is that of sagacity, prudence, and determination.

It is deeply to be regretted that there is no cast of the head of Washington taken from nature. I have examined the common busts and portraits of him, but they show only that the head was large, and that its general proportions were harmonious. I have heard the ques-

(219)

tion discussed both in England and the United States, whether Washington was really a great man; seeing that he did not, in any particular direction, show any extraordinary power. Judging from his conduct and his writings, as well as from what we know of his head, I infer that he was one of those rare specimens of humanity in whom nearly all the mental organs are largely developed, and in harmonious proportions. Such a combination produces a character distinguished for mental power in all directions. His temperament, as already stated, seems to have been sanguine-bilious, giving activity and the capacity of long endurance. He exhibited a constancy which no difficulties could shake, an honesty of purpose and ardor of patriotism which no temptations could overcome or opposition subdue. He placed the welfare of his country on its true basis, that of industry and virtue; and he always regarded its interests before his own. In him there was no important quality of mind deficient, and no quality in excess; there were in his understanding no false lights, and no deficient lights. He gave to every thing its due weight and no more. He was dignified, courteous, and remarkably just. He was brave, yet cautious and politic; quick to perceive and prompt to execute; always acting at the right time, and in the right manner. Those who say that he was not a great man, can merely mean that he displayed no one quality in excess; that he showed no coruscations of isolated talent, and performed no individual acts calculated to dazzle or amaze mankind. But he accomplished a very great achievement, the independence of his country, by a succession of most wise and efficient measures, every one of which showed mental superiority. In short, he displayed in a long career both of adversity and prosperity, that sterling worth of soul, that clear and sound judgment, that grandeur of the whole man, which rendered him far more great and estimable than those geniuses who are endowed with splendid partial talents combined with great defects. In my opinion, Washington was one of the greatest men that ever lived.

GEORGE COMBE, phrenologist, was born near Edinburgh, October 21, 1788, and died at Moor Park, Surrey, England, August 14, 1858. He was bred to the legal profession, but in 1816 devoted himself to the propagation of the science of phrenology, as a writer and lecturer. He visited the United States in 1838, and delivered many lectures on the subject in various parts of the country. His journal kept during the time was published at Philadelphia in 1841, with the title "Notes of the United States of America during a phrenological visit in 1838-40." 2 vols., 12mo. Our, extract is a portion of the entry at Philadelphia, for January 18, 1839.

GUIZOT.

1839.

WASHINGTON had not those brilliant and extraordinary qualities which strike the imagination of men at the first glance. He did not belong to the class of men of vivid genius, who pant for an opportunity of display, are impelled by great thoughts or great passions, and diffuse around them the wealth of their own natures, before any outward occasion or necessity calls for its employment. Free from all internal restlessness and the promptings and pride of ambition, Washington did not seek opportunities to distinguish himself, and never aspired to the admiration of the world. This spirit so resolute, this heart so lofty, was profoundly calm and modest. Capable of rising to a level with the highest destiny, he might have lived in ignorance of his real power without suffering from it, and have found, in the cultivation of his estates, a satisfactory employment for those energetic faculties, which were to be proved equal to the task of commanding armies and founding a government.

But when the opportunity presented itself, when the exigence occurred, without effort on his part, without any surprise on the part of others, indeed rather, as we have just seen, in conformity with their expectations, the prudent planter stood forth a great man. He had, in a remarkable degree, those two qualities which, in active life, make men capable of great things. He could confide strongly in his own

(222)

views, and act resolutely in conformity with them, without fearing to assume the responsibility. * * * *

The same strength of conviction, the same fidelity to his own judgment, which he manifested in his estimate of things generally, attended him in his practical management of business. Possessing a mind of admirable freedom, rather in virtue of the soundness of its views than of its fertility and variety, he never received his opinions at second hand, nor adopted them from any prejudice; but, on every occasion, he formed them himself, by the simple observation or attentive study of facts, unswayed by any bias or prepossession, always acquainting himself personally with the actual truth.

Thus, when he had examined, reflected, and made up his mind, nothing disturbed him; he did not permit himself to be thrown into, and kept in, a state of perpetual doubt and irresolution, either by the opinions of others, or by love of applause, or by fear of opposition. He trusted in God and in himself. "If any power on earth could, or the Great Power above would, erect the standard of infallibility in political opinions, there is no being that inhabits the terrestrial globe, that would resort tò it with more eagerness than myself, so long as I remain a servant of the public. But as I have found no better guide hitherto, than upright intentions, and close investigation, I shall adhere to those maxims, while I keep the watch."*

To this strong and independent understanding, he joined a great courage, always ready to act upon conviction, and fearless of consequences. "What I admire in Christopher Columbus," said Turgot, "is, not his having discovered the new world, but his having gone to

---

* Letter to General Knox, dated Mount Vernon, 20 September, 1795.—ED.

search for it on the faith of an opinion." Whether the occasion was
of great or little moment, whether the consequences were near at hand
or remote, Washington, when once convinced never hesitated to move
onward upon the faith of his conviction. One would have inferred
from his firm and quiet resolution, that it was natural to him to act
with decision, and assume responsibility;—a certain sign of a genius
born to command; an admirable power, when united to a conscientious disinterestedness.

On the list of great men, if there be some who have shone with a
more dazzling lustre, there are none who have been exposed to a more
complete test, in war and in civil government; resisting the king, in
the cause of liberty, and the people, in the cause of legitimate authority;
commencing a revolution and ending it. *   *   *   *

His military capacity has been called in question. He did not
manifest, it is true, those striking displays of it which, in Europe, have
given renown to great captains. Operating with a small army over an
immense space, great manœuvres and great battles were necessarily
unknown to him. But his superiority, acknowledged and declared by
his companions, the continuance of the war during nine years, and its
final success, are also to be taken as proofs of his merit, and may well
justify his reputation. His personal bravery was chivalrous even to
rashness, and he more than once abandoned himself to this impulse in
a manner painful to contemplate. More than once, the American
militia, seized with terror, took to flight, and brave officers sacrificed
their lives to infuse courage into their soldiers. In 1776, on a similar
occasion, Washington indignantly persisted in remaining on the field
of battle, exerting himself to arrest the fugitives by his example and

even by his hand. "We made," wrote General Greene the next day, "a miserable, disorderly retreat from New York, owing to the disorderly conduct of the militia. Fellow's and Parson's brigades ran away from about fifty men, and left his Excellency on the ground within eighty yards of the enemy, so vexed at the infamous conduct of the troops, that he sought death rather than life."*

On more than one occasion, also, when the opportunity appeared favorable, he displayed the boldness of the general as well as the intrepidity of the man. He has been called the *American Fabius*, it being said that the art of avoiding battle, of baffling the enemy, and of temporizing, was his talent as well as his taste. In 1775, before Boston, at the opening of the war, this Fabius wished to bring it to a close by a sudden attack upon the English army, which he flattered himself he should be able to destroy. Three successive councils of war, forced him to abandon his design, but without shaking his conviction, and he expressed bitter regret at the result. In 1776, in the State of New York, when the weather was extremely cold, in the midst of a retreat, with troops half disbanded, the greater part of whom were preparing to leave him and return to their own homes, Washington suddenly assumed an offensive position, attacked, one after another, at Trenton and Princeton, the different corps of the English army, and gained two battles in eight hours.

Moreover, he understood what was even a much higher and much more difficult art, than that of making war; he knew how to control and direct it. War was to him only a means, always kept subordinate

---

* Washington's Writings, Vol. IV, p. 94.

29

to the main and final object,—the success of the cause, the independence of the country. *   *   *   *

A man of experience and a man of action, he had an admirable wisdom, and made no pretension to systematic theories. He took no side beforehand; he made no show of the principles that were to govern him. Thus, there was nothing like a logical harshness in his conduct, no committal of self-love, no struggle of rival talent. When he obtained the victory, his success was not to his adversaries either a stake lost, or a sweeping sentence of condemnation. It was not on the ground of the superiority of his own mind, that he triumphed; but on the ground of the nature of things, and of the inevitable necessity that accompanied them. Still his success was not an event without a moral character, the simple result of skill, strength, or fortune. Uninfluenced by any theory, he had faith in truth, and adopted it as the guide of his conduct. He did not pursue the victory of one opinion against the partisans of another; neither did he act from interest in the event alone, or merely for success. He did nothing which he did not think to be reasonable and just; so that his conduct, which had no systematic character, that might be humbling to his adversaries, had still a moral character, which commanded respect.

Men had, moreover, the most thorough conviction of his disinterestedness; that great light, to which men so willingly trust their fate; that vast power, which draws after it their hearts, while, at the same time, it gives them confidence that their interests will not be surrendered, either as a sacrifice, or as instruments to selfishness and ambition. *   *   *   *

He did the two greatest things which, in politics, man can have the privilege of attempting. He maintained, by peace, that independence of his country, which he had acquired by war. He founded a free government, in the name of the principles of order, and by re-establishing their sway. When he retired from public life, both tasks were accomplished, and he could enjoy the result. For, in such high enterprises, the labor which they have cost matters but little. The sweat of any toil is dried at once on the brow where God places such laurels. * * * *

Government will be, always and everywhere, the greatest exercise of the faculties of man, and consequently that which requires minds of the highest order. It is for the honor, as well as for the interest of society, that such minds should be drawn into the administration of its affairs, and retained there; for no institutions, no securities can supply their place.

And, on the other hand, in men who are worthy of this destiny all weariness, all sadness of spirit, however it might be permitted in others, is a weakness. Their vocation is labor. Their reward is, indeed, the success of their efforts, but still only in labor. Very often they die, bent under the burden, before the day of recompense arrives. Washington lived to receive it. He deserved and enjoyed both success and repose. Of all great men, he was the most virtuous, and the most fortunate. In this world, God has no higher favors to bestow.

Francois Pierre Guillaume Guizot was born of Protestant parentage at Nimes, France, October 4, 1787, and died at Val Richer, Normandy, in September, 1874. Having been educated at Geneva, he went to Paris in 1805 to pursue his studies in the faculty of laws, and was appointed the same year professor of modern history at the Sarbonne; but was suspended from his functions in 1822, because his principles were offensive to the ministry.

He was reinstated in 1828 and elected a member of the French Academy in 1836. He became minister of foreign affairs October 29, 1840, and maintained himself in power until the Revolution of February, 1848, when he escaped to England, returning, however, the following year. M. Guizot supervised a French abridgment of Sparks' "Writings of Washington," Paris, 1839–40, 6 vols., 8vo, preceded by an essay on the character and influence of Washington, written by himself. The essay was published separately at Paris in 1839. A translation was published in London and Paris in 1840, and another by George S. Hillard, in this country, the same year, with a second edition in 1863, 16mo, from which our extracts are made. In the preface, Mr. Hillard says, "nothing has ever been written concerning him (Washington) in Europe, so accurate, so just, and so profound as this; and it will serve to justify and strengthen that admiration, which has been accorded to him in foreign countries, hardly less than in his own."

WILLIAM SMYTH.

1840.

WASHINGTON died in December, 1799, after a short illness, resigning his spirit, with a calm and untroubled mind, to the disposal of that Almighty Being in whose presence he had acted his important part, and to whose kind providence he had so often committed in many an anxious moment, in the cabinet and in the field, the destinies of his beloved country. "He was not," he said, "afraid to die."

To the historian, indeed, there are few characters that appear so little to have shared the common frailties and imperfections of human nature; there are but few particulars that can be mentioned even to his disadvantage. It is understood, for instance, that he was once going to commit an important mistake as a general in the field; but he had at least the very great merit of listening to Lee, (a man whom he could not like, and who was even his rival) and of *not* committing the mistake. Instances may be found where perhaps it may be thought that he was decisive to a degree that partook of severity and harshness, or even more; but how innumerable were the decisions which he had to make! how difficult and how important, through the eventful series of twenty years of command in the cabinet or the field! Let it be considered what it is to have the management of a revolution, and afterwards the maintenance of order. Where is the man that in the history of our race has ever succeeded in attempting successively the

(229)

one and the other? not on a small scale, a petty state in Italy, or among a horde of barbarians, but in an enlightened age, when it is not easy for one man to rise superior to another, and in the eyes of man-kind,—

> " A kingdom for a stage,
> And monarchs to behold the swelling scene."

The plaudits of his country were continually sounding in his ears, and neither the judgment nor the virtues of the man were ever disturbed. Armies were led to the field with all the enterprise of a hero, and then dismissed with all the equanimity of a philosopher. Power was accepted, was exercised, was resigned, precisely at the moment and in the way that duty and patriotism directed. Whatever was the difficulty, the trial, the temptation, or the danger, there stood the soldier and the citizen, eternally the same, without fear and without reproach, and there was the man who was not only at all times virtuous, but at all times wise.

The merit of Washington by no means ceases with his campaigns; it becomes, after the peace of 1783, even more striking than before; for the same man who, for the sake of liberty, was ardent enough to resist the power of Great Britain and hazard every thing on this side the grave, at a later period had to be temperate enough to resist the same spirit of liberty, when it was mistaking its proper objects and transgressing its appointed limits. The American revolution was to approach him, and he was to kindle in the general flame; the French revolution was to reach him and to consume but too many of his countrymen, and his "*own* etherial mould, incapable of stain, was to purge off the baser fire victorious." But all this was done: he might have been pardoned, though he had failed amid the enthusiasm of those around him, and when liberty was the delusion: but the foundations of the moral world were shaken, and not the understanding of Washington.

To those who must necessarily contemplate this remarkable man at a distance, there is a kind of fixed calmness in his character that seems not well fitted to engage our affections (constant superiority we rather venerate than love), but he had those who loved him (his friends and his family), as well as the world and those that admired.

As a ruler of mankind, however, he may be proposed as a model. Deeply impressed with the original rights of human nature, he never forgot that the end, and meaning, and aim of all just government was the happiness of the people, and he never exercised authority till he had first taken care to put himself clearly in the right. His candour, his patience, his love of justice were unexampled; and this, though *naturally* he was not patient,—much otherwise, highly irritable.

He therefore deliberated well, and placed his subject in every point of view before he decided; and his understanding being correct, he was thus rendered, by the nature of his faculties, his strength of mind, and his principles, the man of all others to whom the interests of his fellow-creatures might with most confidence be intrusted; that is, he was the FIRST OF THE RULERS OF MANKIND.

WILLIAM SMYTH was born at Liverpool in 1766, and died at Norwich, England, June 26, 1849. He was educated at Cambridge, where he graduated in 1787, and on March 11, 1807, received the appointment of Professor of Modern History in the University, a post which he retained until his death. His "Lectures on Modern History, from the irruption of the Northern Nations to the close of the American Revolution," from which we quote

 WILLIAM SMYTH.

(Lecture XXXVI), were published in 1840 in 2 vols., 8vo.   London & Cambridge.   Several English and American editions have been issued.   The Preface to the Boston edition of 1841, (from the second London edition,) written by Jared Sparks, contains the following.   "His character of Washington, is happily conceived and well delineated.   In short it would be difficult to find any treatise on the American Revolution comprised within the compass of six lectures, from which so much can be learned, or so accurate an estimate of the merits of both sides of the question can be formed."

CHARLES W. UPHAM.

1840.

It is probable that it would be allowed by all truly liberal and enlightened men, that the Revolution of the North American British colonies, which resulted in the establishment of an independent, republican, and constitutional empire, is one of the greatest and most momentous events in the history of the world. It is, indeed, worthy of being regarded as a perfectly successful political and moral movement. The patriot and the philosophical statesman look back upon it with unmixed approval and unalloyed satisfaction. From the beginning to the end there seems to have been an overruling power guiding all things right, and bringing on the consummation steadily and surely. It is not often that human enterprises and efforts are crowned with results so completely auspicious. When we contemplate its incidents, and follow its vicissitudes to the issue towards which they all tended, we feel that never were the indications of the interposition of a favoring Providence more signal and unquestionable.

This great and glorious event was identified most distinctly with the character and influence of one man. There were many wise, enlightened, patriotic, and powerful spirits, scattered over every part of the country, and laboring most efficiently and nobly in the cause; but whoever traces the course of things, from the commencement of the War of Independence, to the final establishment of the nation

30 (233)

under the Federal Constitution, will not hesitate to say, that at no point could the American Revolution have dispensed with the services, or succeeded without the aid and influence of George Washington. When his career is surveyed, his agency fully explored and considered, his truly wonderful adaptation to the services assigned him discerned and appreciated, and his traits of character are examined, the heart that is not deeply impressed with the belief that he was raised up by a special Providence, will find nothing in history or in Nature to awaken that sentiment.

A concise and plain narrative of his life and actions, of the influence he exerted, the events he controlled, and the course of faithful, trying, and glorious service, through which he passed, will leave upon the mind of the reader a conviction, that neither the actual annals of human experience, nor the creations of poetical fancy, have ever presented a character more worthy of entire respect and admiration. The mind contemplates him with a completeness of satisfaction, such as but few objects, belonging to this present scene of things, suggest. As the military leader of a political revolution, as the ruler of a free, and the father of a great people, he appears stamped with the character of absolute perfection. * * *

General Washington was remarkable for the sobriety, gravity, and dignity of his manners and aspect. In early life, there is reason to believe that he was cheerful and social, even to a more than ordinary degree; but the weight and magnitude of the cares which were afterwards accumulated upon him, gradually imparted to his bearing and mien an appearance of abstraction and reserve. This became the fixed expression of his countenance at the time of the

Revolution. His far-reaching mind discerned the vast importance of the cause intrusted to his hands. He regarded the contest with the deepest solicitude, and was impressed with awe, when he considered the interest at stake. * * * *

The intellect of Washington was of the highest order. His judgment was superlatively clear and strong. His reasoning faculties, in what must unquestionably be considered the surest test of their power, that is, an application to practical questions, of the greatest complexity and the widest comprehension, were wonderfully exact, forcible, and effective in their operations. As a military commander, he succeeded in reaching a perfectly accurate estimate of the character and amount of the resources which his own country could supply, and also of those within the reach of the enemy, and was thus enabled to form a plan for conducting the war which was the only one adapted to the circumstances of the occasion, and which alone could have been crowned with success. The same unerring judgment, grasping every detail, and surveying with the clearest vision the whole ground, led him in safety and in triumph through all the difficulties of his civil administration. It was in consequence of the conviction universally felt of his superior judgment, of the unrivalled strength and efficiency of his reasoning faculties, in all practical applications, that his opinions were clothed with such authority, not only over the great body of the people, but also and equally over the first minds of that day. The same admirable judgment appears in his numerous writings, and, combined with good taste, and a style of remarkable neatness, perspicuity, simplicity, and dignity, has given to the productions of his pen a character and value proportioned to the greatness of his services and the glory of his name. * * * *

Self-control, self-denial, devotion to the welfare of his fellow-men, humility in his estimate of himself, justice and candor towards others, innocence, integrity, and fortitude of heart, and a conscientious and indomitable fidelity and perseverance in the discharge of every trust, were seen in all his actions, constituted the chief lustre of his character, were stamped on every feature, and drawn in every line of his countenance. These moral sentiments were the rules of his thoughts and his life. They were evidently established on the only sure foundation, an habitual and profound reverence of the Divine Being, and an entire subjection of the mind to his will. This appears throughout his private correspondence, as well as in his public productions. His opinions, in reference to the creeds of different churches, and questions of controversial theology, were never made known, and cannot now be ascertained. But his religious character is placed beyond doubt. His life is its evidence. It is seen in all his writings, and is declared by the testimony of those who witnessed his most private and familiar habits and frames of mind. * * * *

The fame of Washington may be safely said to transcend that of all other men. It spreads wider and shines brighter with the lapse of every year. Counties, cities, and towns, political, patriotic, benevolent, literary, and municipal associations, all over America, inscribe his name in their titles. His character is honored, cherished, and understood by all the people of all parties. The day of his birth is held in hallowed remembrance, and commemorated with grateful rejoicings. The slightest actions he ever performed are preserved and embalmed in the hearts of his countrymen. His familiar letters have been published, his most private habits exposed, and his whole life brought to view. Whatever relates to him is regarded with reverence and admiration, and nothing has ever been revealed which has not tended to confirm those sentiments.

The writer of this memoir was disposed to glean and gather all that could be considered as defects in his character, or errors in his conduct. He felt that the picture he had drawn, required some shade to heighten its effect. The only instances in which Washington was known to have yielded to the impulses of passion have been faithfully recorded, and the result of the researches, which have been made in arranging the materials of this biography, is a decided conviction that the subject of it was as habitually, as uniformly, and as constantly under the control of an enlightened conscience as any character within the range of mere human history.

Such, too, is the general sentiment of the world. In this we find the secret of his peculiar glory. It is because it is every where felt that his life was without stain and throughout governed by high moral principle, that his reputation surpasses that of all other military and political leaders. This is the great charm of his character. His unquestionable integrity, and the purity of his personal virtue, have surrounded his name, in the estimation of all nations, with an unrivalled lustre.

This conspicuous and acknowledged rectitude and integrity of character have ever been, and will ever be, to him and to his fame, an all-sufficient shield of defence. They made him, through life, invulnerable to the assults of calumny, and placed him beyond the reach of the vicissitudes of fortune. During his long public career he was, at times, pursued by malice, encompassed by difficulties, and involved in disaster; but never, for a moment, was the brightness of his fame obscured; never, for a moment, did he lose his hold upon the confidence and love of his countrymen.   The clamors of enemies, and the storms of misfortune, passed harmlessly and unheeded beneath the lofty elevation of his bright and spotless honor.   The purity and firmness of his principles were so well known, so visible to the eyes of all beholders, that neither hostile men, nor adverse events, could, even for a moment, cast a shadow over his great and good name.

> "As some tall cliff, that lifts its awful form,
> Swells from the vale, and midway leaves the storm;
> Though round its breast the rolling clouds are spread,
> Eternal sunshine settles on its head."

The memory of Washington is a possession of infinite value to the people of America.   Among the innumerable evidences of the favor of Providence, with which they have been blessed, it is an occasion of especial gratitude, on their part, that such a character was raised up, to lead them to the attainment and enjoyment of their national independence and liberty.   It becomes them, in their thanksgivings to Heaven, to praise and bless God, that when the sword was to be drawn, and embattled hosts to be arrayed, He gave to their fathers a champion and a leader, whom a virtuous and Christian people can safely teach their children to honor and love.   In the progress of civilization and Christianity, war, with all its works, will be done away. Its glories and its horrors will be known only in history;—but in those happy days Washington will still be found worthy of the admiration of mankind.   The future generations of America, and the friends of liberty, to the end of time, while they admire his valor, shown on fields of blood, will also find much more to admire in the private and personal virtues which made his whole life beautiful, noble and grand. The enthusiasm with which they contemplate the hero will be blended with approbation, love, and delight as the patriot, the citizen, the philanthropist rises to view. They may safely give their hearts to the conqueror who feared not man, for their lives will thereby be brought under the power of the example of one who feared God. It will be well for them to linger before the living canvass which delineates his form, for, although the sword of battle is at his side, and his arm rests upon the neck of his war-horse, the spirit of benevolence and of peace beams from his countenance, and the lessons of virtue are proclaimed from his life. Happy indeed is the people, who will for ever call him the FATHER OF HIS COUNTRY!

CHARLES WENTWORTH UPHAM was born at St. John, New Brunswick, May 4, 1802, and died at Salem, Mass., June 15, 1875. He graduated at Harvard College in 1821, and was settled over the First Congregational Church of Salem, December 8, 1824, but relinquished the ministry in 1844, on account of loss of voice. His " Life of Washington in the form of an autobiography, the narrative being to a great extent, conducted by himself, in extracts and selections from his own writings," was published at Boston in 1840, 2 vols., 12mo. The edition having been suppressed by the Circuit Court of the United States, as an invasion of the copyright of Sparks' Life of Washington, the stereotype plates were sent to England, and the work published in London, in 1852, with the title, " The Life of General Washington, First President of the United States, written by himself, comprising his memoirs and correspondence as prepared by him for publication." The materials for this work are judiciously selected and arranged, and the character of Washington, which we quote, ably written.

ARCHIBALD ALISON.

1842.

THE end of the same year (1796), witnessed the resignation of the presidency of the United States of America by General Washington, and his voluntary retirement into private life. Modern history has not a more spotless character to commemorate. Invincible in resolution, firm in conduct, incorruptible in integrity, he brought to the helm of a victorious republic the simplicity and innocence of rural life; he was forced into greatness by circumstances rather than led into it by inclination, and prevailed over his enemies rather by the wisdom of his designs, and the perseverance of his character, than by any extraordinary genius for the art of war. A soldier from necessity and patriotism rather than disposition, he was the first to recommend a return to pacific counsels when the independence of his country was secured; and bequeathed to his countrymen an address on leaving their government, to which there are few compositions of uninspired wisdom which can bear a comparison. He was modest without diffidence; sensible to the voice of fame without vanity; independent and dignified without either asperity or pride. He was a friend to liberty, but not to licentiousness—not to the dreams of enthusiasts, but to those practical ideas which America had inherited from her British descent, and which were opposed to nothing so much as the extravagant love of power in the French democracy. Accordingly, after having signalized his life by a successful resistance to English oppres-

(240)

sion, he closed it by the warmest advice to cultivate the friendship of Great Britain; and exerted his whole influence, shortly before his resignation, to effect the conclusion of a treaty of friendly and commercial intercourse between the mother country and its emancipated offspring.   He was a Cromwell without his ambition; a Sylla without his crimes: and after having raised his country, by his exertions, to the rank of an independent state, he closed his career by a voluntary relinquishment of the power which a grateful people had bestowed. If it is the highest glory of England to have given birth, even amidst Transatlantic wilds, to such a man; and if she cannot number him among those who have extended her provinces or augmented her dominions, she may at least feel a legitimate pride in the victories which he achieved, and the great qualities which he exhibited, in the contest with herself; and indulge with satisfaction in the reflection, that that vast empire, which neither the ambition of Louis XIV nor the power of Napoleon could dismember, received its first shock from the courage which she had communicated to her own offspring; and that, amidst the convulsions and revolutions of other states, real liberty has arisen in that nation alone, which inherited in its veins the genuine principles of British freedom.

SIR ARCHIBALD ALISON was born at Kenley, Shropshire, England, December 29, 1792, and died at Glasgow, Scotland, May 23, 1867. He received his education in Edinburgh; was admitted to the bar in 1814, made Sheriff of Lanarkshire in 1828, Rector of Glasgow University in 1851, and created a baronet, 1852. His "History of Europe from the commencement of the French Revolution to the restoration of the Bourbons," 10 vols., 8vo, 1829-42, from Vol. IV, Chapter XXI, of which we quote, established his reputation as an historian, in Europe and America. Many editions have been published, and it has been translated into French, German, Hindostanee and Arabic.

DANIEL WEBSTER.

1843.

America has furnished to the world the character of Washington! And if our American institutions had done nothing else, that alone would have entitled them to the respect of mankind.

Washington! "First in war, first in peace, and first in the hearts of his countrymen!" Washington is all our own! The enthusiastic veneration and regard in which the people of the United States hold him, prove them to be worthy of such a countryman; while his reputation abroad reflects the highest honor on his country and its institutions. I would cheerfully put the question to-day to the intelligence of Europe and the world, what character of the century, upon the whole, stands out in the relief of history, most pure, most respectable, most sublime; and I doubt not, that, by a suffrage approaching to unanimity, the answer would be Washington!

The structure now standing before us,* by its uprightness, its solidity, its durability, is no unfit emblem of his character. His public virtues and public principles were as firm as the earth on which it stands; his personal motives, as pure as the serene heaven in which its summit is lost. But, indeed, though a fit, it is an inadequate emblem. Towering high above the <u>column</u> which our hands have

---

* Bunker Hill Monument.—Ed.

(242)

builded, <u>beheld</u>, not by the inhabitants of a single city or a single State—but by all the families of man, ascends the colossal grandeur of the character and life of Washington. In all the constituents of the one—in all the acts of the other—in all its <u>titles</u> to immortal love, admiration and renown—it is an American production. It is the embodiment and vindication of our transatlantic liberty. Born upon our soil—of parents also born upon it—never for a moment having had sight of the old world—<u>instructed</u> according to the modes of his time, only in the spare, plain, but wholesome elementary knowledge which our institutions provide for the children of the people—growing up beneath and penetrated by the genuine influences of American society —living from infancy to manhood and age amidst our expanding, but not luxurious civilization—partaking in our great destiny of labor, our long contest with unreclaimed nature and uncivilized man—our agony of glory, the war of Independence—our great victory of peace, the formation of the Union, and the establishment of the Constitution,—he is all—all our own! Washington is ours. That crowded and glorious life—

> " Where multitudes of virtues passed along,
> Each pressing foremost, in the mighty throng
> Ambitious to be seen, then making room
> For greater multitudes that were to come;"—

that life, was the life of an American citizen.

I claim him for America. In all the perils, in every darkened moment of the state, in the midst of the reproaches of enemies and the misgiving of friends—I turn to that transcendent name for courage and for consolation. To him who denies, or doubts whether our fervid liberty can be combined with law, with order, with the security of property, with the pursuits and advancement of happiness—to him who denies that our institutions are capable of producing exaltation of soul, and the passion of true glory—to him who denies that we have contributed any thing to the stock of great lessons and great examples—to all these I reply by pointing to Washington!

DANIEL WEBSTER was born at Salisbury, N. H., January 18, 1782, and died at Marshfield, Mass., October 24, 1852. He graduated at Dartmouth College in 1801, studied law under Christopher Gore of Boston, was admitted to the bar in 1805, and practiced in Portsmouth, N. H., until 1816, when he moved to Boston. He was member of Congress, 1813-17, and 1823-27; United States Senator, 1828-41, and 1845-50; Secretary of State under Presidents Harrison and Tyler, 1841-43, and under President Fillmore, from July 20, 1850, until his death. As an expounder of the powers and functions of the Federal government, as a great pleader, as an eloquent and finished speaker, and as a man, Daniel Webster stands in the front rank of American statesmen, lawyers, orators and patriots. Our extract is from his "Address delivered at Bunker Hill, June 17, 1843, on the completion of the Monument." 8vo., pp. 39. Boston, 1843.

VON RAUMER.

1846.

CONGRESS delivered to General Washington with provident sagacity and noble confidence the supreme command of the army. He was empowered at his discretion to raise and disband troops, to inflict punishment, levy contributions, award compensations, etc. That such a man as Washington was to be found, and that his worth was duly appreciated, were circumstances highly fortunate and highly meritorious. Without his personal influence and exertions, the American revolution could never have succeeded so admirably; in fact none can succed where the excited masses are destitute of wise and virtuous leaders.

George Washington was born in Virginia, in the County of Westmoreland, on the 22d of February, 1732, sound and strong in body, cultivated in mind by industry but still more by his way of life, and distinguished as a leader in the war of 1756 to 1763. He had an intellect powerful but not dazzling. Even in the present day in America, happily for the country, merely brilliant qualities are by no means over-estimated, as is so often the case in France; and rectitude, character, and virtue are never regarded as superfluous unimportant accompaniments. Few men who have earned for themselves a celebrated name in the history of the world exhibit such a harmony, such a concordant symmetry of all the qualities calculated to render himself

(245)

and others happy, as Washington; and it has been very appropriately observed, that, like the master-pieces of ancient art, he must be the more admired in the aggregate, the more closely he is examined in detail. His soul was elevated above party-spirit, prejudice, self-interest, and paltry aims; he acted according to the impulses of a noble heart and a sound understanding, strengthened by impartial observation. By calmly considering things in all their relations and from every point of view, he became master of them, and was able, even in situations of the greatest perplexity, to choose with certainty that which was best. To the greatest firmness he united the mildness and patience equally necessary in the then state of affairs; to prudence and foresight he joined boldness at the right moment; and the power entrusted to him he never abused by the slightest infraction of the laws.

Although it is impossible that an American can ever again perform such services for his country as were then rendered by Washington, his noble, blameless, and spotless image will remain a model and a rallying-point to all, to encourage the good and to deter the bad. How petty do the common race of martial heroes appear in comparison with Washington! how insignificant especially Lord North, who while internally wavering, strove after an appearance of decision, feebly pursued measures of violence, and awakened hatred without instilling fear!

FRIEDRICH LUDWIG GEORG VON RAUMER, a German historian, was born near Dresden, May 14, 1781, and died in 1873. He studied law and financial science at the Universities of Halle and Göttingen, began the practice of law in 1801, and in 1819 became Professor of history and political economy at Berlin. Von Raumer travelled in America in 1843, and wrote "America and the American people," which was translated by William W. Turner, and published in New York in 1846, 8vo, from which we quote.

WILLIAM B. SPRAGUE.

1847.

It is rare to find a perfectly balanced character, even where the qualities which compose it rise not above a humble mediocrity. And it is rarer still to find an assemblage of the loftiest qualities so harmoniously combined, that no one can say that any one quality casts any of the rest into the shade. And who that knows anything o Washington,—who, especially, that reads his farewell address, can doubt for a moment, that he was pre-eminently one of the rarest specimens of human character? Our country can indeed boast many other names that are deservedly called great; but in almost every instance, if you scrutinize closely, you find some doubtful spot that you wish to hide; something to disturb harmony, or mar dignity, or lessen usefulness—Washington, on the other hand, not only possessed every quality that belongs to true greatness, but so far as we can see, possessed all in perfect proportions. The intellectual, the moral, even the physical, are so admirably blended, that every one feels that the elements of his character must have been weighed out in a perfectly even balance; and no one thinks of exalting one of his faculties at the expense of another. I well know that this is not the type of character which multitudes love to contemplate; for many have a passion for the monstrous as well as the marvellous. It is a common remark that genius is eccentric; and hence not a few admire eccentricity from

(247)

its supposed alliance to superior intellect; and some even feign eccentricity, as a means of acquiring an intellectual reputation. But this quality, when it actively exists, always supposes imperfection: a correct taste uniformly condemns it. It may be notorious for a little time; but it is like the transient and startling light of a meteor—not like the clear and steady shining of the sun. Cases indeed there are in which ill-balanced minds possess great strength, and make themselves every where known and always remembered; but the admiration which they excite at first, rarely survives their own generation. Napoleon's name no doubt will live as long as Washington's; but the one will gather around it in the distance, a darkness that can be felt, the other will shrine brighter and brighter unto the perfect day. * * *

I would not indeed be afraid to trust to this unparalled document* to vindicate the claims of its author to the character of the first man of his age—nay, of one of the noblest specimens of the race. I look upon it as that in which his greatness, his goodness, the epitome of all that belongs to his memory, is embalmed; and if it were possible that the time should ever come, when every other witness concerning him was dumb, this of itself would keep his name glorious and glowing to the end of time. Nevertheless in our estimate of him, it is fitting that we include his whole history, instead of limiting ourselves to a single point, no matter how important; and I pledge myself to those who have not already made the experiment, that if they will follow him from the beginning to the close of his career, each successive step will increase their admiration of his character, by throwing into a brighter light some one or more of the exalted qualities that compose it.

* The Farewell Address.—ED.

WILLIAM BUELL SPRAGUE, D.D., was born at Andover, Conn., October 16, 1795, and died May 7, 1876. He graduated at Yale College in 1815, and afterwards studied divinity. He was pastor of the Second Presbyterian Church at Albany, New York, for many years, and the author of numerous publications. Our extract is from "An Address delivered the evening of the 22d of February, 1847, before the Young Men's Association of the City of Albany." 8vo, pp. 51. Albany, 1847.

RUFUS W. GRISWOLD.

1847.

AN attentive examination of the whole subject, and of all that can contribute to the formation of a sound opinion, results in the belief that General Washington's *mental* abilities illustrate the very highest type of greatness. His *mind*, probably, was one of the very greatest that was ever given to mortality. Yet it is impossible to establish that position by a direct analysis of his character, or conduct, or productions. When we look at the incidents or the results of that great career—when we contemplate the qualities by which it is marked, from its beginning to its end—the foresight which never was surprised, the judgment which nothing could deceive, the wisdom whose resources were incapable of exhaustion—combined with a spirit as resolute in its official duties as it was moderate in its private pretensions, as indomitable in its public temper as it was gentle in its personal tone— we are left in wonder and reverence. But when we would enter into the recesses of that mind—when we would discriminate upon its construction, and reason upon its operations—when we would tell how it was composed, and why it excelled—we are entirely at fault. The processes of Washington's understanding are entirely hidden from us. What came from it, in counsel or in action, was the life and glory of his country; what went on within it, is shrouded in impenetrable concealment.

(250)

Such elevation in degree, of wisdom, amounts almost to a change of kind, in nature, and detaches his intelligence from the sympathy of ours. We cannot see him as he was, because we are not like him. The tones of the mighty bell were heard with the certainty of Time itself, and with a force that vibrates still upon the air of life, and will vibrate forever. But the clock-work by which they were regulated and given forth, we can neither see nor understand. In fact, his intellectual abilities did not exist in an analytical and separated form; but in a combined and concrete state. They "moved altogether when they moved at all." They were in no degree speculative, but only practical. They could not act at all in the region of imagination, but only upon the field of reality. The sympathies of his intelligence dwelt exclusively in the national being and action. Its interests and energies were absorbed in them. He was nothing out of that sphere, because he was every thing there. The extent to which he was identified with the country is unexampled in the relations of individual men to the community. During the whole period of his life he was the thinking part of the nation. He was its mind; it was his image and illustration. If we would classify and measure him, it must be with nations, and not with individuals.

This extraordinary nature of Washington's capacities—this impossibility of analyzing and understanding the elements and methods of his wisdom—have led some persons to doubt whether, intellectually, he was of great superiority; but the public—the community—never doubted of the transcendent eminence of Washington's abilities. From the first moment of his appearance as the chief, the recognition of him, from one end of the country to the other, as THE MAN—the leader, the counsellor, the infallible in suggestion and in conduct—was immediate and universal. From that moment to the close of the scene, the national confidence in his capacity was as spontaneous, as enthusiastic, as immovable as it was in his integrity. Particular persons, affected by the untoward course of events, sometimes questioned his sufficiency; but the nation never questioned it, nor would allow it to be questioned. Neither misfortune, nor disappointment, nor accidents, nor delay, nor the protracted gloom of years, could avail to disturb the public trust in him. It was apart from circumstances; it was beside the action of caprice; it was beyond all visionary, and above all changeable feelings. It was founded on nothing extraneous; not upon what he had said or done, but upon what he was. They saw something in the man, which gave them assurance of a nature and destiny of the highest elevation—something inexplicable, but which inspired a complete satisfaction. We feel that this reliance was wise and right; but why it was felt, or why it was right, we are as much to seek as those who came under the direct impression of his personal presence. It is not surprising, that the world recognizing in this man a nature and a greatness which philosophy cannot explain, should revere him almost to religion.

The distance and magnitude of those objects which are too far above us to be estimated directly—such as stars—are determined by their parallax. By some process of that kind we may form an approximate notion of Washington's greatness. We may measure him against the great events in which he moved; and against the great men, among whom, and above whom, his figure stood like a tower. It is agreed that the war of American Independence is one of the most exalted, and honourable, and difficult achievements related in history. Its force was contributed by many; but its grandeur was derived from Washington. His character and wisdom gave unity, and dignity, and effect to the irregular, and often divergent enthusiasm of others. His energy combined the parts; his intelligence guided the whole; his perseverance, and fortitude, and resolution, were the inspiration and support of all. In looking back over that period, his presence seems to fill the whole scene; his influence predominates throughout; his character is reflected from every thing. Perhaps nothing less than his immense weight of mind could have kept the national system, at home, in that position which it held, immovably for seven years; perhaps nothing but the august respectability which his demeanour threw around the American cause abroad, would have induced a foreign nation to enter into an equal alliance with us upon terms that contributed in a most important degree to our final success, or would have caused Great Britain to feel that no great indignity was suffered in admitting the claim to national existence of a people who had such a representative as Washington. What but the most eminent qualities of mind and feeling—discretion superhuman—readiness of invention, and dexterity of means, equal to the most desperate affairs— endurance, self-control, regulated ardour, restrained passion, caution mingled with boldness, and all the contrarieties of moral excellence— could have expanded the life of an individual into a career such as this?

If we compare him with the great men who were his contemporaries throughout the nation; in an age of extraordinary personages, Washington was unquestionably the first man of the time in ability.

Review the correspondence of General Washington—that sublime
monument of intelligence and integrity—scrutinize the public history
and the public men of that era, and you will find that in all the wisdom
that was accomplished or was attempted, Washington was before every
man in his suggestions of the plan, and beyond every one in the
extent to which he contributed to its adoption. In the field, all the
able generals acknowledged his superiority, and looked up to him with
loyalty, reliance, and reverence; the others, who doubted his ability,
or conspired against his sovereignty, illustrated, in their own conduct,
their incapacity to be either his judges or his rivals. In the state,
Adams, Jay, Rutledge, Pinckney, Morris—these are great names; but
there is not one whose wisdom does not vail to his? His superiority
was felt by all these persons, and was felt by Washington himself, as a
simple matter of fact, as little a subject of question, or a cause of vanity,
as the eminence of his personal stature. His appointment as commander-in-chief, was the result of no design on his part, and of no
efforts on the part of his friends; it seemed to take place spontaneously. He moved into position, because there was a vacuum which
no other could supply; in it, he was not sustained by government, by
a party, or by connexions: he sustained himself; and then he sustained every thing else. He sustained Congress against the army,
and the army against the injustice of Congress. The brightest mind
among his contemporaries was Hamilton's; a character which cannot
be contemplated without frequent admiration, and constant affection.
His talents took the form of genius, which Washington's did not.
But active, various, and brilliant, as the faculties of Hamilton were,
whether viewed in the precocity of youth, or in the all-accomplished

elegance of maturer life—lightning-quick as his intelligence was to see through every subject that came before it, and vigorous as it was in constructing the argumentation by which other minds were to be led, as upon a shapely bridge, over the obscure depths across which his had flashed in a moment—fertile and sound in schemes, ready in action, splendid in display, as he was—nothing is more obvious and certain than that when Mr. Hamilton approached Washington, he came into the presence of one who surpassed him in the extent, in the comprehension, the elevation, the sagacity, the force, and the ponderousness of his mind, as much as he did in the majesty of his aspect, and the grandeur of his step. The genius of Hamilton was a flower, which gratifies, surprises, and enchants; the intelligence of Washington was a stately tree, which in the rarity and true dignity of its beauty is as superior, as it is in its dimensions·　＊　＊　＊　＊

In moral qualities, the character of Washington is the most truly dignified that was ever presented to the respect and admiration of mankind. He was one of the few entirely good men in whom goodness had no touch of weakness. He was one of the few rigorously just men whose justice was not commingled with any of the severity of personal temper. The elevation, and strength, and greatness of his feelings were derived from nature; their moderation was the effect of reflection and discipline. His temper, by nature, was ardent, and inclined to action. His passions were quick, and capable of an intensity of motion, which, when it was kindled by either intellectual or moral indignation, amounted almost to fury. But how rarely—how less than rarely—was any thing of this kind exhibited in his public career! How restrained from all excess which reason could reprove, or virtue condemn, or good taste reject, were these earnest impulses, in the accommodation of his nature to "that great line of duty" which he had set up as the course of his life. Seen in his public duties, his attitude and character—the one elevated above familiarity, the other purged of all littlenesses—present a position and an image almost purely sublime.

> No airy and light passion stirs abroad
> To ruffle or to soothe him; all are quelled
> Beneath a mightier, sterner stress of mind:
> Wakeful he sits, and lonely, and unmoved,
> Beyond the arrows, views, or shouts of men;
> As oftentimes an eagle, when the sun
> Throws o'er the varying earth his early ray,
> Stands solitary, stands immovable
> Upon some highest cliff, and rolls his eye,
> Clear, constant, unobservant, unabased,
> In the cold light, above the dews of morn.

But when viewed in the gentler scenes of domestic and friendly relation, there are traits which give loveliness to dignity, and add grace to veneration; like the leaves and twigs which cluster around the trunk and huge branches of the colossal elm, making that beautiful which else were only grand. His sentiments were quick and delicate; his refinement exquisite. His temper was as remote from plebeian, as his principles were opposite to democratic. If his public bearing had something of the solemnity of puritanism, the sources of his social nature were the spirit and maxims of a cavalier. His demeanour towards all men illustrated, in every condition, that "finest sense of justice which the mind can form." IN ALL THINGS ADMIRABLE, IN ALL THINGS TO BE IMITATED; IN SOME THINGS SCARCE IMITABLE AND ONLY TO BE ADMIRED.

RUFUS WILMOT GRISWOLD, D.D., was born at Benson, Rutland County, Vermont, February 15, 1815, and died in New York, August 27, 1857. He was at first apprenticed to a printer, but studied divinity, and became a Baptist preacher. He, however, soon became associated in the literary management of a number of journals in several of the principal cities of the Union, and in 1842–3 edited *Graham's Magazine,* and from 1850 to 1852 the *International Magazine,* in New York. Dr. Griswold was a voluminous writer. "Washington and the Generals of the American Revolution," published at Philadelphia in 1847, 2 vols., 12mo, was edited and partly written by him, assisted by W. G. Simms, E. D. Ingraham, and others. The sketch of Washington in Vol. I, from which we make the extract, is presumed to have been written by Griswold.

JOEL T. HEADLEY.

1847.

THE crowning glory of his character was his patriotism. No man ever before rose out of the mass of the people to such power without abusing it, and history searches in vain for a military leader, so much of whose life had been spent in the camp, and whose will was law to a grateful nation, who voluntarily resigned his rank and chose the humble, peaceful occupation of a farmer. At first the nation, jealous of its liberties, was afraid to pass so much power into his hands; but it soon learned that he watched those liberties with a more anxious eye than itself. From the outset, his honor and his country stood foremost in his affections; the first he guarded with scrupulous care, and for the last he offered up his life and his fortune. His patriotism was so pure, so unmixed with any selfish feeling, that no ingratitude, or suspicions or wrongs, could for a moment weaken its force. It was like the love of a father for his son, notwithstanding his errors and disobedience, and who bends over him with that yearning affection which will still believe and hope on to the end. Men have been found who would sacrifice their lives for their country, and yet would not submit to its injustice or bear with its ingratitude ignorance, and follies. Many have been astonished at the confidence of Washington even in his darkest hours; but it was the faith of strong love. On the nation's heart, let it beat never so wildly, he leaned in solemn trust. * * * *

(258)

But it is not to any *one* striking quality we are to look for a true exponent of Washington—it is to the harmonious whole his character presented. As a warrior he may be surpassed, but as a complete *man*, he is without a parallel. Equal to any crisis, successful in all he undertakes, superior to temptation, faithful in every trial, and without a spot on his name, the history of the race cannot match him. All military men become more or less corrupted by a life in the camp, and many of our best officers were demoralized; but not a stain clung to Washington. Committing his cause to God before battle, and referring the victory to Divine goodness, he remained a religious man through a life on the tented field.

In *moral* elevation, no warrior of ancient or modern times approaches him. Given to no excess himself, he sternly rebuked it in others. The principles of religion were deeply engrafted in his heart, and as there was no stain on his blade, he could go from the fierce-fought field to the sacramental table. That brow which would have awed a Roman Senate in its proudest days, bent in the dust before his Maker. In the darkest night of adversity he leaned in solemn faith on Him who is "mightier than the mightiest." As I see him moving through the wretched hovels of Valley Forge, his heart wrung at the destitution and suffering that meet his eye at every step, slowly making his way to the silent forest, and there kneel in prayer in behalf of his bleeding country—that voice which was never known to falter in the wildest of the conflict, choked with emotion—I seem to behold one on whom God has laid his consecrating hand, and all doubts and fears of ultimate success vanish like morning mist before the uprisen sun. There is no slavish fear of the Deity, which formed so large a part of Cromwell's religion, mingled in that devotion, but an unshaken belief in Truth, and a firm reliance on heaven.

A Brutus in justice, he did not allow personal friendship to sway his decision, or influence him in the bestowment of favors. Fearing neither the carnage of battle nor the hatred of men, threats moved him no more than flatteries; and what is stranger still, the strong aversion to giving pain to his friends never swerved him from the path of duty. Sincere in all his declarations, *his word was never doubted and his promise never broken.* Intrusted finally with almost supreme power, he never abused it, and laid it down at last more cheerfully than he had taken it up. Bonaparte vaulting to supreme command, seized it with avidity, and wielded it without restraint. The Directory obstructing his plans, he broke it up with the bayonet. Cromwell did the same with the Rump Parliament, and installed himself Protector of England, and even hesitated long about the title of king. Washington fettered worse than both, submitted to disgrace and defeat without using even a disrespectful word to Congress, and rejected the offered crown with a sternness and indignation that forever crushed the hopes of those who presented it. Calm and strong in council, untiring in effort, wise in policy, terrible as a storm in battle, unconquered in defeat, and incorruptible in virtue, he rises in moral grandeur so far above the Alexanders, and Cæsars, and Napoleons of the world, that even comparison seems injustice. * * * *

His administration was distinguished by that wisdom and virtue which had ever characterized him. In carrying out the separate requirements of the constitution, he was governed by that pure patriotism which is bound by no personal feelings, or views of self-aggrandizement. Laboring assiduously to master both home and foreign affairs, he succeeded in harmonizing the discordant elements about him, and made his government steady at home and respected abroad. In forming the supreme judiciary—filling the several departments of state—in establishing a national bank—in protecting our frontiers from Indian depredations, and in developing all the resources of the country, he showed himself to be the greatest statesman of the nation, as he was its greatest military leader. When the first four years of his administration closed, he fondly hoped that he would be permitted to retire to private life; but men of all parties who cared for their country, felt that his commanding influence and wisdom were indispensable in order to fix firmly and forever that which he had only settled into repose; and declaring that, if he should not remain, the tottering fabric would fall, they with one voice besought him, by all that was dear to him in the Union, to serve another term. They knew that Washington's only weak side was his patriotism, and this they plied with all the arguments they knew so well how to use. Though he had reached his threescore years, and pined for the rest of a quiet home, he again took on him the burdens of office. The nation prospered under his rule. Words of wisdom and piety dropped from his lips, and stretching out his arms over the Union, both the foundation and topmost stone of which he had laid, he gave it his last blessing. Had his counsels been obeyed, and all his successors followed in his footsteps, this nation would not only have stood first among the powers of the earth, but been the especial favorite of heaven. * * * *

No one, in tracing the history of our struggle, can deny that Providence watched over our interests, and gave us the only man who could have conducted the car of the Revolution to the goal it finally reached. Our revolution brought to a speedy crisis the one that must sooner or later have convulsed France. One was as much needed as the other, and has been productive of equal good. But in tracing the progress of each, how striking is the contrast between the instruments employed—Napoleon and Washington. Heaven and earth are not wider apart than were their moral characters, yet both were sent of Heaven to perform a great work: God acts on more enlarged plans than the bigoted and ignorant have any conception of, and adapts his instruments to the work he wishes to accomplish. To effect the regeneration of a comparatively religious, virtuous and intelligent people, no better man could have been selected than Washington. To rend asunder the feudal system of Europe, which stretched like an iron frame-work over the people, and had rusted so long in its place, that no slow corrosion or steadily wasting power could affect its firmness, there could have been found no better than Bonaparte. Their missions were as different as their characters. Had Bonaparte been put in the place of Washington, he would have overthrown the Congress, as he did the Directory, and taking supreme power into his hands, developed the resources, and kindled the enthusiasm of this country with such astonishing rapidity, that the war would scarcely have begun ere it was ended. But a vast and powerful monarchy instead of a republic, would have occupied this continent. Had Washington been put in the place of Bonaparte, his transcendent virtues and unswerving integrity would not have prevailed against the tyranny of faction, and a prison would have received him, as it did Lafayette. Both were children of a revolution, both rose to the chief command of the army, and eventually to the head of a nation. One led his country step by step to freedom and prosperity, the other arrested at once, and with a strong hand, the earthquake that was rocking France asunder, and sent it rolling under the thrones of Europe. The office of one was to defend and build up Liberty, that of the other to break down the prison walls in which it lay a captive, and rend asunder its century-bound fetters. To suppose that France could have been managed as America was, by any human hand, shows an ignorance as blind as it is culpable. That, and, every other country of Europe will have to pass through successive stages before they can reach the point at which our revolution commenced. Here Liberty needed virtue and patriotism, as well as strength—on the continent it needed simple *power*, concentrated and terrible power. Europe at this day trembles over that volcano Napoleon kindled, and the next eruption will finish what he begun. Thus does Heaven, selecting its own instruments, break up the systems of oppression men deemed eternal, and out of the power and ambition, as well as out of the virtues of men, work the welfare of our race.

JOEL TYLER HEADLEY was born at Walton, Delaware County, New York, December 30, 1814, and graduated at Union College in 1839. He studied at the Auburn Theological Seminary, was licensed to preach, and was pastor for two years of a church at Stockbridge, Mass. Compelled by ill-health to abandon his profession, he travelled in Europe in 1842–3, and upon his return, published his travels in two volumes. He is the author of numerous works. "Washington and his Generals," from which we make the extract, was published at New York in 1847. 2 vols., 12mo.

ROBERT C. WINTHROP.

1848.

IT is, however, the character of Washington, and not the mere part which he played, which I would hold up this day to the world as worthy of endless and universal commemoration. The highest official distinctions may be enjoyed, and the most important public services rendered, by men whose lives will not endure examination. It is the glory of Washington, that the virtues of the man outshone even the brilliancy of his acts, and that the results which he accomplished were only the legitimate exemplifications of the principles which he professed and cherished.

In the whole history of the world it may be doubted whether any man can be found, who has exerted a more controlling influence over men and over events than George Washington. To what did he owe that influence? How did he win, how did he wield, that magic power, that majestic authority, over the minds and hearts of his countrymen and of mankind? In what did the power of Washington consist?

It was not the power of vast learning or varied acquirements. He made no pretensions to scholarship, and had no opportunity for extensive reading.

It was not the power of sparkling wit or glowing rhetoric. Though long associated with deliberative bodies, he never made a set speech in his life, nor ever mingled in a stormy debate.

(264)

It was not the power of personal fascination. There was little about him of that gracious affability which sometimes lends such resistless attraction to men of commanding position. His august presence inspired more of awe than of affection, and his friends, numerous and devoted as they were, were bound to him rather by ties of respect than of love.

It was not the power of a daring and desperate spirit of heroic adventure. "If I ever said so," replied Washington, when asked whether he had said that there was something charming in the sound of a whistling bullet; "if I ever said so, it was when I was young." He had no passion for mere exploits. He sought no bubble reputation in the cannon's mouth. With a courage never questioned, and equal to every exigency, he had yet "a wisdom which did guide his valor to act in safety."

In what, then, did the power of Washington consist? When Patrick Henry returned home from the first Continental Congress, and was asked who was the greatest man in that body, he replied: "If you speak of eloquence, Mr. Rutledge, of South Carolina, is the greatest orator; but if you speak of solid information and sound judgment, Colonel Washington is by far the greatest man on that floor."

When, fifteen years earlier, Washington, at the close of the French war, took his seat, for the first time, in the House of Burgesses of Virginia, and a vote of thanks was presented to him for his military services to the Colony, his hesitation and embarrassment were relieved by the Speaker, who said, "Sit down, Mr. Washington; your modesty equals your valor, and that surpasses the power of any language that I possess."

34

But it was not solid information, or sound judgment, or even that rare combination of surpassing modesty and valor, great as these qualities are, which gave Washington such a hold on the regard, respect, and confidence of the American people. I hazard nothing in saying that it was the high moral element of his character, which imparted to it its preponderating force. His incorruptible honesty, his uncompromising truth, his devout reliance on God, the purity of his life, the scrupulousness of his conscience, the disinterestedness of his purposes, his humanity, generosity, and justice,—these were the ingredients which, blending harmoniously with solid information and sound judgment and a valor only equalled by his modesty, made up a character to which the world may be fearlessly challenged for a parallel.

"Labor to keep alive in your breast that little spark of celestial fire, *conscience*," was one of a series of maxims which Washington framed or copied for his own use when a boy. His rigid adherence to principle; his steadfast discharge of duty; his utter abandonment of self; his unreserved devotion to whatever interests were committed to his care,—attest the more than vestal vigilance with which he observed that maxim. He kept alive that spark. He made it shine before men. He kindled it into a flame which illumined his whole life. No occasion was so momentous, no circumstances so minute, as to absolve him from following its guiding ray.   *   *   *

The Republic may perish; the wide arch of our ranged Union may fall; star by star its glories may expire; stone after stone its columns and its capitol may moulder and crumble; all other names which adorn its annals may be forgotten; but as long as human hearts shall anywhere pant, or human tongues shall any where plead, for a true, rational, constitutional liberty, those hearts shall enshrine the memory, and those tongues prolong the fame, of GEORGE WASHINGTON!

EXTRACT from "An oration pronounced by the Honorable Robert C. Winthrop, Speaker of the House of Representatives of the United States, on the Fourth of July, 1848, on the occasion of laying the corner-stone of the National Monument to the Memory of Washington.", 8vo, pp. 36. Washington: 1848. By a joint resolution of Congress approved May 13, 1884, the delivery of the oration on the *completion* of the Monument, was also assigned to Mr. Winthrop, and although far advanced in his seventy-sixth year, he had substantially prepared what he proposed to say, but falling dangerously ill of pneumonia, two months before the appointed time, his recovery was too slow to admit of the delivery of his oration in person. It was however read for him by the Hon. John Davis Long, late Governor of Massachusetts, and a member of the House of Representatives of the United States. The time fixed by the resolution of Congress for the ceremonies, was the twenty-second of February, 1885, but that day occurring on Sunday, they were held on Saturday the twenty-first. The cap-stone of the monument was set December 6, 1884. Extracts from this oration will be found at the end of the volume.

RICHARD HILDRETH.

1851.

The sudden death of Washington almost entirely swept away, at least for the moment, those feelings of suspicion with which a portion of the Republican party, especially of the leaders, had begun to regard him—now that he was dead, all zealously united to do him honor.

Rare man indeed he was among actors on the military and political stage, possessing in the highest degree the most imposing qualities of a great leader—deliberate and cautious wisdom in judging, promptitude and energy in acting, a steady, firm, indomitable spirit, such as men love to cling to and rely upon; more than all, an unsullied integrity, and a sincere and disinterested devotion to his country's cause, such, indeed, as many public men, or their followers for them, pretend to, but the credit of which very few get and still fewer deserve. History records many names that dazzle the imagination with a greater brilliancy, but few, indeed, that shine with a light so pure, steady, permanent, penetrating, and serene. Washington's character and reputation, as contrasted with those of many other famous men, seem to resemble in effect the Doric architecture as compared with the Gothic and Oriental styles. Those styles often excite, especially in minds peculiarly liable to vivid impressions, the most enthusiastic pitch of admiration, appealing, as they do, not alone or chiefly to the sentiment of the beautiful, but to the powerful emotions, also, of

(268)

surprise and wonder, growing out of novelty, variety, complication, and vastness. But these are emotions, especially if we take into account the mass of men and succeeding generations, liable to great fluctuations, often subsiding into indifference, sometimes sinking into contempt; while the serener sentiments, always and every where inspired by majesty, order, proportion, grace and fitness, are not less · steady, universal, and enduring than the perceptions from which they spring.

RICHARD HILDRETH was born at Deerfield, Mass., June 28, 1807, and died at Florence, Italy, July 11, 1865. He graduated at Harvard College in 1826, studied law at Newburyport, and practised in Boston until he began in 1832, to edit the *Boston Atlas*. He abandoned journalism in 1840. His principal work is, "The History of the United States of America." New York, 1849–52, 6 vols., 8vo., from Vol. V. of which we quote.

JOHN J. CRITTENDEN.

1852.

The character of Washington has ascended above the ordinary language of eulogy. A Cæsar, a Napoleon, a Cromwell may excite the applause of the world, and inflame the passions of men, by the story of their fields and their fame; but the name of Washington occupies a different, a serener, a calmer, a more celestial sphere. There is not in his character, and there is not about his name, any of that turbulence, and excitement, and glare, which constitute glory, in the vulgar and worldly sense of the term. His name has sunk deep into the hearts of mankind, and more especially has it sunk deep into the mind and heart of America, and in that secret and inner temple it will reside, without any of the forms of ostentatious idolatry. It resides in the inner recesses of the hearts of his countrymen; and, like an oracle, is continually whispering lessons of patriotism and of virtue. He never sought or asked for what men call glory. He sought to serve his kind and his country, by his beneficence and his virtues, and he found in that service, and in the performance of his duty, that only and that richest reward which can recompense the patriot and the statesman. That was our Washington. Let all the rest of the world present anything like his parallel.

The verdict of mankind has already assigned to him a pre-eminent and solitary grandeur. In him, all the virtues seem to be combined in the fairest proportions. The elements were so mixed in him, and his blood and judgment were so commingled, that all the virtues

(270)

seemed to be the natural result, and to flow spontaneously from the combination, as water from the purest fountain.   In him, the exercise of the most exalted virtue required no exertion; it was a part, a parcel of his nature, and of the glorious organization "to which every God had seemed to set his seal."   Where was there any error in him?   He was a man; and therefore, in all humility, we who share that humanity must acknowledge that he had his imperfections; but who, through his long and eventful life, can point to an error or to a vice committed, or a duty omitted?

His character was made up and compounded, of all the virtues that constitute the hero, patriot, statesman, and benefactor, and all his achievements were but the practical developments of that character and of those virtues.   He was the same everywhere—in the camp, in the cabinet, at Mount Vernon.   No difference could be distinguished anywhere.   His greatness was of that innate and majestic character that was present with him everywhere.   It was that which gave him his dignity, and not the occasional situations or offices which he held under the Government.   He dignified office—he elevated the highest rank, military or civil, which he ever held.   No rank, military or civil, ever raised him, or could come up to that majesty of character which the God of his nature had implanted in him.   That was our Washington.

JOHN JORDAN CRITTENDEN was born in Woodford County, Kentucky, September 10, 1786, and died at Frankfort, Ky., July 26, 1863.   After studying law he entered the State Legislature, and was subsequently elected United States Senator for several terms.   He was appointed attorney general by President Harrison, but resigned September, 1841, and was appointed again to the same office by President Fillmore in 1850, being at that time Governor of his native State.   Our extract is from some remarks at a Congressional celebration of Washington's birthday, at the seat of Government, Saturday, February 21, 1852.

CAROLINE M. KIRKLAND.

1856.

BUT to record all the praises of Washington, would be a hopeless task. Friends and enemies concur in representing him—the former in their enthusiasm, the latter in their forced admissions, as the greatest and best of men.

So just, so wise, so beneficial, so far above the tone of vulgar heroes, was the Father of our Country, that but a small proportion of what is interesting about him, can be given in any book. His praise is everywhere; he has no competitors, he stands alone. We Americans should strive to know him, and we cannot be grateful enough to the kind Providence that guarded our national infancy, for providing a father whom we need not fear to search out, and whom in all things we may be proud to imitate.

A true warrior, yet no Napoleon, he bore the sword with hands unsoiled, wielded it for peace and not for conquest, laid it down more gladly than he took it up, and used it to make friends even of his enemies.

History, which shows us many a more dazzling character, shows none so grandly consistent, so splendid in disinterestedness, so free from conceit, yet so determined in duty, so true and tender in friendship, yet able to put aside every personal consideration when the good of the country and the great cause of Freedom were in question.

(272)

What manner of people ought we to be in return for this great gift? Let us bless God that America, having produced one such son, may bring forth others like him, when the day of trial shall come, as it may come, even to us, favored as we are above all the nations of the earth. There is more hope, not less, of another Washington, from having had the first.

We say of a great genius, like Shakespeare or Raphael, that he is inimitable. But Washington was not a genius in the ordinary acceptation of that term. His perfections, the growth of nature, circumstances and God's aid and favor combined, are imitable; on an humbler scale.

Resolute integrity, indefatigable industry, the power of deferring self to duty, a feeling of true brotherhood towards mankind, and a sincere and habitual desire to co-operate with God in doing good to the world, may make many a Washington that the world will never hear of; not in man's judgment, perhaps, but to the All-seeing eye, and to the conscious heart of him who is able to devote himself, as Washington did, soul and body, heart and life, to truth, service, and duty.

CAROLINE MATILDA KIRKLAND (Miss Stansbury), was born in New York City, January, 1801, and died there April 6, 1864. Her husband, William Kirkland, was a professor at Hamilton College, and subsequently established a seminary in Goshen on Seneca Lake. We quote from her " Memoirs of Washington," published at New York in 1856. 12mo.

35

GEORGE W. BETHUNE.

1856.

'THUS vividly reminded of him amidst the associations of this day*—the anniversary of our country's birth—it becomes us to meditate with adoring thanks on the wise goodness of God in the gift of Washington. The value of that gift cannot be over estimated, bestowed as it was at the very outset of our national existence. The long vexed question—whether in great crises of human affairs circumstances make the men, or men the circumstances—can never be settled, because each proposition is partly, but neither wholly, true. God makes both. Ordaining the event, he ordains the means and the instruments. The pious reason which ascribes to divine will the formation of the American people and our unprecedented system of government, finds constant cause for wonder in observing the method and the agents, their fitness to each other and adaptedness to the result, that were employed by Providence throughout the long, painful travail; but in nothing so much as the raising up of that elect man. I speak not now of his heroic patience and successes, or of his far-sighted, clear-headed counsels, but of the elements, and especially of their unique combination, constituting the character from which flowed out his deeds and his teachings. That character who can describe? Eulogy is impossible; the superlatives which

---

* July 4, 1856.—ED.

(274)

serve for the best of ordinary humanity are too weak. Comparison
with the most illustrious instances recorded by uninspired pens, shock
us like impertinence. History has not dared to paint him. Delighting to trace the features of her subjects, too often overlooking the
minor lineaments, and shrouding her heroes in a blaze of splendor
lest we should observe too closely, when she gazes on Washington,
drops her pencil. Whence shall she assemble her colors! How
blend them in adequate keeping! Where presume to shade a contrast! Her skill is vain. She seizes the silver mirror of truth,
catches his full reflection, and God's own sunlight fixes it there, so
just, so exquisite, that the most microscopic scrutiny sees only new
beauties the more intimate the perception. Oh, for the same divine
power to impress that image on every American heart!

Searching through the classic ages we discover here and there
a name distinguished by one or more of those commanding qualities
which belong to Washington. Fabius, Cato, Scipio Africanus, Epaminondas, Cincinnatus, rise to our minds as we contemplate him at
different moments; but the likenessess are very partial, and their
lack of other attributes which he had is the more striking. In him
nothing is wanting; yet it is not the parts, but the parts articulated
as a whole, that give him his serene grandeur. Nor may we adopt
the Greek's eclectic expedient, and unite in him what is admirable in
each of all the others, for then should we miss the relative degrees in
which the Almighty hand moulded his peculiar symmetry. Of the
few who have arisen from among the people·to control important
popular revolutions, Washington alone has the honor of having established free principles and of having perpetuated his work. The
power of the rest ceased with their life-time, if it lasted so long.

GEORGE WASHINGTON BETHUNE, D.D., was born in New York City, March, 1805. A graduate of the Princeton Theological Seminary in 1825, he entered the Presbyterian ministry in 1826, but passed to that of the Dutch Reformed the following year. He settled first at Rhinebeck on the Hudson, then in Utica; in Philadelphia in 1834, and in Brooklyn, N. Y., 1849-59. He preached for a time in the American Chapel at Rome (1859-60), then became associate pastor of a church in New York, but was forced by ill health to return to Italy, and died at Florence, April 28, 1862. Dr. Bethune was an accomplished scholar, a learned divine, and an eloquent preacher. Our extract is from his address delivered July 4, 1856, at the unveiling of the equestrian statue of Washington by Henry K. Brown, Union Square, New York.

GENTLEMAN'S MAGAZINE.

1856.

EXTRACT FROM A NOTICE OF VOLUMES I, II AND III, OF IRVING'S LIFE OF WASHINGTON IN THE GENTLEMAN'S MAGAZINE, NOV. 1856.

IT is, indeed impossible to reflect upon the odds against them (the Americans) in the unequal conflict they engaged in, without a feeling of surprise, not simply at their ultimate success, but even at the fact of their being able to prolong the struggle through a single year. And it is just as impossible to doubt, that, more than once during the long interval between the evacuation of Boston and the surrender of Cornwallis, the freedom that his countrymen were striving for was saved by Washington alone. His military skill, alone, was an inestimable assistance to their cause. He has been often called the American Fabius, but he was, when occasion served the American Marcellus also. His cautious policy was often forced upon him by the necessity of holding in check, with means wretchedly inadequate, the well-appointed armies which were opposed to him; and it is only by bearing this in mind—by remembering that the troops which he commanded were exposed, in turn, to almost every mode of hardship and privation; that they were often barefooted, starving, and half-clothed; that they were sometimes destitute of tents and engineers, and sorely enough pinched for arms and ammunition; and that the

(277)

only abundance ever found within the camp was that of zealous, strong, and brave men,—that we can form to ourselves any just conception of the comprehensiveness of that ability for war which enabled Washington, under all these disadvantages, to baffle the finest armies and the ablest generals England could send out, skillfully retreating from them when he could not fight, and fighting well whenever he could find a favourable chance; to take our best commanders by surprise in the very moments of their premature triumph; and finally to teach our rulers, by the bitter lesson of two armies surrendering without a blow, the uselessness of any further efforts to subdue the nation which they had provoked into resistance by oppression and misrule.

But more valuable even than this military genius was that unyielding spirit which animated Washington himself, and with which he inspired both the Congress and the people.   The great practical truth which a modern dramatist teaches from the lips of the younger of the Gracchi, that—

> "————the brave man ne'er despairs,
> And lives where cowards die,"

was never better instanced than in this illustrious example.   His calm, invincible reliance on the ultimate success of the confederate States never waned or wavered in the darkest fortunes they were doomed to undergo.   In the worst emergencies which he experienced, his communications with Congress—however urgent in their tone of recommendation, or remonstrance, or appeal—still breathed a hopefulness which the governing body caught from him, and which they responded to, in spite of factious efforts which were not wanting even there, with constant confidence and love.   The same animating influence seems to have fallen like a refreshing dew, upon those whom business drew about him. The people themselves looked to him with a steady trust which lent alacrity to their exertions, and made the hardest measures of privation more endurable when he was known to sanction or advise them. This was the unavoidable result of his unimpeachable, but yet commanding, character; and if he had done nothing more than this— if he had merely kept alive the sturdy resolution which first shewed itself at Lexington and Bunker's Hill—if, after teaching Congress what the sacrifices were that America was bound to make, and training the Americans to make them, he had left it to some other benefactor to command the armies he had called into the field, and to lead them on to victory and independence—the enduring gratitude of his country-men would still have been his due. But when it is remembered that these distinct services of encouragement, and counsel, and defence were conferred by one man; and that he with a virtue hardly ever paralleled amongst the great generals who have had at their command the means of ruling nations they have freed, permitted no personal ambition to grow up out of his labours, and sought from them no advantages that were not common to him with the meanest citizen of the States; we are tempted to exclaim with the poet,—

> " How shall we rank thee upon glory's page !
> Thou more than soldier ! and just less than sage !
> All that thou art reflects less fame on thee,
> Far less, than all thou hast *forborne to be !* "

GEORGE TUCKER.

1857.

In less than a fortnight after the meeting of Congress, it received the distressing intelligence of Washington's death, after a short illness, brought on by exposure to a cold rain. He died on the fourteenth of December (1799). Both Houses adjourned when the intelligence was first received; and the next day General Marshall, after a brief, but comprehensive eulogy on Washington, offered three resolutions: That the House wait upon the President to condole with him on the occasion; that its members and officers wear mourning the remainder of the session: and that a joint committee of both Houses be appointed to pay due honors to the memory of the man who was "first in war, first in peace, and first in the hearts of his countrymen;" and, lastly, that the House adjourn to the succeeding Monday: which were unanimously adopted.

General Henry Lee, one of the members from Virginia, was appointed to deliver an oration to the Houses; and by another resolution it was recommended to the people, on the next birth-day of Washington, the twenty-second of February, to testify their grief, and to commemorate his virtues and services by eulogies, addresses, and public prayers. These resolutions were passed unanimously, and the House adjourned from Thursday till the succeeding Monday: and though he had, for a year or two before his death, lost much of his former popularity with the more violent of the Republican party, yet those feelings were now all hushed in the grave, and nothing was recollected but his eminent services in the Revolution, his purity, firmness, and disinterestedness in all situations.

The honors he received abroad are such as have no parallel. Napoleon Bonaparte, then First Consul of France, ordered an oration to his honor; and the whole British fleet lowered their colors half-mast.

These unwonted honors were not paid to the elevated station Washington had occupied, as commanding the armies of his country, of presiding in her councils, nor to the unequalled services he had rendered that country in those characters, nor to his singular fortune in having prospered in all his undertakings, and in having obtained an unanimous vote of a free people in every office to which he had been nominated—but to his spotless virtues, which ever sought the noblest ends by the most unexceptionable means, and in whom the virtues of justice and fortitude, prudence and temperance, were so harmoniously blended, that it would be difficult to say which had the predominance. He was regarded not so much as an American, as a man whom all mankind took pleasure in honoring, and who was an honor to the human race.

George Tucker was born in Bermuda, 1775, emigrated to Virginia in 1787, and died at Charlotteville, Va., April 10, 1861. He was a member of Congress in 1819–25, and in 1825–45 was professor of moral philosophy, and political economy in the University of Virginia. His "History of the United States from their colonization to the end of the twenty-sixth Congress in 1841," was published at Philadelphia in 1857. 4 vols., 8vo. Our quotation is from page 104 of Vol. II, in another part of which Mr. Tucker says, "The purity, disinterestedness, and scrupulous regard to justice and propriety of Washington present to us a model which, admired by all, is mistaken by none, and often turns the balance in a mind vacillating between right and wrong, and infuses new life and energy into the virtuous and patriotic."

36

THEODORE PARKER.

1858.

GEORGE WASHINGTON was descended from the common class of Virginia farmers. No ruler of the Anglo-Saxon stock has obtained so great a reputation for the higher qualities of human virtue. For more than one thousand years no statesman or soldier has left a name so much to be coveted. None ever became so dear to the thoughtful of mankind. In the long line of generals, kings, and emperors, from the first monarch to the last president or pope, none ranks so high for the prime excellence of heroic virtue. His name is a watchword of liberty. His example and character are held up as the model for all men in authority. * * * *

The highest moral quality is Integrity, faithfulness to conviction and to all delegated trust. This was his crowning virtue. He had it in the heroic degree. It appears in all his life—from the boy of thirteen, diligently copying his tasks, to the famous man, well nigh threescore and ten. Here I know not who was his superior. I cannot put my finger on a deliberate act of his public or private life which would detract from this high praise. He had no subtility of character, no cunning; he hated duplicity, lying, and liars. He withdrew his confidence from Jefferson when he found him fraudulent; from his secretary, Reed, when he was found false in a small particular. He would not appoint Aaron Burr to any office, because

(282)

he knew him to be an intriguer. He could be silent, he could not feign; simulation and dissimulation formed no part of his character. Reserved, cautious, thinking before he spoke, I can find no act of his civil life which implies the least insincerity, the least want of ingenuousness in the man. * * * *

It has been said Washington was not a great soldier; but certainly he created an army out of the roughest materials, outgeneralled all that Britain could send against him, and in the midst of poverty and distress, organized victory. He was not brilliant and rapid. He was slow, defensive, and victorious. He made "an empty bag stand upright," which Franklin says is "hard." Some men command the world, or hold its admiration by their Ideas or by their Intellect. Washington had neither Original Ideas, nor a deeply cultured mind. He commands by his Integrity, by his Justice. He loved Power by instinct, and strong Government by reflective choice. Twice he was made Dictator, with absolute power, and never abused the awful and despotic trust. The monarchic soldiers and civilians would make him king. He trampled on their offer, and went back to his fields of corn and tobacco at Mount Vernon. The grandest act of his public life was to give up his power; the most magnanimous deed of his private life was to liberate his slaves.

Washington is the first man of his type; when will there be another? As yet the American rhetoricians do not dare tell half his excellence; but the people should not complain.

Cromwell is the greatest Anglo-Saxon who was ever a Ruler on a large scale. In intellect he was immensely superior to Washington; in integrity, immeasurably below him. For one thousand years no king in Christendom has shown such greatness, or gives us so high a type of manly virtue. He never dissembled. He sought nothing for himself. In him there was no unsound spot; nothing little or mean in his character. The whole was clean and presentable. We think better of mankind because he lived, adorning the earth with a life so noble. Shall we make an Idol of him, and worship it with huzzas on the Fourth of July, and with stupid Rhetoric on other days? Shall we build him a great monument, founding it in a slave pen? His glory already covers the Continent. More than two hundred places bear his name. He is revered as the "The Father of his Country." The people are his memorial. The New York Indians hold this tradition of him. "Alone, of all white men," say they, "he has been admitted to the Indian Heaven, because of his justice to the Red Men. He lives in a great palace, built like a fort. All the Indians, as they go to Heaven, pass by, and he himself is in his uniform, a sword at his side, walking to and fro. They bow reverently with great humility. He returns the salute, but says nothing." Such is the reward of his Justice to the Red Men. God be thanked for such a man.

THEODORE PARKER, clergyman and controversialist, was born at Lexington, Mass., August 24, 1810, and died at Florence, Italy, May 10, 1860. He studied divinity at Cambridge, and was settled over the Unitarian Society at West Roxbury, in June, 1837. Mr. Parker was one of the earliest advocates of temperance and anti-slavery, writing and speaking much in the latter cause especially, and was plain, outspoken and uncompromising, in the utterance of his convictions. He published numerous sermons and addresses, and delivered many lectures. Our extracts are from a lecture on Washington prepared in 1858, and published after his decease with three others, on Franklin, John Adams, and Jefferson, under the title "Historic Americans." Boston, 1870. 12mo.

GEORGE BANCROFT.

1858.

On the fifteenth day of June (1775), it was voted to appoint a general. Johnson, of Maryland, nominated George Washington; and as he had been brought forward "at the particular request of the people in New England," he was elected by ballot unanimously.

Washington was then forty-three years of age. In stature he a little exceeded six feet; his limbs were sinewy and well proportioned; his chest broad; his figure stately, blending dignity of presence with ease. His robust constitution had been tried and invigorated by his early life in the wilderness, his habit of occupation out of doors, and his rigid temperance; so that few equalled him in strength of arm or power of endurance. His complexion was florid; his hair dark brown; his head in its shape perfectly round. His broad nostrils seemed formed to give expression and escape to scornful anger. His dark blue eyes, which were deeply set, had an expression of resignation, and an earnestness that was almost sadness. * * * *

His faculties were so well balanced and combined, that his constitution, free from excess, was tempered evenly with all the elements of activity, and his mind resembled a well ordered commonwealth; his passions, which had the intensest vigor, owned allegiance to reason; and, with all the fiery quickness of his spirit, his impetuous and massive will was held in check by consummate judgment. He had in his

(285)

composition a calm, which gave him in moments of highest excitement
the power of self-control, and enabled him to excel in patience, even
when he had most cause for disgust.   Washington was offered a command when there was little to bring out the unorganized resources of
the continent but his own influence, and authority was connected with
the people by the most frail, most attenuated, scarcely discernible
threads; yet vehement as was his nature, impassioned as was his
courage, he so restrained his ardor, that he never failed continuously
to exert the attracting power of that influence, and never exerted it so
sharply as to break its force.

In secrecy he was unsurpassed; but his secrecy had the character
of prudent reserve, not of cunning or concealment.

His understanding was lucid, and his judgment accurate; so that
his conduct never betrayed hurry or confusion.   No detail was too
minute for his personal inquiry and continued supervision; and at the
same time he comprehended events in their widest aspects and relations.   He never seemed above the object that engaged his attention,
and he was always equal, without an effort, to the solution of the
highest questions, even when there existed no precedents to guide his
decision.

In this way he never drew to himself admiration for the possession
of any one quality in excess, never made in council any one suggestion
that was sublime but impracticable, never in action took to himself the
praise or the blame of undertakings astonishing in conception, but
beyond his means of execution.   It was the most wonderful accomplishment of this man that placed upon the largest theatre of events,
at the head of the greatest revolution in human affairs, he never failed

to observe all that was possible, and at the same time to bound his aspirations by that which was possible.

A slight tinge in his character, perceptible only to the close observer, revealed the region from which he sprung, and he might be described as the best specimen of manhood as developed in the south; but his qualities were so faultlessly proportioned, that his whole country rather claimed him as its choicest representative, the most complete expression of all its attainments and aspirations. He studied his country and conformed to it. His countrymen felt that he was the best type of America, and rejoiced in it, and were proud of it. They lived in his life, and made his success and his praise their own.

Profoundly impressed with confidence in God's Providence, and exemplary in his respect for the forms of public worship, no philosopher of the eighteenth century was more firm in the support of freedom of religious opinion; none more tolerant, or more remote from bigotry; but belief in God and trust in His overruling power, formed the essence of his character. Divine wisdom not only illumines the spirit, it inspires the will. Washington was a man of action, and not of theory or words; his creed appears in his life, not in his professions, which burst from him very rarely, and only at those great moments of crisis in the fortunes of his country, when earth and heaven seemed actually to meet, and his emotions became too intense for suppression; but his whole being was one continued act of faith in the eternal, intelligent, moral order of the universe. Integrity was so completely the law of his nature, that a planet would sooner have shot from its sphere, than he have departed from his uprightness, which was so constant, that it often seemed to be almost impersonal.

They say of Giotto, that he introduced goodness into the art of painting; Washington carried it with him to the camp and the cabinet, and established a new criterion of human greatness. The purity of his will confirmed his fortitude; and as he never faltered in his faith in virtue, he stood fast by that which he knew to be just; free from illusions; never dejected by the apprehension of the difficulties and perils that went before him, and drawing the promise of success from the justice of his cause. Hence he was persevering, leaving nothing unfinished; free from all taint of obstinacy in his firmness; seeking, and gladly receiving advice, but immovable in his devotedness to right.

Of a "retiring modesty and habitual reserve," his ambition was no more than the consciousness of his power, and was subordinate to his sense of duty; he took the foremost place, for he knew from inborn magnanimity that it belonged to him, and he dared not withhold the service required of him; so that with all his humility, he was by necessity the first, though never for himself or for private ends. He loved fame, the approval of coming generations, the good opinion of his fellow-men of his own time, and he desired to make his conduct coincide with their wishes; but not fear of censure, not the prospect of applause, could tempt him to swerve from rectitude, and the praise which he coveted, was the sympathy of that moral sentiment which exists in every human breast, and goes forth only to the welcome of virtue.

There have been soldiers who have achieved mightier victories in the field, and made conquests more nearly corresponding to the boundlessness of selfish ambition; statesmen who have been connected with more startling upheavals of society; but it is the greatness

of Washington, that in public trusts he used power solely for the
public good; that he was the life, and moderator, and stay of the
most momentous revolution in human affairs, its moving impulse and
its restraining power.   Combining the centripetal and the centrifugal
forces in their utmost strength and in perfect relations, with creative
grandeur of instinct he held ruin in check, and renewed and perfected
the institutions of his country.   Finding the colonies disconnected
and dependent, he left them such a united and well ordered commonwealth as no visionary had believed to be possible.   So that it has
been truly said, "he was as fortunate as great and good."*

This also is the praise of Washington; that never in the tide of
time has any man lived who had in so great a degree the almost
divine faculty to command the confidence of his fellow-men and rule
the willing.   Wherever he became known, in his family, his neighborhood, his county, his native state, the continent, the camp, civil life,
the United States, among the common people, in foreign courts,
throughout the civilized world of the human race, and even among
the savages, he, beyond all other men, had the confidence of his kind.

GEORGE BANCROFT, son of the Rev. Aaron Bancroft, D.D., (page 154,) was born in
Worcester, Mass., October 3, 1800. He entered Harvard College at the early age of thirteen,
and graduated in 1817; he also studied at the German Universities, and held for a short
time (1822) the post of Greek tutor in Harvard. Mr. Bancroft was appointed Secretary of
the Navy in 1845, his administration being marked by the establishment of the naval school
at Annapolis, and during 1846–9 was minister plenipotentiary to Great Britain. As early as
. 1823 he began collecting materials for his " History of the United States," the first volume
appearing in 1834, the seventh, from which we quote, in 1858, and the tenth and last in 1874,
since supplemented by the "History of the formation of the Constitution of the United States."

* Aaron Bancroft, page 153.—ED.

37

2 vols., 8vo., 1882.   In a review by WILLIAM H. PRESCOTT of the third volume, (*North Am. Review*, January, 1841,) that writer says, "What Mr. Bancroft has done for the Colonial history is, after all, but preparation for a richer theme, the history of the War for Independence; a subject which finds its origin in the remote past, its results in the infinite future; which finds a central point of unity in the ennobling principle of independence, that gives dignity and grandeur to the most petty details of the conflict, and which has its foreground occupied by a single character, to which all others converge as to a centre—the character of Washington, in war, in peace, and in private life the most sublime on historical record."

HENRY T. TUCKERMAN.

1859.

THE world has yet to understand the intellectual efficiency derived from moral qualities,—how the candor of an honest and the clearness of an unperverted mind attain results beyond the reach of mere intelligence and adroitness,—how conscious integrity gives both insight and directness to mental operations, and elevation above the plane of selfish motives affords a more comprehensive, and therefore a more available view of affairs, than the keenest examination based exclusively on personal ability. It becomes apparent, when illustrated by a life and its results, that the cunning of a Talleyrand, the military genius of a Napoleon, the fascinating qualities of a Fox, and other similar endowments of statesmen and soldiers, are essentially limited and temporary in their influence; whereas a good average intellect, sublimated by self-forgetting intrepidity, allies itself for ever to the central and permanent interests of humanity. The mind of Washington was eminently practical; his perceptive faculties were strongly developed; the sense of beauty and the power of expression, those endowments so large in the scholar and the poet, were the least active in his nature; but the observant powers whereby space is measured at a glance, and the physical qualities noted correctly,—the reflective instincts through which just ideas of facts and circumstances are realized,—the sentiment of order which regulates the most chaotic elements of duty and

(291)

work, thus securing despatch and precision,—the openness to right
impressions characteristic of an intellect, over which the visionary
tendencies of imagination cast no delusion, and whose chief affinity is
for absolute truth,—these noble and efficient qualities eminently distinguished his mental organization, and were exhibited as its normal
traits from childhood to age. To them we refer his prescience in regard
to the agricultural promise of wild tracts, the future growth of locali-
ties, the improvement of estates, the facilities of communication, the
adaptation of soils, and other branches of economics. By means of
them he read character with extraordinary success. They led him to
methodize his life and labors, to plan with wisdom and execute with
judgment, to use the most appropriate terms in conversation and
writing, to keep the most exact accounts, to seek useful information
from every source, to weigh prudently and decide firmly, to measure
his words and manner with singular adaptation to the company and
the occasion, to keep tranquil within his own brain perplexities, doubts,
projects, anxieties, cares, and hopes enough to bewilder the most
capacious intellect and to sink the boldest heart. His mental features
beam through his correspondence. We say this advisedly, notwithstanding the formal and apparently cold tenor of many of his letters;
for so grand is the sincerity of purpose, so magnanimous the spirit, so
patient, reverent, and devoted the sentiment underlying these brief
and unadorned epistles, whether of business or courtesy, that a moral
glow interfuses their plain and direct language, often noble enough to
awaken a thrill of admiration, together with a latent pathos that starts
tears in the reader of true sensibility. The unconsciousness of self, the
consideration for others, the moderation in success, the calmness in dis-

aster, the singleness of purpose, the heroic self-reliance, the immaculate patriotism, the sense of God and humanity, the wise, fearless, truthful soul that is thus revealed, in self-possessed energy in the midst of the heaviest responsibilities that ever pressed on mortal heart, with the highest earthly good in view, and the most complicated obstacles around,—serene, baffled, yet never overcome, and never oblivious of self-respect or neglectful of the minutest details of official and personal duty,—is manifest to our consciousness as we read, and we seem to behold the benign and dignified countenance of the writer through the transparent medium of his unpretending letters.* Compare, as illustrations of character, the authenticity of which is beyond dispute, the correspondence of Washington and that between Napoleon and his brother Joseph, recently published at Paris. All the romance of spurious memoirs, all the dazzling *prestige* of military genius, fails to obviate the impression the emperor's own pen conveys, in the honest utterance of fraternal correspondence, of his obtuse egotism, arrogant self-will, and heartless ambition. In Washington's letters, whether expostulating, in the name of our common humanity, with Gage, striving to reconcile Schuyler to the mortifications of a

* "The publication of the correspondence of Washington is, without doubt, the noblest monument which could have been raised to his glory. In it is truly shown this great character, so original in its simplicity. Little to astonish, few special characteristics, but a striking whole. Little fertility with little conciseness; monotony in construction, and the winning power of genius; a penetration and a breadth of view amounting to eloquence; a sincere propriety, without extravagance or prudery; a quick temper, but regulated and restrained, against which none were tempted to guard themselves, and which moved and attracted the coldest spirits without disturbing minds more thoughtful."—CORNELIS DE WITT. *Histoire de Washington, etc. Paris,* 1855. *8vo.*—ED.

service he threatened to quit in disgust, freely describing his own trials to Reed, pleading with Congress for supplies, directing the management of his estate from amid the gloomy cares of the camp, acknowledging a gift from some foreign nobleman, or a copy of verses from poor Phillis Wheatley, the same perspicuity and propriety, wisdom and kindliness, self-respect and remembrance of every personal obligation, are obvious.   *   *   *   *

Is not the absence of brilliant mental qualities one of the chief benefactions to man of Washington's example? He conspicuously illustrated a truth in the philosophy of life, often appreciated in the domestic circle and the intimacies of private society, but rarely in history,—the genius of character, the absolute efficiency of the will and the sentiments independently of extraordinary intellectual gifts. Not that these were not superior also in the man; but it was through their alliance with moral energy, and not by virtue of any transcendent and intrinsic force in themselves, that he was great. It requires no analytical insight to distinguish between the traits which insured success and renown to Washington, and those whereby Alexander, Cæsar, and Napoleon, achieved their triumphs; and it is precisely because the popular heart so clearly and universally beholds in the American hero the simple majesty of truth, the power of moral consistency, the beauty and grandeur of disinterestedness and magnanimity, that his name and fame are inexpressibly dear to humanity. Never before nor since has it been so memorably demonstrated that unselfish devotion and patient self-respect are the great reconciling principles of civic as well as of social and domestic life; that they are the nucleus around which all the elements of national integrity, however scattered and perverted, inevitably crystallize; that men thus severely true to themselves and duty, become not dazzling meteors to lure armies to victory, nor triumphant leaders to dazzle and win mankind to the superstitious abrogation of their rights, but oracles of public faith, representatives of what is highest in our common nature, and therefore an authority which it is noble and ennobling to recognise. The appellative so heartily, and by common instinct, bestowed upon Washington, is a striking proof of this, and gives a deep significance to the beautiful idea, that "Providence left him childless, that his country might call him—Father."

HENRY THEODORE TUCKERMAN was born at Boston, April 20, 1813, and died in New York City, December 17, 1871. He received his education in Boston, and after visiting Europe, moved to New York. He was the author of numerous works, biographies, essays and art criticisms, and frequently contributed to the periodicals of the day. His "Character and Portraits of Washington," from which we make the extracts, was published at New York, in 1859, 4to; the essay on the character, pronounced by Everett as "extremely judicious," originally appeared in the *North American Review*, July, 1856.

WASHINGTON IRVING.

1859.

In regard to the character and conduct of Washington, we have endeavored to place his deeds in the clearest light, and left them to speak for themselves, generally avoiding comment or eulogium. We have quoted his own words and writings largely, to explain his feelings and motives, and give the true key to his policy; for never did man leave a more truthful mirror of his heart and mind, and a more thorough exponent of his conduct than he has left in his copious correspondence. There his character is to be found in all its majestic simplicity, its massive grandeur, and quiet colossal strength. He was no hero of romance; there was nothing of romantic heroism in his nature. As a warrior, he was incapable of fear, but made no merit of defying danger. He fought for a cause, but not for personal renown. Gladly, when he had won the cause, he hung up his sword never again to take it down. Glory, that blatant word, which haunts some military minds like the bray of the trumpet, formed no part of his aspirations. To act justly was his instinct, to promote the public weal his constant effort, to deserve the "affections of good men" his ambition. With such qualifications for the pure exercise of sound judgment and comprehensive wisdom, he ascended the presidential chair. * * * *

The character of Washington may want some of those poetical elements which dazzle and delight the multitude, but it possessed

(296)

fewer inequalities, and a rarer union of virtues than perhaps ever fell to the lot of one man. Prudence, firmness, sagacity, moderation, an overruling judgment, an immovable justice, courage that never faltered, patience that never wearied, truth that disdained all artifice, magnanimity without alloy. It seems as if Providence had endowed him in a preëminent degree with the qualities requisite to fit him for the high destiny he was called upon to fulfil—to conduct a momentous revolution which was to form an era in the history of the world, and to inaugurate a new and untried government, which, to use his own words, was to lay the foundation "for the enjoyment of much purer civil liberty, and greater public happiness, than have hitherto been the portion of mankind."

The fame of Washington stands apart from every other in history; shining with a truer lustre and a more benignant glory. With us his memory remains a national property, where all sympathies throughout our widely-extended and diversified empire meet in unison. Under all dissensions and amid all the storms of party, his precepts and example speak to us from the grave with a paternal appeal; and his name—by all revered—forms a universal tie of brotherhood—a watchword of our Union.

"It will be the duty of the historian and the sage of all nations," writes an eminent British statesman, "to let no occasion pass of commemorating this illustrious man, and until time shall be no more, will a test of the progress which our race has made in wisdom and virtue, be derived from the veneration paid to the immortal name of Washington."*

* Lord Brougham, page 210.—ED.

38

Washington Irving was born in New York City, April 3, 1783, and died at Sunnyside on the Hudson river, November 28, 1859. He studied law and was admitted to the bar, but did not enter into its practice. His earliest contribution to the Republic of Letters was a series of articles on the drama, the social customs of New York, etc., under the *nom-de-plume* of "Jonathan Oldstyle," published in the *Morning Chronicle*, edited by his brother, Peter Irving. The productions of his pen, replete with talent, and the finest utterances our language is capable of, have caused his name to be known to the entire civilized world, and stamped him as the American classic. His "Life of Washington," published at New York, 1855-9, 5 vols., 8vo, from Vols. IV and V of which we quote, was his last production, a fitting close to the labors of a life, as free from stain, and as pure, as his own beautiful writings.

WILLIAM M. THACKERAY.

1859.

IN reading over our American campaigns from their unhappy commencement to their inglorious end, now that we are able to see the enemy's movements and condition as well as our own, I fancy we can see how an advance, a march, might have put enemies into our power who had no means to withstand it, and changed the entire issue of the struggle. But is was ordained by heaven, and for the good, as we can now have no doubt, of both empires, that the great Western Republic should separate from us: and the gallant soldiers who fought on her side, their indomitable Chief above all, had the glory of facing and overcoming, not only veterans amply provided and inured to war, but wretchedness, cold, hunger, dissensions, treason within their own camp, where all must have gone to rack, but for the pure unquenchable flame of patriotism that was ever burning in the bosom of the heroic leader. What a constancy, what a magnanimity, what a surprising persistence against fortune! Washington before the enemy was no better nor braver than hundreds who fought with him or against him (who has not heard the repeated sneers against "Fabius" in which his factious captains were accustomed to indulge?) but Washington the Chief of a nation in arms, doing battle with distracted parties; calm in the midst of conspiracy; serene against the open foe before him and the darker enemies at his back; Washington inspiring

(299)

order and spirit into troops hungry and in rags ; stung by ingratitude, but betraying no anger, and ever ready to forgive; in defeat invincible, magnanimous in conquest, and never so sublime as on that day when he laid down his victorious sword and sought his noble retirement:— here indeed is a character to admire and revere; a life without a stain, a fame without a flaw. *Quando invenies parem?*

WILLIAM MAKEPEACE THACKERAY, one of the most eminent of modern English novelists and essayists, was born at Calcutta in 1811, and died in London, December 24, 1863. He was sent to England at seven years of age, and received his education at the Charter-House School, and at the University of Cambridge. "The Virginians," from which we quote, was published at London, in 1858-59. 2 vols., 8vo.

EDWARD EVERETT.

1860.

GENERAL WASHINGTON'S personal appearance was in harmony with his character; it was a model of manly strength and beauty. He was about six feet two inches in height, and his person well proportioned,—in the earlier part of life rather spare, and never too stout for active and graceful movement. The complexion inclined to the florid; the eyes were blue and remarkably far apart; a profusion of brown hair was drawn back from the forehead, highly powdered according to the fashion of the day, and gathered in a bag behind. He was scrupulously neat in his dress, and while in camp, though he habitually left his tent at sunrise, he was usually dressed for the day. His strength of arm, and his skill and grace as a horseman, have been already mentioned. His power of endurance was great, and there were occasions, as at the retreat from Long Island and the battle of Princeton, when he was scarcely out of his saddle for two days. * * * *

Washington's religious impressions were in harmony with the rest of his character,—deep, rational, and practical. . . . . He was at all times a regular attendant on public worship, and an occasional partaker of the communion; and is believed habitually to have begun the day with the reading of the Scriptures and prayer in his closet. His private correspondence, his general orders, and his public acts of

(301)

all kinds contain devout recognitions of a divine Providence in the government of the world, and his whole life bears witness to the influence of a prevailing sense of religious responsibility.　＊　＊　＊

Posterity will not be left without a faithful representation of his person. The statue by Houdon in the capitol at Richmond, modelled at the age of fifty-three, is the accepted embodiment of his countenance and form, and has been followed substantially by all his successors, in several monumental works of distinguished merit. A series of portraits by able artists, from the age of thirty-eight onwards, delineate him under all the modifications of feature and person gradually induced by the advance of years.*

In the final contemplation of his character, we shall not hesitate to pronounce Washington, of all men that have ever lived, THE GREATEST OF GOOD MEN AND THE BEST OF GREAT MEN. Nor let this judgment be attributed to national partiality. In the year 1797, Mr. Rufus King, then the American minister in London, wrote to General Hamilton, " No one who has not been in England, can have a just idea of the admiration expressed among all parties for General Washington. It is a common observation, that he is not only the most illustrious, but

---

* One of these portraits—a full length—was painted from life at Philadelphia, in 1796, by Gilbert Stuart, at the instance of William Bingham of that city, for presentation to the Marquis of Lansdowne. This picture is still in England, but is known in this country by copies made by Stuart, one of which, painted for Mr. Bingham, is now owned by the " Pennsylvania Academy of the Fine Arts." The Marquis, in a letter to Major William Jackson, dated London, March 5th, 1797, after alluding to the picture as " in every respect worthy of the original," writes: "General Washington's conduct is above all praise. He has left a noble example to sovereigns and nations, present and to come. I beg you will mention both me and my sons to him in the most respectful terms possible. If I was not too old, I would go to Virginia to do him homage."—ED.

the most meritorious character that has yet appeared." Lord Erskine, in writing to Washington about the same time, says, " You are the only human being for whom I ever felt an awful reverence."* Mr. Charles James Fox remarks of him, that " A character of virtues, so happily tempered by one another and so wholly unalloyed by any vices, as that of Washington, is hardly to be found on the pages of history."† Lord Brougham, in his brilliant comparative sketch of Napoleon and Washington, after a glowing picture of the virtues and vices of the great modern conqueror, exclaims, " How grateful the relief, which the friend of mankind, the lover of virtue, experiences, when, turning from the contemplation of such a character, his eye rests upon the greatest man of our own or of any age, the only one upon whom an epithet, so thoughtlessly lavished by men, may be innocently and justly bestowed !"† Nor are these testimonies confined to Englishmen, in whom they might be supposed to be inspired, in some degree, by Anglo-Saxon sympathy. When the news of his death reached France, Fontanes, by direction of Napoleon, delivered an eloquent eulogium, in which he declared him to be "a character worthy the best days of antiquity."† M. Guizot,† a far higher authority, in his admirable essay on the character of Washington, pronounces that

* The letter from Erskine to Washington, dated London, 15 March, 1797, said to have been written on a blank page of his pamphlet, entitled *A View of the Causes and Consequences of the present War with France,* is as follows : " I have taken the liberty to introduce your august and immortal name in a short sentence which is to be found in the book I send to you. I have a large acquaintance among the most valuable and exalted classes of men ; but you are the only human being for whom I ever felt an awful reverence. I sincerely pray God to grant a long and serene evening to a life so gloriously devoted to the universal happiness of the world."—ED.,

† See pages 46, 206, 97, 227.—ED.

"Of all great men he was the most virtuous and the most fortunate."*

The comparison of Napoleon and Washington suggests a remark on the military character of the latter, who is frequently disparaged in contrast with the great chieftains of ancient and modern times. But no comparison can be instituted to any valuable purpose between individuals, which does not extend to the countries and periods in which they lived and to the means at their command. When these circumstances are taken into the account, Washington, as a chieftain, I am inclined to think, will sustain the comparison with any other of ancient or modern time. A recent judicious French writer (M. Edouard Laboulaye), though greatly admiring the character of Washington, denies him the brilliant military genius of Julius Cæsar. It is, to say the least, as certain that Julius Cæsar, remaining in other respects what he was, could not have conducted the American Revolution to a successful issue, as that Washington could not have subdued Gaul, thrown an army into Great Britain, or gained the battle of Pharsalia. No one has ever denied to Washington the possession of the highest

---

* This foreign appreciation is gracefully alluded to by Benjamin Franklin, in a letter to Washington, dated Passy, 5. March, 1780, in which he urges him to visit Europe should peace arrive after another campaign or two, and then says: "You would, on this side of the sea, enjoy the great reputation you have acquired, pure and free from those little shades that the jealousy and envy of a man's countrymen and contemporaries are ever endeavoring to cast over living merit. Here you would know, and enjoy, what posterity will say of Washington. For a thousand leagues have nearly the same effect with a thousand years. The feeble voice of those grovelling passions cannot extend so far either in time or distance. At present I enjoy that pleasure for you; as I frequently hear the old generals of this martial country, who study the maps of America, and mark upon them all your operations, speak with sincere approbation and great applause of your conduct; and join in giving you the character of one of the greatest captains of the age."—ED.

degree of physical and moral courage; no one has ever accused him of missing an opportunity to strike a bold blow; no one has pointed out a want of vigor in the moment of action, or of forethought in the plans of his campaigns; in short, no one has alleged a fact, from which it can be made even probable that Napoleon or Cæsar, working with his means and on his field of action, could have wrought out greater or better results than he did, or that, if he had been placed on a field of action and with a command of means like theirs, he would have shown himself unequal to the position.

There is, in this respect, a great mistake on the subject of Washington's temperament, which was naturally sanguine. Traditionary accounts, which must, however, be received with great caution as far as particular anecdotes are concerned, authorize the belief that, in early life at least, he habitually waged a strenuous warfare with his own ardent temper. At all events, while he was placed in circumstances, in both his wars, which forced upon him the Fabian policy, there were occasions, as we have seen in the narration, when.he seized the opportunity of making what, if it had failed, would have been called a rash movement. This showed him the possessor of an expansive capacity; conforming patiently to straits, and keeping good heart in adversity, but ready at a moment of change to move with vigor and power. When we add to this an unquestioned fondness for the military profession, who can doubt that, if he had been trained in the great wars of Europe, he would have proved himself equal to their severest tests? It is a remarkable fact, that from his youth upward he evinced military capacity beyond that of all the trained and experienced officers, with whom he was associated or brought in conflict.

39

The neglect of his advice in 1755 cost the veteran Braddock his army and his life, and threw the valley of the Ohio into the power of the French; and all the skill and energy visible in the operations of General Forbes by which it was recovered. in 1758, were infused into them by Washington.

Akin to the argument against his military capacity, is the question whether, generally speaking, Washington was a man of genius, —a question not to be answered till that word is explained. Dr. Johnson calls it, "that power which constitutes a poet," and in that acceptation Washington certainly was not endowed with it. As little did he possess the genius of the orator, the man of letters, the sculptor, the painter, the musician. The term is so habitually, not to say exclusively, appropriated to that native power which enables men to excel in science, literature, and the fine arts, that those who are destitute of it in these departments are often declared to want it altogether. But there is a genius of political and military skill; of social influence, of personal ascendency, of government;—a genius for practical utility; a moral genius of true heroism, of unselfish patriotism, and of stern public integrity, which is as strongly marked an endowment as those gifts of intellect, imagination, and taste, which constitute the poet or the artist. Without adopting Virgil's magnificent but scornful contrast between scientific and literary skill, on the one hand, and those masterful arts on the other, by which victories are gained and nations are governed, we must still admit, that the chieftain who, in spite of obstacles the most formidable, and vicissitudes the most distressing, conducts great wars to successful issues,—that the statesman who harmonizes angry parties in peace, skilfully moderates the counsels of constituent assemblies, and, without the resources of rhetoric but by influence mightier than authority, secures the formation and organization of governments, and in their administration establishes the model of official conduct for all following time, is endowed with a divine principle of thought and action, as distinct in its kind as that of Demosthenes or Milton. It is the genius of a consummate manhood. Analysis may describe its manifestations in either case, but cannot define the ulterior principle. It is a final element of character. We may speak of prudence, punctuality, and self-control, of bravery and disinterestedness, as we speak of an eye for color and a perception of the graceful in the painter, a sensibility to the sublime, the pathetic, and the beautiful in discourse; but behind and above all these there must be a creative and animating principle; at least as much in character as in intellect or art. The qualities which pertain to genius are not the whole of genius in the one case any more than the other. The arteries, the lungs, and the nerves are essential to life, but they are not life itself,—that higher something, which puts all the organic functions of the frame in motion. In the possession of that mysterious quality of character, manifested in a long life of unambitious service, which, called by whatever name, inspires the confidence, commands the respect, and wins the affection of contemporaries, and grows upon the admiration of successive generations, forming a standard to which the merit of other men is referred, and a living proof that pure patriotism is not a delusion, nor virtue an empty name, no one of the sons of men has equalled George Washington.

EDWARD EVERETT, scholar and orator, was born at Dorchester, Mass., April 11, 1794, and died at Boston, January 15, 1865. He graduated at Harvard College in 1811, and after two years preparatory study was ordained (Feb. 9, 1814,) at the early age of nineteen, pastor of the Brattle Street, (Boston) Unitarian Church. In 1815 he was elected professor of Greek language and literature in Harvard, and became president of the university in 1846, serving for three years. Mr. Everett was a member of Congress 1825–35, governor of Mass, 1836–40, minister to England 1841–45, secretary of state from Nov. 1852 to March 1853, and U. S. Senator from that time until May 1854, when he retired to private life on account of ill health. His practical assistance in aid of the movement for the purchase of Mount Vernon, is one of the most notable features in the history of its acquisition by "The Mount Vernon Ladies' Association," the present custodians. His oration on "The Character of Washington," first delivered before the "Mercantile Library Association of Boston," February 22, 1856, and afterwards repeated at intervals till the spring of 1861, in all the principal towns and cities of the country, together with his contributions to the *New York Ledger* in 1858, realized for the fund nearly seventy thousand dollars. Taking into consideration the labor and discomfort inseparable to such an undertaking, the lecture having been delivered at least one hundred and thirty times, it is extremely doubtful whether a greater example of unwearied industry, and unselfish devotion, can be cited. The "Life of George Washington," from which we quote, published at Boston in 1860, 12mo, was written by Mr. Everett at the suggestion of Lord Macaulay, for the eighth edition of the "Encyclopædia Britannica," in which it appears.

GEORGE W. P. CUSTIS.

1860.

THE person of Washington, always graceful, dignified, and commanding, showed to peculiar advantage when mounted; it exhibited, indeed, the very *beau ideal* of a perfect cavalier. The good Lafayette, during his last visit to America, delighted to discourse of the "times that tried men's souls." From the venerated friend of our country we derived a most graphic description of Washington and the field of battle. Lafayette said, "At Monmouth I commanded a division, and, it may be supposed, I was pretty well occupied; still I took time, amid the roar and confusion of the conflict, to admire our beloved chief, who, mounted on a splendid charger, rode along the ranks amid the shouts of the soldiers, cheering them by his voice and example, and restoring to our standard the fortunes of the fight. I thought then as now," continued Lafayette, "that never had I beheld so *superb a man.*" * * * *

At the grand dinner given at the headquarters (Yorktown) to the officers of the three armies, Washington filled his glass, and, after his invariable toast, whether in peace or war, of "All our friends," gave "The British Army," with some complimentary remarks upon its chief, his proud career in arms, and his gallant defence of Yorktown. When it came to Cornwallis's turn, he prefaced his toast by saying that the war was virtually at an end, and the contending parties would

(309)

soon embrace as friends; there might be affairs of posts, but nothing on a more enlarged scale, as it was scarcely to be expected that the ministry would send another army to America. Then turning to Washington, his lordship continued: "And when the illustrious part that your excellency has borne in this long and arduous contest becomes matter of history, fame will gather your brightest laurels rather from the banks of the Delaware than from those of the Chesapeake."

GEORGE WASHINGTON PARKE CUSTIS, grandson of Mrs. Washington, and adopted son of Washington, was born April 30, 1781, and died at Arlington, October 10, 1857. His early home was at Mount Vernon. Mr. Custis wrote some orations and plays, and executed some paintings of Revolutionary battles. His "Recollections and private Memoirs of Washington," from which we quote, were published at New York in 1860. 8vo.

THE ATHENÆUM.

1860.

Extract from a Notice of Recollections and Private Memoirs of Washington, by his adopted son George Washington Parke Custis, in The Athenæum, London, May 5, 1860.

ALL the many attempts to throw a halo of romance about the private life of Washington have failed. Apart from his public career, he was as uninteresting a character as one can easily conceive. Cold, prudent, plodding, a painstaking farmer, fond of field-sports, and highly respectable, he was a type of a sober, well-disposed country gentleman. His appearance was very imposing, and on horseback he looked "a king of men." But notwithstanding his "grand air," he was little calculated to shine in society. His early education had been picked up at inferior schools, and he had not done much to supply the deficiencies of juvenile training. He had no wit, no humour, no readiness in conversation. Sound common sense (as we are wont to name about the most uncommon of faculties) was his distinguishing mental characteristic, just as inflexible probity was his great moral endowment. He had not the genius requisite for a brilliant speaker; but as he never spoke on any subject until he had conscientiously considered it from every point of view, and as he brought to the consideration of a public question the same practical sagacity which he displayed so success-

(311)

fully in the management of his private affairs, he never opened his lips in debate without exercising great influence on his hearers.

The secret of his glory lies in the fact that his sterling honesty placed him high above the pettiness of personal ambition. Raised in the troublous times of revolution to the position of Dictator to a powerful people, he kept unbroken the trust reposed in him by his fellow citizens. It is no detraction from his merit to say that any other course would have led him to ruin,—that a career of successful usurpation was an impossibility to any adventurer amongst the American colonists,—and that had any set of infatuated partizans succeeded for a day in establishing a Washington dynasty, it would have been speedily swept away by the combined forces of the Republican and Tory parties, and the cause of liberty in the revolted colonies would have lost that invaluable moral support which it enjoyed in every civilized country of the world. But honour, not less than prudence, precluded Washington from entertaining any foolish design of personal aggrandizement. After a long experience Jefferson said of him, "His integrity was most pure; his justice the most inflexible I have ever known,—no motives of interest or consanguinity, of friendship or hatred, being able to bias his decision."* And in consequence of this integrity, he was "the only man in the United States who possessed the confidence of all, there being no other man who was considered as anything more than a party leader." He was surrounded by more brilliant men, but out of them all—orators, wits, scholars—there was not one so fit to be trusted. Politicans of every school knew

---

* See page 168.—Ed.

that he was a plain, sober, guileless gentleman, who would to the best of his ability fulfil his instructions, but could be induced to exceed them by no bribe of fame, or power, or flattery.

Few public characters have been so fortunate as Washington. The sympathy which men of generous natures throughout Europe felt for his cause took the form of enthusiastic admiration of the man; and when, his work accomplished, he returned to the position of a private citizen, in every quarter were resounded the praises of one who, with unprecedented magnanimity, had declined to seize a crown that he might (as it was erroneously imagined) safely have grasped. Lord Erskine said that he could not reflect on such a character without a sensation "of awe;" and Lord Brougham has spoken of him as "the greatest of great men." The philosophic moderation, however, that elicited these eulogies, consisted solely in freedom from a foolish ambition, that could never have obtained its object.

SAMUEL M. SMUCKER.

1860.

THE personal qualities of this illustrious man have so often been delineated, that it seems almost a superfluous task to attempt a description of them. His best and most accurate portrait is to be derived from the examination of the actions which he performed, and of the results which he accomplished. The intellectual character of Washington was peculiar. Though he became the triumphant hero of a long and arduous war, his military talents were not of the highest order. In this respect he was inferior to many men who, in the career of arms, have achieved far less renown than he. He possessed little power of strategy, little of that promptness and intuitive sagacity which enables a commander to adapt himself to the sudden and unexpected emergencies which occur in the crises of great engagements. In this respect, if his plan of battle was once deranged by unforseen accidents, he was unable to readjust the machinery of his army, or to confront and confound the operations of the foe by new and instantaneous combinations adapted to the emergency.* In this respect Marlborough, Saxe, Prince Eugene, Frederick the Great, Napoleon, were all infinitely his superiors.

The chief *military* ability of Washington consisted in the prudence

---

* Compare Thomas Jefferson, page 168.—ED.

(314)

and skill with which he adjusted the details of an assault on an enemy who was posted in a firm position; and the energy and perseverance with which he persisted in the subsequent attack. Thus he was triumphant over the British at Boston and Yorktown, and achieved brilliant successes there, because he was enabled to prepare his plans of attack, and to adhere to them, without the possibility of having them disarranged by sudden and unforseen movements of the enemy. His personal bravery was unquestionable; and he faced danger and death with the most perfect fortitude and indifference, when honor and duty required him so to do. His most prominent characteristic as a military commander, was his prudence; and it is probable that this solid quality was more available, under the existing circumstances, in weakening the foe by long delays, by harassing evasions, by cautious postponements of decisive actions, than by those more brilliant and showy talents which would have risked the fate of vast and important interests upon the issue of a few rash and imprudent conflicts.

A prominent element in the greatness of Washington consisted in the fact that, with respectable military talents, he combined far higher and greater abilities for the administration of government. He was placed at the head of this Confederacy at the most difficult and perilous period of its past career; when a thousand hostile and rival interests among the States, and between the separate States and the Federal Government, and between the Federal Government and the continental troops, and between several political factions in the Government, rendered it impossible so to steer as fully to meet the views and satisfy the demands of all parties. Yet that result was attained by Washington in a remarkable degree; and when, after an administration of eight eventful years, he retired from the Presidency, he left the Republic in a compact and united condition; the community at large flourishing and prosperous; and their reputation among foreign nations as a young and vigorous empire, unspotted, greatly respected, and destined to achieve with the lapse of time, a high and glorious position among the oldest communities on the globe. The triumphs of Washington as a civil and executive officer were far more honorable than even those attained by him on the battle-field.

Taken as a whole, therefore, his character was one of the most remarkable and estimable that ever existed among men. His predominating political attribute was Patriotism. His leading intellectual faculty was Sagacity. His chief social characteristics were Prudence and Self-control. His prominent moral qualities were Honesty and Conscientiousness. And all the several parts of his nature were combined together and proportioned in so admirable and equitable a measure, that he constituted a grand and harmonious *Whole*, such as is rarely exhibited in the chequered annals of this world's history. Many great and illustrious men have equalled George Washington in some one or other single quality; but scarcely any man of ancient or modern times possessed a mental and moral constitution of such admirable proportions, or of such beautiful, complete, and uniform development. Nature formed him truly great; but the peculiar circumstances in which he was placed—first of war and then of peace—conspired to render him, as possessing such faculties, greater still; until his position became at length firmly fixed among the few mortals whose majestic forms loom up sublimely through all times and ages, as specimens of spotless, peerless and almost perfect Humanity.

SAMUEL M. SMUCKER was born at Newmarket, Virginia, January 12, 1823, and died at Philadelphia, May 12, 1863. He graduated at Washington College, Pa., in 1840, studied theology in the Gettysburg Theological Seminary, and in 1842 was licensed by the Lutheran Synod, to preach at Bloomfield. He afterwards preached at Lewistown, Pa., and in German-town, 1845–48. He then studied law, and was admitted to the Philadelphia bar in January, 1850, but occupied himself chiefly in literature. His "Life of George Washington," from which we quote, was published at Philadelphia in 1860. 12mo.

HENRY ARMITT BROWN.

1878.

And what shall I say of him who bears on his heart the weight of all? Who can measure the anxieties that afflict his mind? Who weigh the burdens that he has to bear? Who but himself can ever know the responsibilities that rest upon his soul? Behold him in yonder cottage, his lamp burning steadily through half the winter night, his brain never at rest, his hand always busy, his pen ever at work; now counselling with Greene how to clothe and feed the troops, or with Steuben how to reorganize the service; now writing to Howe about exchanges, or to Livingston about the relief of prisoners, or to Clinton about supplies, or to Congress about enlistments or promotions or finances or the French Alliance; opposing foolish and rash counsels to-day, urging prompt and rigorous policies to-morrow; now calming the jealousy of Congress, now soothing the wounded pride of ill-used officers; now answering the complaints of the civil authority, and now those of the starving soldiers, whose sufferings he shares, and by his cheerful courage keeping up the hearts of both; repressing the zeal of friends to-day, and overcoming with steadfast rectitude the intrigues of enemies in Congress and in camp to-morrow; bearing criticism with patience, and calumny with fortitude, and, lest his country should suffer, answering both only with plans for her defence, of which others are to reap the glory; guarding the long coast with

(318)

ceaseless vigilance, and watching with sleepless eye a chance to strike the enemy in front a blow; a soldier, subordinating the military to the civil power; a dictator, as mindful of the rights of Tories as of the wrongs of Whigs; a statesman, commanding a revolutionary army; a patriot, forgetful of nothing but himself; this is he whose extraordinary virtues only have kept the army from disbanding, and saved his country's cause. Modest in the midst of Pride; Wise in the midst of Folly; Calm in the midst of Passion; Cheerful in the midst of Gloom; Steadfast among the Wavering; Hopeful among the Despondent; Bold among the Timid; Prudent among the Rash; Generous among the Selfish; True among the Faithless; Greatest among good men, and Best among the Great—such was George Washington at Valley Forge.

HENRY ARMITT BROWN was born at Philadelphia, December 1, 1844, and died there August 21, 1878. He graduated at Yale College in 1865, and after studying law was admitted to the Philadelphia bar December 18, 1869. Mr. Brown delivered several important historical addresses, was a ripe scholar, a forcible writer, and an accomplished orator. Our extract is from his "Oration at Valley Forge, June 19, 1878, the one hundredth anniversary of the departure of the Army of the Revolution from winter quarters at that place." This oration while showing the careful student, and earnest patriot, is remarkable for its graphic descriptions and historical information. It is printed in the Memoirs of the author by J. M. Hoppin, published at Philadelphia in 1880. 8vo. In a previous oration delivered in Carpenters' Hall, Philadelphia, September 5, 1874, in commemoration of the one hundredth anniversary of the meeting of the Congress of 1774, Mr. Brown in alluding to Washington, as a member, said: "This is he who has just made in the Virginia Convention that speech which Lynch of Carolina says is the most eloquent that ever was made: 'I will raise a thousand men, subsist them at my own expense, and march with them, at their head, for the relief of Boston.' These were his words—and his name is Washington."

JOHN RICHARD GREEN.

1880.

WITH the rejection of these efforts for conciliation,* began the great struggle which ended eight years later in the severance of the American Colonies from the British Crown. The Congress of delegates from the Colonial Legislatures at once voted measures for general defence, ordered the levy of an army, and set George Washington at its head. No nobler figure ever stood in the forefront of a nation's life. Washington was grave and courteous in address; his manners were simple and unpretending; his silence and the serene calmness of his temper spoke of a perfect self-mastery. But there was little in his outer bearing to reveal the grandeur of soul which lifts his figure with all the simple majesty of an ancient statue out of the smaller passions, the meaner impulses of the world around him. What recommended him for command was simply his weight among his fellow landowners of Virginia, and the experience of war which he had gained by service in border contests with the French and the Indians, as well as in Braddock's luckless expedition against Fort Duquesne. It was only as the weary fight went on that the colonists discovered, however slowly and imperfectly, the greatness of their leader, his clear judgment, his heroic endurance, his silence under

---

* Measures advocated by William Pitt, Earl of Chatham, in the House of Lords, and by Edmund Burke in the House of Commons.—ED.

(320)

difficulties, his calmness in the hour of danger or defeat, the patience with which he waited, the quickness and hardness with which he struck, the lofty and serene sense of duty that never swerved from its task through resentment or jealousy, that never through war or peace felt the touch of a meaner ambition, that knew no aim save that of guarding the freedom of his fellow countrymen, and no personal longing save that of returning to his own fireside when their freedom was secured. It was almost unconsciously that men learned to cling to Washington with a trust and faith such as few other men have won, and to regard him with a reverence which still hushes us in presence of his memory. But even America hardly recognized his real greatness while he lived. It was only when death set its seal on him that the voice of those whom he had served so long proclaimed him "the man first in war, first in peace, and first in the hearts of his fellow countrymen."

JOHN RICHARD GREEN was born at Oxford, England, in 1837, and died at Menton, France, March 7, 1883. He was educated at Magdalen College School, and when about eighteen, entered for a scholarship at Jesus College. After taking his degree in 1860, he entered the Ministry, and filled several charges. In 1868 he commenced collecting materials for his "History of the English People." The work appeared about 1874 in one volume, but was afterwards recast on a larger scale, and published at intervals from 1877 to 1880, in 4 vols., 8vo, from Chapter ii, Book ix, of which we quote.

WILLIAM E. H. LECKY.

1882.

To the appointment of Washington, far more than to any other
single circumstance, is due the ultimate success of the American
Revolution, though in purely intellectual powers, Washington was
certainly inferior to Franklin, and perhaps to two or three other of his
colleagues. There is a theory which once received the countenance
of some considerable physiologists, though it is now, I believe, completely discarded, that one of the great lines of division among men
may be traced to the comparative development of the cerebrum and
the cerebellum. To the first organ it was supposed belong those
special gifts or powers which make men poets, orators, thinkers, artists,
conquerors, or wits. To the second belong the superintending,
restraining, discerning, and directing faculties which enable men to
employ their several talents with sanity and wisdom, which maintain
the balance and the proportion of intellect and character, and make
sound judgments and well-regulated lives. The theory, however untrue
in its physiological aspect, corresponds to a real distinction in human
minds and characters, and it was especially in the second order of
faculties that Washington excelled. His mind was not quick or
remarkably original. His conversation had no brilliancy or wit. He
was entirely without the gift of eloquence, and he had very few
accomplishments. He knew no language but his own, and except for

(322)

a rather strong turn for mathematics, he had no taste which can be called purely intellectual. There was nothing in him of the meteor or the cataract, nothing that either dazzled or overpowered. A courteous and hospitable country gentleman, a skilful farmer, a very keen sportsman, he probably differed little in tastes and habits from the better members of the class to which he belonged; and it was in a great degree in the administration of a large estate and in assiduous attention to county and provincial business that he acquired his rare skill in reading and managing men.

As a soldier the circumstances of his career brought him into the blaze not only of domestic, but of foreign criticism, and it was only very gradually that his superiority was fully recognised. Lee, who of all American soldiers had seen most service in the English army, and Conway, who had risen to great repute in the French army, were both accustomed to speak of his military talents with extreme disparagement; but personal jealousy and animosity undoubtedly coloured their judgments. Kalb, who had been trained in the best military schools of the Continent, at first pronounced him to be very deficient in the strength, decision, and promptitude of a general; and, although he soon learnt to form the highest estimate of his military capacity, he continued to lament that an excessive modesty led him too frequently to act upon the opinion of inferior men, rather than upon his own most excellent judgment. In the army and the Congress more than one rival was opposed to him. He had his full share of disaster; the operations which he conducted, if compared with great European wars, were on a very small scale; and he had the immense advantage of encountering in most cases generals of singular incapacity. It may, however, be truly said of him that his military reputation steadily rose through many successive campaigns, and before the end of the struggle he had outlived all rivalry, and almost all envy. He had a thorough knowledge of the technical part of his profession, a good eye for military combinations, an extraordinary gift of military administration. Punctual, methodical, and exact in the highest degree, he excelled in managing those minute details which are so essential to the efficiency of an army, and he possessed to an eminent degree not only the common courage of a soldier, but also that much rarer form of courage which can endure long-continued suspense, bear the weight of great responsibility, and encounter the risks of misrepresentation and unpopularity. For several years, and usually in the neighborhood of superior forces, he commanded a perpetually fluctuating army, almost wholly destitute of discipline and respect for authority, torn by the most violent personal and provincial jealousies, wretchedly armed, wretchedly clothed, and sometimes in imminent danger of starvation. Unsupported for the most part by the population among whom he was quartered, and incessantly thwarted by the jealousy of Congress, he kept his army together by a combination of skill, firmness, patience, and judgment which has rarely been surpassed, and he led it at last to a signal triumph.

In civil as in military life, he was pre-eminent among his contemporaries for the clearness and soundness of his judgment, for his perfect moderation and self-control, for the quiet dignity and the indomitable firmness with which he pursued every path which he had deliberately chosen. Of all the great men in history he was the most invariably judicious, and there is scarcely a rash word or action or judgment recorded of him. Those who knew him well, noticed that he had keen sensibilities and strong passions; but his power of self-command never failed him, and no act of his public life can be traced to personal caprice, ambition, or resentment. In the despondency of long-continued failure, in the elation of sudden success, at times when his soldiers were deserting by hundreds and when malignant plots were formed against his reputation, amid the constant quarrels, rivalries, and jealousies of his subordinates, in the dark hour of national ingratitude, and in the midst of the most universal and intoxicating flattery, he was always the same calm, wise, just, and single-minded man, pursuing the course which he believed to be right, without fear or' favour or fanaticism; equally free from the passions that spring from interest, and from the passions that spring from imagination. He never acted on the impulse of an absorbing or uncalculating enthusiasm, and he valued very highly fortune, position, and reputation; but at the command of duty he was ready to risk and sacrifice them all. He was in the highest sense of the words a gentleman and a man of honour, and he carried into public life the severest standard of private morals. It was at first the constant dread of large sections of the American people, that if the old Government were overthrown, they would fall into the hands of military adventurers, and undergo the yoke of military despotism. It was mainly the transparent integrity of the character of Washington that dispelled the fear. It was always known by his friends, and it was soon acknowledged by the whole nation and by the English themselves, that in Washington America had found a leader who could be induced by no earthly motive to tell a falsehood, or to break an engagement, or to commit any dishonourable act. Men of this moral type are happily not rare, and we have all met them in our experience; but there is scarcely another instance in history of such a man having reached and maintained the highest position in the convulsions of civil war and of a great popular agitation.

WILLIAM EDWARD HARTPOLE LECKY was born in the neighborhood of Dublin, Ireland, March 26, 1838, and was educated at Trinity College, where he graduated B.A. in 1859, and M.A. in 1863. Devoting himself to literature, he soon gained great distinction as an author. His "History of England in the Eighteenth Century," from which we quote, was published at London and New York in 1878–82, 4 vols., 8vo. A critic (*London Spectator*) says of the author and this work, " He has written the best history of the century, has corrected many errors of his predecessors, and his manner of treatment is large, philosophical, and impartial." All of his works have been translated into German, and some of them into other languages.

GEORGE WILLIAM CURTIS.

1883.

Doubtless the American Revolution was the work of the people, but it seems the work of a man. How can we conceive its heroic prosecution, its triumphant issue, without its leader? Had he fallen at Trenton; had he been captured by Clinton; had intrigues of selfish ambition prevailed against him; had he not nerved—he alone—the hesitating army at Newburgh, who dare doubt that the vision of the "one far off divine event" that drew the country through the war, would still have been fulfilled? But what American does not know, and proudly own, that the perpetual and inspiring assurance of that event, the cheer of the weary march, the joy of the victory, the confidence of Congress, the pride and hope of America, was the character of Washington? *   *   *   *

To lead a people in revolution wisely and successfully, without ambition and without a crime, demands, indeed, lofty genius and unbending virtue. But to build their state,—amid the angry conflict of passion and prejudice and unreasonable apprehension, the incredulity of many, and the grave doubt of all, to organize for them and peacefully to inaugurate a complete and satisfactory government,— this is the greatest service that a man can render to mankind. But this, also, is the glory of Washington. The power of his personal character, his penetrating foresight, and the wisdom of his judgment, in composing the myriad elements that threatened to overwhelm the mighty undertaking, are all unparalleled. "Nothing but harmony, honesty, industry and frugality," he said to Lafayette, "are necessary to make us a great and happy people." But he was not a man of phrases, nor did he suppose that government could be established or maintained by lofty professions of virtue. No man's perception of the indispensability of great principles to the successful conduct of great affairs was ever more unclouded than his, but no man had ever learned by a more prolonged or arduous experience that infinite patience, sagacity, forbearance, and wise concession must attend inflexible principle, if great affairs are to be greatly administered. His countrymen are charged with fond idolatry of his memory, and his greatness is pleasantly depreciated as a mythologic exaggeration. But no church ever canonized a saint more worthily than he is canonized by the national affection, and to no ancient hero, benefactor, or lawgiver, were divine honors ever so justly decreed as to Washington the homage of the world.

With the sure sagacity of a leader of men, he selected at once, for the highest and most responsible stations, the three chief Americans who represented the three forces in the Nation which alone could command success in the institution of the government. Hamilton was the head, Jefferson was the heart, and John Jay was the conscience. Washington's just and serene ascendency was the lambent flame in which these beneficent powers were fused; and nothing less than that ascendency could have ridden the whirlwind and directed the storm that burst around him. Party spirit blazed into fury; John Jay was hung in effigy; Hamilton was stoned; insurrection raised its head in the West; Washington himself was denounced; and suddenly the French Revolution, the ghastly spectre rising from delirium and despair, the avenging fury of intolerable oppression, at once hopeful and heart-rending, seized modern civilization, shook Europe to the centre, divided the sympathy of America, and, as the child of liberty, appealed to Washington. But the great soul, amidst battle, and defeat, and long retreat, and the sinking heart of a people, undismayed, was not appalled by the convulsion of the world. Amidst the uproar of Christendom he knew liberty too well to be deluded by its mad pretence. Without a beacon, without a chart, but with unwavering eye and steady hand, he guided his country safe through darkness and through storm. In the angry shock of domestic parties, "there is but one character which keeps them in awe," wrote Edmund Randolph. "The foundations of the moral world," said a wise teacher in Cambridge University, bidding young Englishmen mark the matchless man,—"the foundations of the moral world were shaken, but not the understanding of Washington."* He held his steadfast way, like the sun across the firmament, giving life, and health, and strength to the new nation; and upon a searching survey of his administration, which established the fundamental principles of American policy in every department of the Government, there is no great act which his country would annul, no word spoken, no line written, no deed done by him, which justice would reverse or wisdom deplore.

GEORGE WILLIAM CURTIS was born at Providence, R. I., February 24, 1824, and received his early education at Jamaica Plain, Mass. He visited Europe in 1846, studied for

---

* William Smyth, page 231.—ED.

some time in the University of Berlin, and after making an extensive tour in the Levant, returned to the United States in 1850. Mr. Curtis edited *Harper's Monthly* for many years, has acquired a high reputation as an orator and lecturer, and since 1857, has been the managing editor of *Harper's Weekly*. Our extract is from an "Address at the unveiling of the Statue of Washington, upon the spot where he took the oath as First President of the United States, delivered on the 26th of November 1883." 8vo, pp. 35. New York: 1883. The statue, by John Q. A. Ward, erected by the citizens of New York to commemorate the event, stands on the steps of the Sub-Treasury Building, Wall Street, the site of the second City Hall, on the balcony of which Washington took the oath, April 30, 1789.

ROBERT C. WINTHROP.

1885.

THE character of Washington! Who can delineate it worthily? Who can describe that priceless gift of America to the world, in terms which may do it any sort of justice, or afford any degree of satisfaction to his hearers or to himself?

Modest, disinterested, generous, just,—of clean hands and a pure heart,—self-denying and self-sacrificing, seeking nothing for himself, declining all remuneration beyond the reimbursement of his outlays, scrupulous to a farthing in keeping his accounts, of spotless integrity, scorning gifts, charitable to the needy, forgiving injuries and injustices, brave, fearless, heroic, with a prudence ever governing his impulses and a wisdom ever guiding his valor,—true to his friends, true to his whole country, true to himself,—fearing God, believing in Christ, no stranger to private devotion or public worship, or to the holiest offices of the Church to which he belonged, but ever gratefully recognizing a Divine aid and direction in all that he attempted and in all that he accomplished,—what epithet, what attribute, could be added to that consummate character to commend it as an example above all other characters in merely human history!

From first to last, he never solicited, or sought, an office, military or civil. Every office stood candidate for him, and was ennobled by his acceptance of it. Honors clustered around him as if by the force

(331)

of "first intention."   Responsibilities heaped themselves on his shoulders as if by the law of gravitation.   They could rest safely nowhere else, and they found him ever ready to bear them all, ever equal to discharge them all.   To what is called personal magnetism he could have had little pretension.   A vein of dignified reserve, which Houdon and Stuart have rightly made his peculiar characteristic in marble and on canvas, repressed all familiarities with him.   His magnetism was that of merit,—superior, surpassing merit,—the merit of spotless integrity, of recognized ability, and of unwearied willingness to spend and be spent in the service of his country.   That was sufficient to attract irresistibly to his support, not only the great mass of the people, but the wisest and best of his contemporaries in all quarters of the Union, and from them he selected, with signal discrimination, such advisers and counsellors, in War and in Peace, as have never surrounded any other American leader.   No jealousy of their abilities and accomplishments ever ruffled his breast, and with them he achieved our Independence, organized our Constitutional Government, and stamped his name indelibly on the age in which he lived as the Age of Washington!

Well did Chief Justice Marshall, in that admirable Preface to the biography of his revered and illustrious friend, sum up with judicial precision the services he was about to describe in detail.   Well and truly did he say, "As if the chosen instrument of Heaven, selected for the purpose of effecting the great designs of Providence respecting this our Western Hemisphere, it was the peculiar lot ot this distinguished man, at every epoch when the destinies of his country seemed dependent on the measures adopted, to be called by the united voice of his fellow-citizens to those high stations on which the success of those measures principally depended."

And not less justly has Bancroft said, when describing Washington's first inauguration as President; "But for him the Country could not have achieved its Independence; but for him it could not have formed its Union; and now but for him it could not set the Federal .Government in successful motion."*

I do not forget that there have been other men, in other days, in other lands, and in our own land, who have been called to command larger armies, to preside over more distracted councils, to administer more extended governments, and to grapple with as complicated and critical affairs. Gratitude and honor wait ever on their persons and their names! But we do not estimate Miltiades at Marathon, or Pausanias at Platæa, or Themistocles at Salamis, or Epaminondas at Mantinea or Leuctra, or Leonidas at Thermopylæ, by the number of the forces which they led on land or on sea. Nor do we gauge the glory of Columbus by the size of the little fleet with which he ventured so heroically upon the perils of a mighty unknown deep. There are

---

* Count Moustier, the French minister to the United States, at the time of the inception of the new government, writing from New York, 5 June, 1789, to Count Montmorin, thus expresses himself: "It is already beyond doubt that, in spite of the asserted beauty of the plan which has been adopted, it would have been necessary to renounce its introduction if the same man who presided over its formation had not been placed at the head of the enterprise. The opinion of General Washington was of such weight that it alone contributed more than any other measure to cause the present constitution to be adopted. The extreme confidence in his patriotism, his integrity, and his intelligence forms to-day its principal support. It has become popular much more out of respect for the chief of the republic than by any merit of its own. All is hushed in presence of the trust of the people in the savior of the country."— *Bancroft's History of the Constitution.* Vol. II, p. 495. *Appendix.*—ED.

some circumstances which cannot occur twice; some occasions of which there can be no repetition; some names which will always assert their individual pre-eminence, and will admit of no rivalry or comparison. The glory of Columbus can never be eclipsed, never approached, till our New World shall require a fresh discovery; and the glory of Washington will remain unique and peerless until American Independence shall require to be again achieved, or the foundations of Constitutional Liberty to be laid anew.

Think not that I am claiming an immaculate perfection for any mortal man. One Being only has ever walked this earth of ours without sin. Washington had his infirmities and his passions like the rest of us; and he would have been more or less than human had he never been overcome by them. There were young officers around him, in camp and elsewhere, not unlikely to have thrown temptations in his path. There were treacherous men, also,—downright traitors, some of them,—whose words in council, or conduct in battle, or secret plottings behind his back, aroused his righteous indignation, and gave occasion for memorable bursts of anger. Now and then, too, there was a disaster, like that of St. Clair's expedition against the Indians in 1791, the first tidings of which stirred the very depths of his soul, and betrayed him into a momentary outbreak of mingled grief and rage, which only proved how violent were the emotions he was so generally able to control.

While, however, not even the polluted breath of slander has left a shadow upon the purity of his life, or a doubt of his eminent power of self-command, he made no boast of virtue or of valor, and no amount of flattery ever led him to be otherwise than distrustful of his own

ability and merits.   As early as 1757, when only twenty-five years of
age, he wrote to Governor Dinwiddie: "That I have foibles, and perhaps many of them, I shall not deny; I should esteem myself, as the
world also would, vain and empty were I to arrogate perfection."
On accepting the command of the Army of the Revolution, in 1775,
he said to Congress: "I beg it may be remembered by every gentleman in the room, that I this day declare, with the utmost sincerity, I
do not think myself equal to the command I am honored with." And,
in 1777, when informed that anonymous accusations against him had
been sent to Laurens, then President of Congress, he wrote privately to
beg that the paper might at once be submitted to the body to which
it was addressed, adding these frank and noble words: "Why should
I be exempt from censure,—the unfailing lot of an elevated station?
Merit and talents which I cannot pretend to rival have ever been subject to it.   My heart tells me it has been my unremitted aim to do
the best which circumstances would permit; yet I may have been
very often mistaken in my judgment of the means, and may, in many
instances, deserve the imputation of error."   And when, at last, he
was contemplating a final retirement from the Presidency, and, in one
of the drafts of his Farewell Address, had written that he withdrew
"with a pure heart and undefiled hands," or words to that effect, he
suppressed the passage and all other similar expressions, lest, as he
suggested, he should seem to claim for himself a measure of perfection which all the world now unites in according to him.   For I
hazard little in asserting that all the world does now accord to Washington a tribute, which has the indorsement of the Encyclopædia
Britannica, that, "of all men that have ever lived, he was the greatest

of good men, and the best of great men."* Or, let me borrow the same idea from a renowned English poet, who gave his young life and brilliant genius to the cause of Liberty in modern Greece. "Where," wrote Byron,—

> "Where may the wearied eye repose
>   When gazing on the great,
> Where neither guilty glory glows,
>   Nor despicable state!
> Yes, one—the first, the last, the best,
> The Cincinnatus of the West,
>   Whom envy dared not hate—
> Bequeathed the name of Washington,
> To make men blush there was but One!"†

To what other name have such tributes ever been paid by great and good men, abroad as well as at home? You have not forgotten the language of Lord Erskine, in his inscription of one of his productions to Washington himself: "You are the only being for whom I have an awful reverence!"‡ You have not forgotten the language of Charles James Fox, in the House of Commons: "Illustrious Man, before whom all borrowed greatness sinks into insignificance."‡ You have not forgotten the language of Lord Brougham, twice uttered, at long intervals, and with a purpose, as Brougham himself once told me, to impress and enforce those emphatic words as his fixed and final judgment: "Until time shall be no more will a test of the progress which our race has made in Wisdom and Virtue be derived from the veneration paid to the immortal name of Washington!"‡

---

* Edward Everett, page 302.—ED.

† Ode to Napoleon Bonaparte, April 10, 1814.—ED.   ‡ See pages 303, 44, 210.—ED.

Nor can I fail to welcome the crowning tribute, perhaps, from our mother land,—reaching me, as it has, at the last moment of revising what I had prepared for this occasion,—in a published letter from Gladstone,* her great Prime Minister, who, after saying, in casual conversation, that Washington was "the purest figure in history," writes deliberately, "that if, among all the pedestals supplied by history for public characters of extraordinary nobility and purity, I saw one higher than all the rest, and if I were required, at a moment's notice, to name the fittest occupant for it, I think my choice, at any time during the last forty-five years, would have lighted, and it would now light upon Washington!"

But if any one would get a full impression of the affection and veneration in which Washington was held by his contemporaries, let him turn, almost at random, to the letters which were addressed to him, or which were written about him, by the eminent men, military or civil, American or European, who were privileged to correspond with him, or who ever so casually found occasion to allude to his career and character. And let him by no means forget, as he reads them, that those letters were written a hundred years ago, when language was more measured, if not more sincere, than now, and before the indiscriminate use of the superlative, and the exaggerations and adulations of flatterers and parasites, sending great and small alike down to posterity as patterns of every virtue under Heaven, had tended to render such tributes as suspicious as they often are worthless.

---

* To G. W. Smalley, dated 10 Downing St., Whitehall, October 4, 1884. Mr. Smalley was the London correspondent of the *New York Tribune*, and the letter was published in that paper, February 1, 1885.—ED.

43

What, for instance, said plain-speaking old Benjamin Franklin? "My fine crab-tree walking-stick, with a gold head curiously wrought in the form of the cap of Liberty,"—these are the words of his Will, in 1789,—"I give to my friend and the friend of mankind, George Washington. If it were a sceptre, he has merited it, and would become it."

"Happy, happy America," wrote Gouverneur Morris from Paris, in 1793, when the French Revolution was making such terrific progress,—"happy, happy America, governed by reason, by law, by the man whom she loves, whom she almost adores! It is the pride of my life to consider that man as my friend, and I hope long to be honored with that title."

"I have always admired," wrote to him Count Herzburg, from Berlin,* where he had presided for thirty years over the Ministry of Foreign Affairs, under Frederick the Great,—"I have always admired your great virtues and qualities, your disinterested patriotism, your unshaken courage and simplicity of manners,—qualifications by which you surpass men even the most celebrated of antiquity."

"I am sorry," wrote Patrick Henry, then Governor of Virginia, in allusion to the accusations of one of the notorious faction of 1777, —"I am sorry there should be one man who counts himself my friend who is not yours."

Thomas Jefferson, who, we all know, sometimes differed from him, took pains, at a later period of his life, to say of him in a record for posterity: "His integrity was most pure; his justice the most inflexible I have ever known; no motives of interest or consanguinity, of friend-

---

* June 14, 1793.—ED.

ship or hatred, being able to bias his decision. He was, indeed, in every sense of the word, a wise, a good, and a great man."* And when it was once suggested to him, not long before his own death, that the fame of Washington might lessen with the lapse of years, Jefferson, looking up to the sky, and in a tone which betrayed deep emotion, is said to have replied: "Washington's fame will go on increasing until the brightest constellation in yonder heavens is called by his name."†

"If I could now present myself," wrote Edmund Randolph, who had made injurious imputations on Washington before and after his dismissal from the Cabinet in 1795,—"if I could now present myself before your venerated uncle," he wrote most touchingly to Judge Bushrod Washington in 1810, "it would be my pride to confess my contrition, that I suffered my irritation, let the cause be what it might, to use some of those expressions respecting him, which, at this moment of indifference to the world, I wish to recall, as being inconsistent with my subsequent conviction. My life will, I hope, be sufficiently extended for the recording of my sincere opinion of his virtues and merit, in a style which is not the result of a mind merely debilitated by misfortune, but of that Christian Philosophy on which alone I depend for inward tranquillity."

And far more touching and more telling still is the fact, that even Thomas Conway, the leader of that despicable cabal at Valley Forge, but who lived to redeem his name in other lands, if not in our own,— when believing himself to be mortally wounded in a duel, in 1778,

---

* See page 168.—Ed.

† Randall's Life of Thomas Jefferson. Vol. II, p. 375.—Ed.

and "just able," as he said, "to hold the pen for a few minutes,"—employed those few minutes in writing to Washington to express his "sincere grief for having done, written, or said anything disagreeable" to him, adding these memorable words: "You are, in my eyes, the great and good man. May you long enjoy the love, veneration, and esteem of these States, whose liberties you have asserted by your virtues."

From his illustrious friend, Alexander Hamilton, I need not cite a word. His whole life bore testimony, more impressive than words, to an admiration and affection for his great chief, which could not be exceeded, and which no momentary misunderstandings could shake.

But listen once more, and only once more, to Lafayette, writing to Washington from Cadiz in 1783, when the glad tidings of the Treaty of Peace had just reached him: "Were you but such a man as Julius Cæsar, or the King of Prussia, I should almost be sorry for you at the end of the great tragedy where you are acting such a part. But, with my dear General, I rejoice at the blessings of a Peace in which our noble ends have been secured. . . . . As for you, who truly can say you have done all this, what must your virtuous and good heart feel in the happy moment when the Revolution you have made is now firmly established!" Rightly and truly did Lafayette say that his beloved General was of another spirit and of a different mould from Cæsar and Frederick. Washington had little, or nothing, in common with the great military heroes of his own or any other age,—conquering for the sake of conquest,—" wading through slaughter to a throne,"—and overrunning the world, at a countless cost of blood and treasure, to gratify their own ambition, or to realize some mad dream of universal empire. No ancient Plutarch has furnished any just parallel for him in this respect. No modern Plutarch will find one. In all history, ancient and modern alike, he stands, in this respect, as individual and unique as yonder majestic Needle.*

In his Eulogy on Washington before the Legislature of Massachusetts, the eloquent Fisher Ames, my earliest predecessor in Congress from the Boston district, said, eighty-five years ago, that, in contemplating his career and character, "Mankind perceived some change in their ideas of greatness. . . . The splendor of power, and even the name of Conqueror, had grown dim in their eyes. . . . They knew and felt that the world's wealth, and its empire too, would be a bribe far beneath his acceptance." Yes, they all saw that he bore ever in his mind and in his heart, as he said at Philadelphia on his way to Cambridge, in 1775, that "as the Sword was the last resort for the preservation of our liberties, so it ought to be the first thing laid aside when those liberties were firmly established." And they saw him lay down his sword at the earliest moment, and retire to the pursuits of peace, only returning again to public service at the unanimous call of his country, to preside for a limited period over a free Constitutional Republic, and then eagerly resuming the rank of an American Citizen. That was the example which changed the ideas of mankind as to what constituted real greatness. And that example was exhibited for all nations and for all ages, never to be forgotten or overlooked, by him who was born, one hundred and fifty-three years ago to-morrow, in that primitive little Virginia farm-house!

I am myself a New-Englander by birth, a son of Massachusetts,

---

* The National Monument to Washington.—Ed.

bound by the strongest ties of affection and of blood to honor and venerate the earlier and the later Worthies of the old Puritan Commonwealth, jealous of their fair fame, and every ready to assert and vindicate their just renown.   But I turn reverently to the Old Dominion to-day, and salute her as the mother of the pre-eminent and incomparable American, the Father of his Country, and the foremost figure in all merely human history.   In the words of our own poet, Lowell,

> "Virginia gave us this imperial man,
> Cast in the massive mould
> Of those high-statured ages old
> Which into grander forms our mortal metal ran;
> She gave us this unblemished gentleman :
> What shall we give her back but love and praise ?"[*]

Virginia has had other noble sons, whom I will not name, but whom I do not forget.   When I remember how many they are, and how great they have been, and how much our country has owed them, I may well exclaim, "*Felix prole virûm.*"   But, as I think of her Washington,—of our Washington, let me rather say,—I am almost ready to add, "*Læta Deûm partu!*" [†]

A celebrated philosopher of antiquity, who was nearly contempo-

---

[*] Poem read at the Cambridge Centennial, July 3, 1875.—Ed.

[†] Mr. Winthrop referring to Virginia on a previous occasion, "Oration before the New England Society of New York, December 23, 1839," said : "Nor let me omit to allude to a peculiar distinction which belongs to Virginia alone.   It is her preëminent honor and pride, that the name which the whole country acknowledges as that of a father, she can claim as that of a son—a name at which comparison ceases—to which there is nothing similar, nothing second :—a name combining in its associations all that was most pure and godly in the nature of the Pilgrims, with all that was most brave and manly in the character of the Patriots :—A NAME ABOVE EVERY NAME IN THE ANNALS OF HUMAN LIBERTY ! "—ED.

rary with Christ, but who could have known nothing of what was going on in Judæa, and who, alas! did not always "reck his own rede,"—wrote thus to a younger friend, as a precept for a worthy life: "Some good man must be singled out and kept ever before our eyes, that we may live as if he were looking on, and do everything as if he could see it." *

Let me borrow the spirit, if not the exact letter, of that precept, and address it to the young men of my Country: "Keep ever in your mind, and before your mind's eye, the loftiest standard of character. You have it, I need not say, supremely and unapproachably, in Him who spake as never man spake, and lived as never man lived, and who died for the sins of the world. That character stands apart and alone. But of merely mortal men the monument we have dedicated to-day points out the one for all Americans to study, to imitate, and, as far as may be, to emulate. Keep his example and his character ever before your eyes and in your hearts. Live and act as if he were seeing and judging your personal conduct and your public career. Strive to approximate that lofty standard, and measure your integrity and your patriotism by your nearness to it, or your departure from it. The prime meridian of universal longitude, on sea or land, may be at Greenwich, or at Paris, or where you will. But the prime meridian of pure, disinterested, patriotic, exalted human character will be marked forever by yonder Washington obelisk!" * * * * *

Our matchless Obelisk stands proudly before us to-day, and we

* *"Aliquis vir bonus nobis eligendus est, ac semper ante oculos habendus, ut sic tanquam illo spectante vivamus, et omnia tanquam illo vidente faciamus.*—Senecae Epistola ad Lucilium XI.

hail it with the exultations of a united and glorious Nation. It may, or may not, be proof against the cavils of critics, but nothing of human construction is proof against the casualities of time. The storms of winter must blow and beat upon it. The action of the elements must soil and discolor it. The lightnings of Heaven may scar and blacken it. An earthquake may shake its foundations. Some mighty tornado, or resistless cyclone, may rend its massive blocks asunder and hurl huge fragments to the ground. But the character which it commemorates and illustrates is secure. It will remain unchanged and unchangeable in all its consummate purity and splendor, and will more and more command the homage of succeeding ages in all regions of the Earth.

GOD BE PRAISED, THAT CHARACTER IS OURS FOREVER!

ROBERT CHARLES WINTHROP was born in Boston, May 12, 1809, graduated at Harvard College in 1828, and studied law with Daniel Webster. He entered the state legislature in 1835, and was speaker in 1838-40; member of Congress 1840-50, speaker in 1847-8, and United States Senator 1850-1. Mr. Winthrop has published several memoirs, delivered many historical addresses, is a ripe scholar, and an eloquent speaker. Our extract is from the second edition of his "Oration on the completion of the National Monument to Washington agreeably to the appointment of Congress, February 21, 1885." 8vo, pp. 39. Boston: 1885. Extracts from Mr. Winthrop's oration on the occasion of laying the *corner-stone* of the monument, July 4, 1848, are given on page 264.

INDEX.